PRAISE FOR
Kid Magic Unlocked

"*Kid Magic Unlocked* is a must-read for every educator and caregiver! It brilliantly connects neuroscience with everyday practice, helping adults truly understand and support the way children learn, move, and grow. It reminds us that to reach children, we must first understand the remarkable brains and bodies behind their behaviors. It's a compassionate, science-based guide that helps adults see kids not as small adults, but as developing humans full of potential. *Kid Magic Unlocked* is smart, engaging, and full of practical takeaways for anyone who works with children."
—*Ashley Donnelly, Grade School Teacher*

"Dr. Miller's philosophy pushes educators not to just think 'outside the box,' but to not see 'a box' at all. She guides educators on a journey of the connection between brain science and classroom practice, something not fully addressed in teacher preparation programs. The *How To Be A Kid*™ framework is the epitome of what education should be: child-centered and empowering for the adults that surround them."
—*Emily Moran, Teacher, Assistant Principal, Lifelong Learner*

"My son faces many learning challenges and often struggles with anxiety, but on the days he works with Dr. Miller, he is happy and excited for school. She looks at the whole child, weaving classroom learning into her sessions to make them fun and engaging. Her dedication has boosted his confidence and made him truly look forward to learning."
—*C.B., Mom, Special Education Teacher*

"As both mom and educator, *Kid Magic Unlocked* gives eye-opening insight into how children truly learn and offers practical strategies I can use at home and in the classroom."
—*E.R. Keeney, Mom, Middle School Teacher*

Kid Magic Unlocked

A GROWN-UP'S GUIDE
for Re-Imagining Education to Cultivate
the Limitless Potential of Every Child

Dr. Crystal T. Miller

First edition

ISBN (paperback): 979-8-9931001-9-7
ISBN (hardcover): 979-8-9931001-8-0

Editing by Megan Tatreau
Cover design and interior layout by David Provolo
Illustrations by Dr. Crystal T. Miller
Illustration of Mr. Homunculus by Eszter Czap-Tóth

Published by How To Be A Kid LLC 2025

Howtobeakid.com

For inquiries contact kidmagic@howtobeakid.com
United States of America

For my children:
Jackson, Zachary, and Cameron

You are my reason for being, my whole heart, my everything!
You are living proof that Magic truly exists and
that kids have endless, unlimited potential.
It is through you that my own Magic shines.
Your Kid Magic continues to grow and is creating a better world!
I love you infinity... always.

To my kids:

Joey, Dean, Jason, Alexis, Zoey, Kellen, Gavin, David, Christina,
Patricia, Obinna, Chauncey, Grace, Brian, Haylie, James, Ellie,
Daniel, and ALL the kids I have worked with over the years,
the How To Be A Kid™ program was made with you in mind.
You will find pieces of you all throughout this book as
those pieces have filled my heart and helped shape who I am.
You are Magical and limitless and you make this world beautiful!

Contents

Bridging the Gap Between the Worlds of Education and Neuroscience

Forewords by Dr. Robert Melillo & Travis Davey

I met Dr. Crystal Miller a few years ago when she came to my office and introduced herself. From our first conversation, I was impressed by her credentials—she holds a Doctorate in Physical Therapy and has extensive experience working directly in schools, developing curricula, and training both teachers and therapists. Crystal's approach was distinct from the standard methods employed in schools nationwide; she offered a deeper understanding of the root issues affecting the children she worked with and had developed specific tools to address these challenges. She was not satisfied with merely addressing symptoms or behaviors—her interventions were purposeful and intentional, not just routine.

Crystal began taking some of my courses, and our conversations grew to include everything she was learning, how it related to her work in schools, and the ways she was integrating these ideas into her practice. I was continually impressed by her unique perspective and her ability to apply these concepts in educational settings. While I had focused on building practices and centers and teaching parents to implement my work at home, I had not done much to adapt my ideas for schools and teachers. This was Crystal's area of expertise; her deep understanding of school environments and the mindset of teachers was unparalleled. She not only grasped the neuroscience but also developed new, practical activities and interventions to address core issues within the classroom. Crystal's presence and her connection to this pivotal moment in my career seems more than mere coincidence—it feels meaningful.

Eventually, Crystal told me she was writing a book about her work. Many people express the intention to write a book, but few actually complete one. Several months later, she shared an early draft with me, and I was once again impressed.

Fifteen years ago, while writing my first book, *Disconnected Kids*, my main goal was to provide parents with real information and concrete answers to their questions about their children. As a health care practitioner specializing in neurology and rehabilitation—and as a parent of children with neurological and developmental delays—I understood firsthand the frustration parents experience when doctors and therapists cannot offer clear explanations about what is happening in their child's brain or how to address the root of the problem. Parents want to know: What is the root cause, and what can be done? I have dedicated my life to understanding and perfecting my approach to answering these questions.

Crystal's completed book, *Kid Magic Unlocked*, is filled with practical and useful information. I was struck by her clear, concise, engaging, and relatable writing style—qualities I am certain readers will appreciate. When Crystal mentioned that she had also created all the illustrations herself, I was truly amazed.

For any teacher, parent, or therapist seeking real answers and practical activities to help children, I highly recommend this remarkable book, *Kid Magic Unlocked: A Grown-up's Guide For Reimagining Education to Cultivate The Limitless Potential in Every Child.*

Dr. Robert Melillo
Author, Disconnected Kids, Founder of The Melillo Method
and Brain Balance Achievement Centers
PhD Developmental Cognitive Neuroscience

As superintendent and principal of a small PK–6 school district nestled within the protected beauty of a National Seashore in New York, I have the privilege of working each day with a community that treasures both childhood and learning. My mission has always been to help create and sustain the optimal school experience for children: places where curiosity, joy, and belonging are the norm rather than the exception.

As a husband to a lifelong educator and a father of four, family is the heartbeat of my life. Professionally, that same sense of care extends to the children and adults I serve. Over twenty-five years in education—from the classrooms of southern Mississippi to the inner cities of North Carolina, the bustle of midtown Manhattan, and now to my coastal district—I've been guided by one enduring belief: Schools should be sanctuaries for the wonder of childhood. I have tried to build communities that challenge the tired narratives of over-testing, labeling, and constraint, replacing them with cultures that think like children—curious, creative, and full of possibility. My aim has always been to lead schools where both students and the educators who dedicate their lives to them feel seen, supported, and inspired.

It was within this shared mission that I first met Dr. Crystal Miller. Returning to elementary leadership after several years at the middle school level, I discovered that among our parent community was a brilliant thinker, a practicing doctor of physical therapy, and someone whose devotion to children was as deep as it was authentic. One evening after a back-to-school event, she approached me with an idea—one that would become the seed of *Kid Magic Unlocked*. Her questions were incisive yet filled with that rare combination of curiosity and conviction that reminds me of how children approach the world: open, fearless, and full of wonder. What followed was years of inquiry, collaboration, and creation. Dr. Miller immersed herself in understanding education from within, bridging her medical background and her belief in the whole child to craft a framework that empowers educators to rediscover the essence of their calling.

Kid Magic Unlocked is exactly what its title promises: an enchanting blend of wisdom, practicality, and heart that reminds us why we entered education in the first place. Unlike so many professional texts that bury us in methods and metrics, this book begins where every good story should—with the child at the center.

Dr. Miller's M.A.G.I.C framework—Meet, Assess, Guide, Incorporate, Create—is both clever and compelling. It's more than an acronym; it's a movement, a call to action for educators, parents, and communities to rekindle the joy, imagination, and moral purpose that define great schools. She equips us with tangible strategies we can use immediately, but even more importantly, she reignites the hope and humanity that make those strategies meaningful.

Kid Magic Unlocked deserves a place not only on teachers' desks or graduate syllabi, but in the hands of PTAs, community book clubs, and anyone who believes in the transformative power of spirited, child-centered learning communities. With equal parts expertise and love, Dr. Miller reminds us that the real magic happens when adults choose to truly see, listen to, and celebrate children. This book is a gift—and a spark—that will continue to light the way for years to come.

Travis Davey
Superintendent of Fire Island School District

INTRODUCTION

Childhood is under siege. What was once a sacred time of wonder, movement, mess, and magic is now being crowded out by screens, stress, and standards. We're watching play be replaced by pressure. Laughter replaced by anxiety. Curiosity replaced by compliance. And while the grown-up world keeps spinning faster, our kids are paying the price—with their minds, their bodies, and their joy.

You may have sensed it already—that feeling deep down that something isn't right. That childhood today feels… off. That it's harder than ever to be a kid—and maybe even harder to be the grown-up responsible for them. You're not imagining it. Childhood is in trouble.

Just ask my five-year-old niece. She spent the summer counting down the days to kindergarten, bubbling with excitement. She talked endlessly about how fun it was going to be—new friends, games, songs, learning new things in magical ways. It was all she could talk about. But just a few weeks into the school year, she looked up at her mom with confusion and disappointment and said, "Kindergarten isn't fun. It's just boring work. We don't even get to play." She wanted to go back to preschool. Or better yet—just stay home and play with her sister, her cousins, and her friends.

Her words gutted me. Not because they were unusual—but because they weren't. Children across the country, and around the world, are saying the same thing in different ways: "This isn't what I thought growing up would feel like."

But here's the good news: There's still time to reclaim the magic of learning.

Kid Magic Unlocked is not just a guide—it's a call to action. A roadmap back to what childhood is meant to be. It's for parents, teachers, caregivers, and anyone else who knows that children deserve more than a world of diagnoses, data points, and disconnected days.

The most amazing part of the M.A.G.I.C. Model is that it is for ALL children. All children deserve wonder. They deserve movement. They deserve connection. They deserve a childhood. For the past eleven years, I've had the privilege of working with students with special needs. These incredible children have enriched my life in ways I never imagined and have helped me become who I am today. Their raw, unfiltered presence brings an unmatched beauty to the world, and they challenge us to rethink what education and inclusion really mean. The M.A.G.I.C. Model isn't just valuable for them—it's even more essential. In fact, it was designed with my kids in mind—yes, *my kids*!

It was in working with my kids each day that I was able to truly let *my* magic run free! I had to dig to the deepest parts of myself to connect with each and every one of them. There was no faking it—they can *feel* me! My methods had to connect with them on their unique, individual levels. We had to learn each other and trust each other. I had to put myself out there. On any given day, I was singing "Chicken Fried" at the top of my lungs while jogging on a treadmill, or "Baby, I Love Your Way" during bridges. I held them in my arms while they cried or just because they needed a hug. We worked inside, outside, in classrooms, stairwells, and hallways. They told me that PT (physical therapy) was the best part of their day or that my programs were the worst ever—and they had to "redesign" them (which I let them). No sugar coating and no holding back! I learned about every back-up racer in Pixar's *Cars* as well as everything there is to know about soccer. I have listened to every showtune that ever was. I learned to improvise, "sneak in" exercise to their fun, and work by their rules.

You see, the entire How To Be A Kid™ program I created began with these kids. It started with wanting to do more than have them do ten jumping jacks to "achieve their PT goals." It came from recognizing the potential they carried inside themselves—not just for them, but for everyone around them. I have seen these kids break down barriers like you would never believe!

Working with these students has shown me that our responsibility as educators, parents, and caregivers is to continuously learn about child development and to understand that every child's journey is different. By embracing their differences and creating spaces that honor each child's unique magic, we not only transform their lives—we change our own perspectives on what it means to learn and grow. We create and enhance a nurturing environment for everyone. The M.A.G.I.C. Model is more than a tool; it's a commitment to unlocking the brilliance in *every* child and, in doing so, enriching our collective future.

HOW THIS BOOK WORKS

This book is broken into three parts, each one helping you unlock a piece of the puzzle:

Part One: The Lost Art of Childhood

We'll start by pulling back the curtain on what's happening to childhood today. We'll look at how our fast-paced, screen-saturated, test-obsessed culture is reshaping development—and not in a good way. Before we can fix the problem, we need to fully see it.

Part Two: Using the M.A.G.I.C. Model to Help Our Children

Here, we'll explore a new framework for recalibrating development and restoring what's been lost. The M.A.G.I.C. Model gives you practical tools to meet kids where they are, assess what they need, and guide them toward growth—through movement, connection, play, and creativity. It's not make-believe magic. It's the real kind that happens when we stop fighting against human nature and start working with it.

Part Three: Creating a New Story: Re-imagining Childhood

Finally, we'll look ahead—because the future isn't written yet. What if we could rewrite the story of childhood? What if we created schools that felt more like playgrounds and less like pressure cookers? What if we trusted joy and curiosity to lead the way? This section invites you to imagine—and help build—a better world for our kids.

A NOTE BEFORE WE BEGIN

First and foremost, this book is a guide. This is not meant to contain all the answers, but, instead, to let you know there are answers. It is not meant to fix all the problems presented, but rather to let you know there are solutions. It is not meant to scare you with a feeling of impending doom, but rather to validate your feelings that something feels off.

It is to share with you the brilliance in those who are fighting for solutions and to help bring more attention to that brilliance. It's about trusting in the magic of our human potential and using creativity, imagination, and innovation to make a new story for us.

So let's get back to where all stories start: Once upon a time…

Part I

The Lost Art of Childhood

1

Where is the Magic?

"But all the magic I have known, I've had to make."

—Shel Silverstein

Once upon a time, there was a child with big, beautiful eyes full of wonder. This child had the greatest imagination, dreams that spanned the universe, and the curiosity to understand the world around him. But as time went on and this child grew older, the world around him began to dim that spark. Adults told him to "be realistic," to "grow up," to stop letting his "imagination run wild." "Start taking responsibility," they said.

Sound familiar? Let me start over.

Once upon a time, there was a child with big, beautiful eyes full of wonder. This child had the greatest imagination, dreams that spanned the universe, and the curiosity to understand the world around him. Adults supported this child and encouraged him to follow his dreams. Adults guided him, nurtured his spirit, and honored his questions. He used his wild imagination to solve problems. Life wasn't always easy, but the adults around him tended to and protected his imagination, his joy, and his dreams.

Every child's story starts with "Once upon a time," but what comes next? That part is still being written—and you, whether you are a parent, teacher, grandparent, coach, aunt, uncle, counselor, doctor, neighbor, or friend, are a co-author of that story. Your role in raising a happy, healthy child is essential.

We all carry our own beliefs about what it takes to raise a "successful" human being—someone who is "ready" for adulthood, whatever that means. But before we talk about raising kids, guiding them, or educating them, we need to answer one deceptively simple question:

What is a kid?

This question sounds easy enough, doesn't it? But the truth is, it's more complicated than we might think.

The Boring Definition

Kid (n.)—a child or young person. A young goat.

Child (n.)—a young human being below the age of puberty or below the legal age of majority. A human being below the age of eighteen.

OK, sure. Technically accurate—but it's missing something. A lot of somethings. It doesn't mention the spark in their eyes, the creative explosions that happen mid-sentence, the way their legs twitch with energy they can't contain, or the way they see the world as if it's a giant, mysterious playground. It doesn't speak to the way they're wired to learn through movement, touch, trial and error, imagination, and wonder. The formal definition leaves out the very soul of what a kid truly is.

So, I decided to go to the real experts: actual kids. Here's how they define a kid:

Advice from the Experts:

"A kid is a person who is small and still has small person magic." —Boy, age 9

"When you're a kid you can play more and you don't have as many injuries." —Boy, age 9

"Kids have more energy than grown-ups because we are smaller." —Boy, age 7

"A kid is technically anyone between the ages of toddler and 18 years old, but my heart tells me it is someone with a childlike mind, someone creative, someone with energy and creativity, a joyful heart." —Girl, age 13

"A kid is someone who isn't fully developed and hasn't had experience in 'the real world' because, you know, we are in school." —Boy, age 14

"There are different levels of kid - elementary then high school, who knows more but is still developing." —Boy, age 15

"A person who is not fully grown yet." —Boy, age 9

"A young human." —Boy, age 10

"A kid is a creative person that still has magic." —Boy, age 11

"A magical human." —Boy, age 7

"I don't know, we didn't learn that in school." —Girl, age 5

"[My big sister's] friend." —Girl, age 2

"A kid is like a smaller person than a grown-up. Kids usually play and grown-ups usually clean." —Girl, age 7

"What's a kid?... a kid is a baby goat." —Girl, age 10

"A kid, I am a kid!" —Girl, age 7

"A kid is a crazy thing that likes to do fun things. Like if there was a giant cookie, they would try to steal it. A kid also does bad things (sometimes) and they also want to drive and that's all." —Boy, age 7

"A kid likes when you play, have fun, do stuff nice and play." —Girl, age 5

"A kid is to be happy." —Boy, age 8

"Like a young person, someone who still goes to school. Under 18 or when you stop growing." —Girl, age 12

"It's hard to explain! A young person without brains that needs to learn. Someone who likes playing, but you can have kid traits when you're an adult." —Girl, age 10

"Kids learn. Grown ups can be kids, too, if they're learning." —Girl, age 6

Figure 1.1 Advice from the experts

These definitions are gold—not because they're precise, but because they are honest. They reveal the thread that runs through all kids: a deep sense of possibility, creativity, playfulness, and growth.

Have you ever paused to think about what your definition of a kid is? What would you say if someone asked?

For the purpose of this book, here's the working definition we'll go with:

Kid (n.)—A young human (not a baby goat) who is in the early stages of development. This period includes infancy, early childhood, middle childhood, and adolescence. Kids are characterized by rapid growth, learning, and development—physically, cognitively, emotionally, and socially. They are curious, imaginative, full of energy, and in the process of acquiring the knowledge, skills, and confidence they need to navigate their world. Oh—and they have boundless potential.

A kid is not just a small adult. They're undergoing a period of rapid, astonishing transformation—physically, emotionally, and neurologically. Their brains are building pathways with every experience, every touch, every emotion, every challenge and triumph. They are learning not just facts, but how the world works. They are learning how relationships work. How they work. Kids need room to explore, to mess up, to create, to cry, to climb, to imagine, to rest, to grow, to connect, to play.

Let's protect this. Let's nurture it. Because the story we help write for the kids in our lives matters.

How Childhood Has Changed

Childhood used to be simple. After school and on weekends, kids spilled out into their neighborhoods to play. It didn't matter what the game was. It didn't matter who was there—big kids, little kids, boys, girls, kids from different backgrounds—everyone played. Some games had rules all the kids knew, some were made up on the spot. The older kids helped the younger ones, and the younger kids did everything they could to keep up. There is no question that childhood looks different today. We now live in an era of scheduled playdates and overbooked calendars filled with structured activities—soccer practice, piano lessons, travel leagues, tutoring sessions, enrichment classes. Family time is shrinking, and connection is fading into the background of our chaos. When kids do get downtime, it's often filled with screens—video games, TV, YouTube, and endless scrolling. Meanwhile, formal education starts earlier and earlier. Kindergarten is the new first grade, preschool is the new kindergarten, and some kids are enrolled in structured learning as young as two years old.

Even play isn't really play anymore. It's organized by adults, structured by rules, and controlled by an underlying need to keep everything safe, clean, and predictable.

Figure 1.2 Over-structuring childhood may keep them clean, but it costs them their creativity, their imagination, and their magic.

What is this difference doing to our kids? It's creating less exploration. Less risk-taking. Less creativity, curiosity, and imagination. Less freedom to figure things out—to problem solve, to negotiate, to adapt. The very experiences that once helped kids grow—physically, cognitively, socially—are vanishing.

And the consequences? They're impossible to ignore.

We have lost our way, and for our children's sake, we don't just need to find our way back—we need to build a better path forward.

Times Are Crazy

We are in a CRAZY time. (I know people have said that at different points in history, but seriously, this time it's true.) We are living through a historically critical moment, especially when it comes to our children. Suicide is now the second leading cause of death for kids ages ten to twenty-four—and the leading cause of death for fourteen- and fifteen-year-olds.[1] Developmental and learning disabilities are not only at an all-time high—they're still rising. Mental health issues among children (and adults) continue to climb. The United States ranks among the lowest worldwide in literacy, numeracy, and problem solving in technology-rich environments. Teachers are leaving education at an alarming rate of 8 percent per year. School attendance is declining. Funding for schools is uncertain. Social programs are being cut. College graduates are struggling to find their place in the world. Parents don't trust schools. Schools don't trust parents. Like I said—crazy times.

The numbers speak for themselves.[2] Some argue these numbers simply reflect better diagnostic tools. And while it's true that criteria and awareness have improved, that statement is not only not the full story, but also blatantly not true. Many of the children now diagnosed with autism or other disabilities may have carried different diagnoses in the past, but looking at the big picture, childhood developmental disabilities as a whole are on the rise. The reality is supported by research, by statistics, and by the daily experience of educators: We are seeing a dramatic, measurable rise in developmental differences and learning challenges. Teachers who've been in classrooms for decades say it plainly: "Kids are different than they used to be." "They're struggling with basic skills." "They're more physically delayed." "They can't sit still." "They're constantly distracted." "Many of my students can't even throw or catch."

Looking at **the Numbers**

1 in 6 Kids are Diagnosed with a Developmental Disability

384 %

Increase in prevalence of Autism Spectrum Disorder from 2000 and over **3000%** increase from **1980**

1 in 31

children are diagnosed with Autism Spectrum Disorder
1 in 20 Boys

1 in 9 with ADHD

In California, 1 in 22 children and 1 in 12.5 boys have **ASD** (Autism Spectrum Disorder)

1 in 5

Kids are diagnosed with a mental, emotional or behavioral health condition

SUICIDE is the **2****ND**

Leading cause of death for kids 10-24 yo and number one for 14 and 15 yo.

***According to the US Center for Disease Control and Prevention (CDC)

Figure 1.3 A look at the numbers

And here's where it gets even more challenging. The support systems within schools—special education staff, school psychologists, counselors, mental health professionals—are completely overwhelmed. They're doing everything they can, but they can't keep up with the rising needs. And while they are doing their best, they're doing it largely on their own—without the resources, training, or capacity to meet every need in the room. As a result, many general education teachers are left to support students with clear and significant needs who haven't yet been formally identified or evaluated.

This doesn't just affect the students who are struggling. It also means that students who are typical, average, or even exceptional are often overlooked. In a system that is stretched too thin, no one is getting what they need. The current structure of education simply cannot support the current state of our children. And yet—education is still a powerful place to begin. Why? It's simple: Education is the foundation of growth. As Nelson Mandela once said, "Education is the most powerful tool you can use to change the world."

When we talk about what threatens childhood, education sits at the center—not as the root cause, but as the greatest opportunity. Because when we truly understand how children grow and learn, we can design environments that support their development. We can build systems grounded in connection, curiosity, and compassion—systems that don't just serve some children, but all children.

Think back for a minute. Has our education system ever truly been where it needed to be? Did it prepare us for the world we were entering, or did it fall short? Did your education shape your success—or did you succeed despite it? Did school prepare you for the "real world," or did you have to unlearn before you could thrive? I've asked these questions to many people, and I rarely hear stories of triumph rooted in test scores or curriculum standards. Instead, people often share stories about the adults (whether teacher, coach, parent, etc.) who made a difference, the moments of real-world learning, "overcoming" their schooling, or the times someone paused long enough to see something in them they hadn't seen in themselves. This isn't about nostalgia or returning to the "good old days" of education. It's about recognizing that the system has long had shortcomings—and now, those gaps have widened into chasms. We're not aiming to revert to a past model; we're striving to learn from its persistent flaws and reimagine a better future.

We Didn't Fix It—We Made It More Broken

In our attempt to repair the consequences of an over-structured, disconnected childhood, we didn't fix it—we made it even more broken. Our previous efforts to address these challenges have often resulted in doubling down on outdated methods. Instead of embracing creativity and play, we leaned into standardization and testing. In trying to fix the system, we inadvertently made it more rigid and less responsive to the needs of our children. Rather than recognizing that children need more play, movement, creativity, and time to develop naturally,[3] we doubled down on the very elements that were causing harm. We raised academic stakes, started structured learning even earlier, and pushed out the remnants of unstructured childhood. When children inevitably struggled, the response was to push them harder, assign more homework, and send them to tutoring.

We have constructed an education system on false premises and are now witnessing its collapse in real-time. The evidence is all around us: missed developmental milestones, declining literacy and numeracy rates, escalating mental health issues, and an overwhelming number of children struggling to keep up.[4] The system is failing them—not the other way around. A quick look at the Finnish education system, often hailed as one of the best in the world, shows us a different approach. In Finland, childhood is not rushed—it is honored. According to Pasi Sahlberg, author of *Finnish Lessons 3.0*[5], formal schooling doesn't begin until the age of eight. Before that, childhood is centered around family bonding, play, exploration, and connection. Their education system prioritizes developmental milestones, not standardized assessments. Students are seen as individuals, not as test scores. Finland shows us that an education model that celebrates childhood, values individuality, and aligns with natural development is not only possible—it works.

In contrast, the US has increased academic rigor and standards without a foundational understanding of child development and learning. Initiatives like Common Core have been implemented without adequately considering how children grow and absorb information. And then we wonder why the system isn't working.

The late Sir Ken Robinson captured this dilemma in his renowned TED Talk, "Do Schools Kill Creativity?"[6] He stated, "All kids have tremendous talents, and we squander them quite ruthlessly." Robinson highlighted an academic hierarchy that neglects the needs of the child, the individual, and basic developmental science. Our modern education system remains rooted in the Industrial Revolution's demands—designed to produce compliant workers, not curious thinkers.

He further observed, "Every education system on earth has the same hierarchy of subjects… at the top are mathematics and languages, then the humanities, and then the arts… As children grow up, we start to educate them from the neck up and slightly to one side." This approach has effectively removed the body and senses from the learning process, despite the brain's need for full-body engagement to truly absorb information.

We see this pattern extending beyond education and into youth sports. Gone are the days of spontaneous games at the park; now, children are funneled into highly structured leagues and specialized training from as early as preschool. Their movements are no longer natural but trained—designed for performance rather than development. Yet, parents feel compelled to enroll them because that's where the children are. Free play has been replaced with organized competition.

And then there are the Arts, our most fundamental form of human expression and connection, which have been relegated to electives— treated as extras rather than essentials. Yet, they engage our senses, stimulate cognitive growth, and foster deep emotional connections. They are the universal language of humanity. Ignoring the overwhelming research supporting their critical role in learning and development is a disservice to our children.[7]

We cannot afford to wait for policymakers or institutions to rectify this. While systemic change is necessary, we don't need permission to do what's right for our kids. We don't have that kind of time. We must start now—in our homes, classrooms, and communities. By applying what research, experience, and common sense tell us, we can begin to make a difference.

The answers are here. The solutions exist. But it will require an open mind, a paradigm shift, and a measure of bravery to break the cycle.

The Hope

I hope I haven't scared you—too much. If I have, I hope I've also ignited a fire within you. A fire that fuels a burning desire to be part of the change. Let's face it: Childhood is at risk. And at this point, you're either part of the problem or part of the solution. The truth is, there is hope. There is a way forward. And there are already people fighting for it. A growing grassroots movement is rising to meet this moment.

All true revolutionary change starts at the grassroots level—so welcome to the revolution! By taking the time to read this book, to educate yourself, and to apply what you learn, you are standing up for our future. And not just in theory—in action. We need you. Because the more people who join this movement, the faster change will come and the stronger it will be. As you continue this journey, you'll see that we are not alone. In fact, we are part of a vast and growing community, working together for a better education system, a better childhood, and ultimately, a better future for all of us.

Change doesn't happen overnight. But it does happen when enough of us refuse to sit still and wait for someone else to fix what's broken. But how do we begin?

2

The Quest for Magic and Rediscovery of Childhood

"The world is full of magic things, patiently waiting for our senses to grow sharper."

—W.B. Yeats

Do you believe in magic?

I don't mean magic involving potions or wands. I mean the amazing light show of the aurora borealis, the vibrant hues of a sunrise, or the miraculous birth of a child. Magic is all around us—if we take the time to notice.

For a child, this magic is even more real. They see and feel it in countless ways, and they are intrinsically connected to it. In our home, *magic* has always been an important word. I've told my children since they were little that they were born with **Kid Magic**. I explained that their magic lives deep within them, and their responsibility is to discover it, nurture it, and use it to positively impact the world around them. This lesson has extended beyond my family to my students—and, truthfully, to myself.

Initially, it was innocent and fun. My oldest believed he had "electrical powers" because he could "make" the lights flicker in our home (our house is over one hundred years old). My middle child claimed he could communicate with animals. As they've grown, their understanding has evolved and they are able to zero in on their own true magic. Our youngest channels his creativity into building and art that brings joy to others. Our oldest, an aspiring chef, spreads happiness through his culinary creations. Our middle child, a natural problem solver, applies his playful energy and determination across all areas of his life.

What is your Kid Magic?

Why start with magic? Because it's crucial. Every child possesses incredible, boundless potential. Yet, our educational model often celebrates only one form of intelligence, setting it as the benchmark for all achievement. By recognizing and nurturing the unique magic within each child, we can help them grow into their full potential. We can move away from arbitrary universal standards that make children feel inferior if their magic doesn't align with society's narrow view of "achievement."

"Everybody is a genius. But if you judge a fish by its ability to climb a tree, it will live its whole life believing that it is stupid."

—Albert Einstein[8]

The quest for magic isn't a fantasy; it's the next step in our "once upon a time." The magic is there, and as adults and caretakers of these beautiful, tiny humans, we are entrusted with the task of helping them discover their magic—through play, imagination, creativity, and curiosity. We are responsible for helping their Kid Magic grow.

As our quest for magic continues, it seems only natural to use it as both a tool and a theme for the next step in our journey. Welcome to M.A.G.I.C.—an acronym to guide us in supporting children's unique gifts:

M
Meet the Child Where They Are.

Begin by understanding the child's current emotional, physical, and developmental state. Recognize their unique situations, challenges, and abilities so you can connect with them judgment free, on their level— wherever that may be.

A
Assess Developmental Needs.

Observe and evaluate the child's specific needs, including social skills, physical development, and emotional well-being. Identify any other areas where they may need support. Focus on developmental standards rather than solely academic ones, and seek support if you're unfamiliar with typical development.

G
Guide Using Whole-Body Strategies.

Engage the child's entire body and mind through activities that incorporate movement, play, and hands-on learning. Pay particular attention to areas needing additional support while highlighting their unique strengths.

I
Incorporate Strategies into the Child's Program
Based on Individual Assessments.

Customize the child's learning or development plan by integrating strategies that work best for them. This ensures that the support they receive is tailored to their specific needs.

C

Create a Nurturing Environment that Highlights the Magic in Each Child.

Build a supportive, loving, and positive space where the child feels connected, valued, and appreciated. Such an environment enables the child to thrive and allows their unique qualities to shine and grow.

Figure 2.1 The Magic Model

Utilizing the M.A.G.I.C. Model to discover and grow their Kid Magic is poetic, easy to remember, and, well, kind of fun! Throughout this guide, I will share information, inspiration, and strategies to help you initiate the process of transforming at least one (but hopefully many) young lives. We'll delve into child development and the significance of childhood in that process. Moreover, while celebrating each child's magic, we'll also learn to recognize when development is interrupted or atypical, ensuring that every child has access to the appropriate resources to maximize their potential while preserving their magical gift.

What does childhood have to do with learning?

Well… EVERYTHING!

Childhood is learning. It's not just a stage of life—it's the engine of development. Have you ever stopped to think about how kids actually learn? Sure, we adults teach, model, and guide them. But in our absence, would they stop learning?

Not a chance.

I hate to burst your grown-up bubble, but even children who never attend school or receive any "formal" education will still learn. They'll learn to survive, to adapt, to communicate, to navigate their environment—whatever that environment may be. Because kids are wired to learn. It's built in. They learn by observing, experimenting, making mistakes, trying again, exploring, engaging their senses, and simply living. They don't need a midterm exam to figure out how to crawl, walk, eat, or speak. There's no pop quiz for jumping in puddles.

As a mom of three boys, I can confirm that my kids mastered the science of gravity before they turned two—the proof is in the pudding… that I cleaned up from the floor, repeatedly, along with everything else they threw from their high chair.

Learning happens through engagement with the world around us. And here's the fascinating part: When kids experience something new, their brains change. Novel experiences help form new neurological pathways—tiny connections between neurons that lay the foundation for all future learning. At first, a pathway is like a narrow trail through the woods—there, but not well-traveled. The more a child repeats that experience, the more that trail gets used. Eventually, that footpath becomes a road. And if it's repeated with enough frequency, emotional relevance, and context, it becomes a superhighway.

This ability of the brain to reorganize, grow, and adapt by creating new connections is called neuroplasticity. Childhood is the golden window where this ability is most powerful. What starts as wobbly and awkward (like a toddler taking their first step) can, over time, become automatic and effortless—like that same child running and jumping through fields by preschool.[9]

"Scientists have discovered that it takes approximately 400 repetitions to create a new synapse in the brain, unless it's done in play, in which case it only takes 10–20 repetitions."—Dr. Karyn Purvis (Director of Texas Christian University's Child Developmental Centre)

Play isn't just fun. It's rocket fuel for the brain. It combines several of the most powerful elements needed for real learning: novelty, emotional connection, repetition, multisensory input, and meaningful context. Novelty—something new or unexpected—is especially important because it captures attention. Novelty triggers the brain's natural curiosity, and with it, the release of **dopamine**—a neurotransmitter that boosts motivation and reinforces memory. That's why kids learn so much when they're excited, playful, or genuinely curious. They're not just memorizing— they're living the learning.

Play also naturally involves repetition—because when kids enjoy something, they want to do it again and again. And unlike rote memorization, this kind of repetition happens in an emotionally rich, joyful state. On top of that, play often engages multiple senses—what kids see, hear, touch, smell, and even how they move their bodies. This lights up several areas of the brain at once, strengthening the neural pathways involved. Add to that a meaningful context (something that makes sense to them or feels important), and the brain begins making connections between the new experience and what it already knows. The more connections it makes— emotional, sensory, contextual, experiential—the more "hooks" there are to anchor that memory and make it easier to retrieve later. This is how deep, lasting learning is built—not through repetition alone, but through experiences that are engaging, rich, and memorable.[10]

But let's be clear: Not all repetition is created equal. The kind of repetition that leads to superhighways is meaningful, emotionally engaging, and contextually relevant. Repetition without novelty—like cramming flashcards or memorizing facts for a test—might get something into short-term memory, but it doesn't tend to stick. That kind of repetition is often emotionally flat, or worse, stressful. And when stress enters the picture, another chemical shows up: **cortisol**. It interferes with memory formation, reduces the brain's ability to build flexible pathways, and can make learning feel tedious or even painful. So while forced repetition might result in better test scores, it rarely builds the kind of durable, flexible understanding that real learning requires. You can ace a test and still forget everything a week later.

And this is exactly where we begin to see the difference between schooling and learning. Schooling often leans heavily on the memorization of facts, procedures, and correct answers—typically aimed at short-term performance, like passing a test. But learning—real, lasting learning—happens when new ideas are actively constructed through experience, curiosity, and connection. A child might "know" something well enough to choose the right answer on a multiple-choice exam, but unless that knowledge has been felt, lived, explored, or made personally meaningful, it's unlikely to be deeply understood or remembered. The brain is efficient—if it doesn't see a reason to hold onto information, it clears it out to make space. In other words, it ends up in the memory dump.

I saw this firsthand when I asked my middle schooler what he learned in social studies in the previous year. His response? "I did really good—I got at least one hundred on every test."

I followed up: "That's great! But what did you learn?"

He paused. "Umm… I don't remember. But I got all A's!"

But then I asked, "Do you remember the fourth grade lesson on taxation without representation?"

Suddenly, his eyes lit up. "Yes! My teacher gave us all Skittles. Then she made one kid the king, and we had to give our Skittles to the king. At the end, the king got to eat ALL of them… we didn't get them back!"

I laughed. "So, what does taxation without representation mean?"

He launched into a full explanation—how the colonies felt, what it led to, how it impacted the revolution. That memory had stuck.

Not because he memorized it. But because he lived it. Felt it. Got emotionally robbed of his Skittles. And that emotional connection made the concept stick.[11]

So how do we avoid the memory dump? We give the brain more "hooks." For example, if you try to explain to a young child how to ride a bike, you may say something like, "Sit on the seat, keep your balance, pedal forward, steer where you want to go, and brake when you want to stop." You can ask the child to study the steps and repeat them back to you until they can ace a written exam on bike riding 101, but does that mean they have learned to ride a bike? No—not until they hop on, have to feel for their balance, fall off a few times, feel the wind in their face, hear the clicking of the chain, understand how hard they have to pedal uphill vs. downhill, and can hop on a bike after not riding it for ten years, did they truly learn how to ride a bike.[12] The multiple senses in combination with the emotional connections, such as freedom, independence, or biking with your friends to get pizza, create a deeper connection with more "hooks" or anchors. That combination of multiple senses and emotional connection acts like glue, binding the memory more deeply into long-term memory and thus, we have REAL learning.[13]

This is why creating rich, meaningful, and playful learning environments matters—because the brain doesn't store facts in neat little folders alphabetized in a mental library. Memories aren't filed away in some numerical order. They're formed through webs of connection—anchored to sensory experiences, emotions, context, and prior knowledge. The more meaningful those connections, the more "hooks" the brain has to retrieve that memory later—especially when it matters.

When learning is meaningful or relatable, the brain doesn't just process isolated facts; it connects that learning to a broader network of experiences, emotions, and knowledge. For example, learning about geometry through worksheets might teach definitions. But learning about angles and shapes while building a fort outside? That involves spatial reasoning, problem solving, teamwork, creativity, movement, and hands-on engagement. That's not just learning—it's superhighway construction.

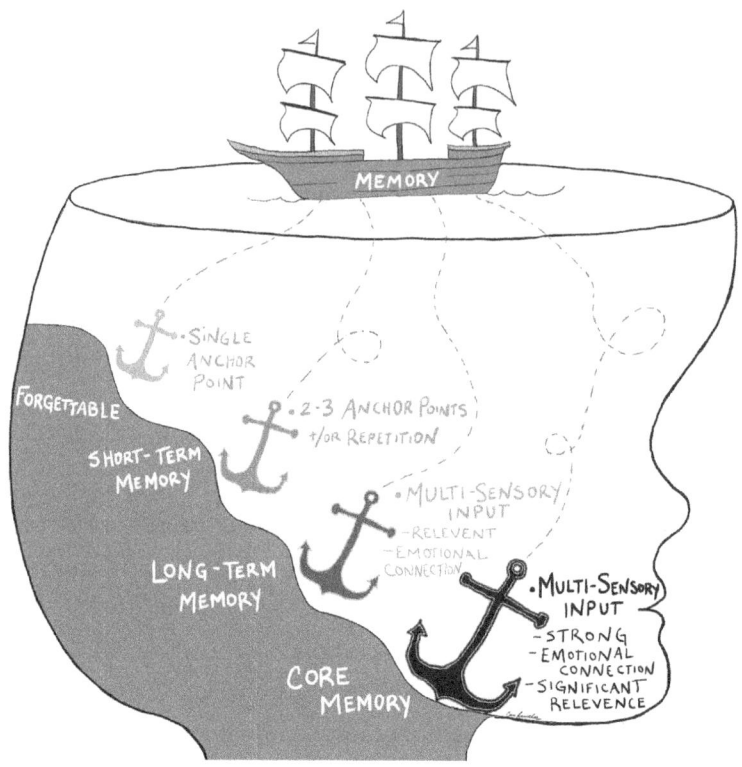

Figure 2.2 This illustration demonstrates how memories are more effectively stored when anchored by multiple points. A single sensory input may fade quickly, while multisensory experiences with emotional relevance create stronger anchor points that secure information into long-term and core memory.

So here's the heart of the message: Children don't need school to learn—it happens through living. But this does NOT mean that schooling isn't necessary (obviously, or this book would be useless). It just means that our approach and understanding of the purpose of education is even MORE important. How we teach and how we do "formal education" can be significantly enhanced by understanding how a child's developing brain works.

If we remember the importance of helping each kid discover their Kid Magic, we can start with the very important element of meeting each child where they are—the "M" in our M.A.G.I.C. Model.

Part II

Using the M.A.G.I.C. Model to Help Our Children

3

Meet the Child Where They Are

"See the child before you, not the one in your mind."

—Dr. Crystal T. Miller

When I say, "meet the child where they are," I'm not talking about finding them in the hallway or bumping into them in art class. I mean getting to know them—who they really are. Start by truly connecting and understanding where the child is in their emotional, physical, social, and developmental journey. This means recognizing their unique situation, challenges, and abilities, without any preconceived notions or judgments. They could have loads of baggage, or not. Maybe they've had a tough morning, or maybe they're bubbling over with excitement about something you don't even know about yet. Whatever their state, meet them there—on their level, with openness and curiosity. It's not about where you think they should be (we'll get to that in the "A" section); it's about honoring where they are in this moment.[14]

Seek to understand their quirky little personalities—what lights them up and what makes them nervous. Learn their passions, their fears, those one-of-a-kind traits that make them uniquely them. You need to know their triggers, their "safe space," and how they react when the going gets tough. Dig deeper than just academics—meet them emotionally, socially, and artistically.[15]

Each child is a blend of their home life, their social world, and their experiences—including what happened last school year (which could have been amazing, or not so much). We are getting to know them as a whole child—on all levels—so we can create a caring and trusting human connection. Sure, we can take in information from previous teachers and staff, academic performance, parental concerns, or reports. But at this point, we are just learning about them. We are taking in the information without judgment and adding in our own observations to create a real-time picture of our starting point.

This is not the part where we label them as "a typical third grader" or a "normal fifth grader." We are not assessing if they are "neurotypical" or "neurodiverse." This is the part where we simply get to know the child as they are. *See the child before you, not the one in your mind.*[16]

We do need to talk about developmental milestones and we do

have academic goals to hit by the end of the year. I get it. But before we jump ahead, we need to take a breath and a step back. Because here's the truth: If you don't meet the child where they are—if you don't genuinely see them and make a connection—those milestones and goals become much harder to achieve. Real learning only happens when a child is truly engaged, and true engagement begins with genuine human connection. That's where the magic is.

By seeing the child as they are right now, you create space for trust, connection, and the kind of growth that can't be forced or rushed. It's the foundation for everything else. Only once you've met them where they are can you guide them forward, encouraging them to stretch, learn, and achieve in ways that feel both possible and exciting. And when that connection is made and you feel that spark, the magic follows right behind.[17]

Human Connection

Let's talk more about that human connection part. In a time when technology has us more connected than ever, we live in a society that is more disconnected with the people around us (and nature) than ever before. I had a middle schooler say to me, "I don't even know what I need school for. I can just Google anything I need to know." Our students are not looking to us for information the same way we may have looked to our teachers or adults in our life. But they still need us. Even though technology has hijacked many of our opportunities, their hearts still yearn for human connection. Not the kind you get through social media and text messaging, but the kind you get through eye contact, high fives, a listening ear, a pat on the back, a warm hug, and even birthday punches. The kind of connection that builds trust and rapport. They need the kind of human relationship created when you listen to their fears, their concerns, and their passions and interests.[18]

I recently enjoyed a TED Talk about the importance of human connection for child development. It was given by a brilliant young speaker, and by young, I mean seven-year-old Molly Wright.[19] If you have not had the opportunity to hear Molly school all of us adults in brain science, well, you are missing out! Molly speaks about how our brain develops faster in our early years than any other time in life. She talks about the importance of human connection early and often. Molly highlights the fact that children are hard-wired to seek meaningful connections and that talking and playing with kids is essential for their brain development and laying the foundation for cognitive and social development.

It is important to show genuine interest in the things that interest them, even if you don't have any interest. It has always been hard for me to engage in conversations about *Fortnite*, *Minecraft*, and anything having to do with video games and YouTubers. I would always redirect the conversation to, "What did you do outside?" or "What kind of things did you do with friends or family?" I thought I was doing the right thing by encouraging connection and outdoor play instead of video games. What I was missing is that I closed off access to a trusting relationship by creating a barrier to things that truly interested them and unknowingly let them know they were being judged for their interests. I noticed where I had made my mistake when I allowed my students (and then my own children) to freely tell me all about the gaming world and showed genuine interest, asked good questions, and remembered to bring it up during the next conversation. I cannot positively influence anyone if I haven't created the trusting relationship. It was a true turning point for me. And I actually learned a thing or two about their world and became genuinely interested and fascinated with aspects I was previously unaware of.[20]

It is also important to share with them. Trust is a two-way street. How do we expect them to trust us if we don't show our kids we trust them? Kids get excited when you tell them about you. Share your favorite color, your sports team, your hobbies, your family. Tell them about your weekend, your vacation, or that one time you accidentally wore two different shoes to work. Let them in on your fear of spiders or the dark and how you manage the best you can.

My children tell me stories about their favorite teachers all the time. It is those teachers that make them want to go to school and learn.[21] They never say, "Wow, I really love the way my teacher taught me that lesson." They typically say, "My teacher's favorite color is pink," "We have to get that for my teacher; she loves cats," "Mom, don't change the channel. This is my teacher's favorite team—she loves Penn State," "My teacher loves Harry Potter, just like you, Mom, but she is a Ravenclaw!" My kids will never forget going to their teacher's wedding and seeing the things they made proudly displayed.

We are social beings, from the moment we are born. It is innate; it's for survival. Babies are born looking for connection through eye contact, touch, and sound. Research shows that babies recognize the sound of their mama's voice at birth (and even in the womb). The positive relationships with the grown-ups in their lives are essential to the brain development of our children.[22] Some of the challenges we are overcoming as a society include recognizing that these relationships are not just important, but that they are one of the most important things—they are foundational to everything!

Seeing the Magic in Them

Before we move on to the "A" in the M.A.G.I.C. framework— Assessment—I want to pause and shine a light on one more dimension of "Meet them where they are." Because sometimes—actually, more often than not—we are able to see something in someone before they are able to see it in themselves.

Has anyone ever pointed out something wonderful about you— something you hadn't even noticed yet? A strength, a spark, a piece of your potential that had been there all along, just waiting for someone else to see it?

Two people who had an enormous influence on my life were my high school drama director, Mr. David Kramer, and our choreographer, Miss Jean. But the story actually begins earlier, back in sixth grade, when auditions were announced for the children's chorus in the high school production of *Joseph and the Amazing Technicolor Dreamcoat*.

At that time, I was quiet, small, and incredibly shy. I was definitely not a theater kid. I wanted absolutely nothing to do with the spotlight. So when my dad mentioned the auditions, I responded immediately: "Nope. Drama is not my thing."

But then he did something that was completely out of character—he asked me to do it anyway. Just this once. For him. He told me that *Joseph* was his and my grandma's favorite musical, and that it would mean a lot to him. My dad rarely asked me for anything. So... I auditioned.

I sang "Happy Birthday" to Mr. Kramer, who also happened to be my third-grade music teacher. Though tryouts were required, no one was ever cut. Mr. Kramer always made it clear that there was room for everyone. And that wasn't just a nice sentiment—he meant it. He held us all to high expectations and less than your best was not tolerated. He made sure we knew that every role, whether lead or ensemble, stage crew or lighting, mattered equally. We were all responsible for helping build the set, and later, breaking it down. Everyone pitched in. Everyone belonged. He taught us character, grit, teamwork, and responsibility. He empowered us and pushed us to grow.

That first show lit a spark in me. I joined the children's chorus that year, and I stayed in theater through all of high school—as did my siblings. Not because I had suddenly become a "theater person," but because something inside of me had been awakened. Each production helped me discover more of who I was. I was never a lead (honestly, I'd be cast as ensemble in a one-person show), but it didn't matter. I found my voice. I became comfortable in my own skin. I found confidence on that stage.

Mr. Kramer and Miss Jean were a perfect pair—sugar and spice. Kind and supportive, but with extremely high expectations. Miss Jean didn't just teach us to dance with our bodies—she taught us to dance with our hearts, our expressions, and our whole selves.

In our small district, our productions regularly involved over one hundred students. Most of us didn't go on to careers in the performing arts, but we all carried the lessons with us. We learned to show up for something bigger than ourselves. We learned that every role matters in a production—and in life. We learned to see and value the people behind the scenes. We learned that being part of something meaningful helps you discover things you didn't know were inside you.

Years later, I asked my dad why he had pushed me so hard to audition. He smiled and said, "Yes, it was Grandma's and my favorite show—but really, I saw something in you. Something that hadn't yet surfaced. And I believed that if it had the chance to come out, you could use it to help people." Mr. Kramer and Miss Jean took it from there. In fact, what I am doing today can to some degree be traced back to that divergent point in my life.

I've been incredibly fortunate. The grown-ups in my life helped me discover and develop a kind of magic I didn't know I had. And now, I get to do the same for others. I get to be the one who notices the spark, even when it's buried under layers of doubt, distraction, or difficulty.

It takes patience. It takes the ability to look past labels and judgments and see the whole child. But when you practice this kind of seeing—when you truly meet a child where they are—you step into the role of a magic-maker.

Let me share one more story.

I was working with a sixth-grade girl in physical therapy. She had been diagnosed with ADHD, and she struggled with motor coordination, sensory processing, and frequent injuries—including falling down the school stairs twice. She was often clumsy and embarrassed, but she always showed up and tried. Still, there was a tone of defeat beneath her efforts. You could hear it in her voice when she said things like, "I know I'm different... I know I'm limited because of my disability."

This time, I decided to respond differently. I looked her in the eyes and said, "Sweetheart, you don't have a disability—you have a superpower. And I'm not here to 'fix' you. I'm here to help you learn how to control your superpower."

Something shifted immediately. We talked about the unique abilities she had and how building strength in other areas could help her harness her natural gifts. After that conversation, everything changed. She became more engaged. She started walking taller—literally and figuratively. She began taking on more responsibilities at home. Her confidence grew. And her mom even called me later to share just how much her daughter's outlook on life had transformed.

In that moment, I got to witness a miracle… a real-time transformation sparked by human connection. And I discovered one of my own superpowers: helping others find their Kid Magic.

"What do you want to be when you grow up?"

I needed this section to be separate for an important reason. Sometimes things we are so accustomed to saying or a way of thinking can turn out to be the mindset that is the exact challenge we are working to overcome. Let's start with something that seems so simple, so benign. Have you ever heard or ever asked your students or children, "What do you want to be when you grow up?"

I was giving a presentation to group of middle school kids—yup, tiny me and a whole room full of seventh and eighth graders (for those who don't know me, I stand at a whopping 4 feet, 11.5 inches tall). It was a fun presentation, and I was excited to get into it. I started off with what I thought to be a super simple slide that read: "You've heard at least 1000 times, 'What do you want to be when you grow up?', but who asks, 'Who are you now?'" The reaction I received not only startled me, but it also changed me! The room FULL of twelve- and thirteen-year-old students threw their fists in the air and screamed, "NOBODY!" Wow! Did that hit you in the center of your heart? Well, it sure hit me!

Whether true or not, these kids truly felt that nobody cared about who they are, only about what they would become. How do you even know what you will become if you don't know who you are? This pivotal experience in my life is the ENTIRE reason for this whole chapter; it is the reason behind the "M" in the M.A.G.I.C.

Meet the Child Where They Are. Ask them who they are now and truly listen to the answer. I now do this not only with my own children, regularly, but with every single student and with the adults I teach in my professional development courses. At one of my recent workshops, we started with this question as an activity where everyone took a minute or two to write down who they are. The result? A shift in course to a half-hour group therapy session as one of the teachers broke down in tears, sharing that no one has asked her who she is and she truly doesn't know anymore. It was one of the most heartbreaking but beautiful human experiences to watch every other person in the room come hug her and engage in meaningful human connection. Fortunately for all of us, this was day one of a two-day workshop, and we were all blessed with the beneficial experience of seeing her come in the next session expressing how that moment had changed her life!

It is a gift to work with children, but with that gift comes tremendous responsibility. Helping others discover the magic inside themselves, taking the time to ask who they are (not what they will be), and truly meeting the child where they are is step one in changing the actual world!

4

Assess Developmental Needs

"The child must know that he is a miracle, that since the beginning
of the world there hasn't been, and until the end of the world
there will not be, another child like him."

—Pablo Casals

Now that I have you all emotional and in a state of personal reflection, it's time to shift gears and dive into the "A" in the M.A.G.I.C. framework: Assessing developmental needs. Before we can assess developmental needs, though, we need to understand development itself. So let's begin at, well, the beginning.

I know I said that kids are born with boundless potential—and they are—but they're also born extremely vulnerable and dependent for their early years. When I had my oldest son, I'll never forget something his first pediatrician told me: "Nothing you really do matters for the first five years." Fortunately, I had both medical training and common sense on my side. But I often think about the parents who heard that same advice and didn't realize how wrong it was.

In reality, more brain development occurs in the first five years of life than at any other time. If you had a chance to watch seven-year-old Molly Wright's TED Talk, you may remember she highlights that a baby's brain doubles in size during the first year, and by age five, it reaches about 90 percent of its adult volume. While this information is readily available in medical journals and textbooks, it is much more powerful coming from a child. She also outlines the simple but powerful ways grown-ups can support healthy development—advice that might have been helpful for my son's first pediatrician.

So what makes humans so special?

Unlike many other species in the animal kingdom, human babies are born, frankly, pretty helpless. Most other mammals arrive in the world with at least basic survival skills. Take the baby giraffe, for example: Within just a few hours of birth, it's already wobbly but standing, ready to explore the savannah. Meanwhile, human babies are still trying to figure out how to keep their heads from flopping around like little bobbleheads. Why the difference?

It all comes back to the brain. Human brains are extremely complex and enormous relative to body size. Because humans are bipedal (we stand up on two feet), we have small birth canals relative to the head size of our offspring. If we stayed in the womb until our brains were fully developed, well, let's just say labor and delivery would be a much bigger ordeal—and our poor mothers might not be too thrilled about giving birth to toddler-sized infants. So, instead, humans are born early, giving our brains space and time to finish developing outside the womb, in an environment filled with rich sensory and social experiences. In fact, from birth to age six, the brain has a four-fold increase in size, reaching 90 percent of adult volume. Much of that occurs in the first year of life, with the brain growing from 36 percent of adult size at birth to 70 percent of adult size at one year old.[23] Those early years are responsible for creating connections between neurons (specialized cells that make up the brain and nervous system). Each neuron can make connections with more than one thousand other neurons—leading to an estimated 60 trillion neural connections in the adult brain.[24] To put that in perspective, there are more connections in your brain than there are stars in the Milky Way Galaxy (which has an estimated 400 billion stars—so your brain's wiring outnumbers those stars by over two hundred times).

Now, here's a key point: Movement is essential for brain development. In fact, the brain cannot fully develop without coordinated effort from the entire body. Our brains are not just passive sponges soaking up information—they actively wire themselves through movement and interaction with the environment. The majority of that growth that occurs shortly after birth is in the brain's neural connections and creation of neural circuits. Movement and experiences shape the brain's connectivity and circuitry.[25]

However, babies don't have voluntary, coordinated motor control at first. Moving their arms and legs, lifting their heads, and rolling over are huge challenges. To overcome this, babies are born with a set of automatic movement patterns called primitive reflexes. These reflexes are nature's way of getting the developmental ball rolling.

Primitive reflexes help babies perform the basic, repetitive movements that begin to lay the foundation for more complex brain and body development. They form our earliest movement patterns, begin building tiny muscles, and stimulate sensory and motor pathways critical for future learning, behavior, and self-regulation. As the brain matures, these primitive reflexes should gradually be replaced by more complex, voluntary movement patterns. When that transition happens on time, it's a sign that brain development is progressing as expected. However, when primitive reflexes persist beyond infancy—or if they aren't properly integrated—it can be a sign of developmental delay or dysfunction. Early recognition of these signs is important as early intervention can significantly alter a child's developmental path for the better.[26]

So, while it might seem like human babies may be lagging behind compared to baby giraffes and the rest of the animal kingdom, what is actually happening is nature's way of accommodating for how incredibly unique the human mind and body are. Our extended "training period" allows for the development of the most advanced control center known to life on Earth—the human brain.

And while it's an incredible opportunity, it also means that grown-up interactions and influences are not just helpful—they're critical to healthy brain development. No pressure, right? Gaining a basic understanding of what goes into the creation of a kid—and how children transition through the stages of growth—gives us the insight we need to better assess developmental needs.[27] It also helps us recognize when development might be getting off track, and when and where to seek support or intervention.

We are about to dive into a little brain science—not a deep dive, more like a snorkel. This understanding will help us assess our kids' developmental needs, recognize when they are off track, as well as when and where to look for support and assistance.

A Snorkel into Brain Science

Now for a bit of brain science—just a little bit, I promise! We are going to start by breaking the brain up into easy to understand sections; for now, we will talk about three main areas. The concept of "three brains in one" is a fascinating way to understand the layers of complexity in our brain's make-up. It's like thinking of the brain as an onion, with each layer representing a different developmental complexity. Here's a breakdown of these three layers[28]:

The Brainstem (Reptilian Brain): This is the oldest and deepest part of our brain. It is our most primitive area, sitting at the very base and core. It's often called the "lizard brain" because it's similar to the entire brain of reptiles. This brain is all about survival. It connects to the spinal cord and is responsible for life-sustaining automatic processes like heart rate, breathing, blood pressure, swallowing, coughing, and sleeping. It's our autopilot system that keeps us alive without conscious effort. This part of our brain contains areas that are involved in motor control, procedural learning, and habits to help coordinate movements necessary for maintaining routine behavior and is essential for rituals and basic survival functions. It is also made up of a network of neurons that regulates arousal, consciousness, and sleep-wake cycles.

The Limbic System (Mammalian Brain): Surrounding the Reptilian Brain is the limbic system, often referred to as the Mammalian Brain. This part of the brain is what makes mammals social creatures and is a bit more advanced than the Reptilian Brain. The Mammalian Brain brings meaning and connection to life. It is a critical network in the brain that manages our emotions, memories, and certain physiological responses. It's responsible for feelings like love, fear, anger, and pleasure. It's also involved in memory formation and helps us form social bonds. Think of it as the part of the brain that makes us care about our relationships, feel happy when we see someone we love, or get anxious before a big event. It's also where we process rewards and punishments, helping us learn from our experiences. The Mammalian Brain contains the thalamus, which is our switchboard that integrates sensory input and processes it so we can understand and interact with the world around us. It contains our amygdala, which is responsible for our fight-or-flight response, helping us to react to danger. This area also manages emotions, forms memories, and regulates basic needs, creating a complex network that supports both survival and social interactions. The Mammalian Brain adds a layer of emotional depth to our behavior. It's not just about survival—it's about thriving in a social world, forming attachments, interacting with the world around us, and learning from our experiences and environment.

The Neocortex (Human Brain): This is the outermost layer of our brain. This part sets us apart from other animals. The neocortex is where all the high-level thinking happens. It's responsible for language, reasoning, planning, abstract thinking, and moral judgment. This is the part of the brain that allows us to write a novel, solve a complex math problem, or imagine the future. It is where executive function[29] lives and thrives. It is also where we can reflect on our actions, make decisions based on long-term goals, and understand complex social dynamics. This is where creativity and imagination exist with limitless possibilities! For example, when a kid jumps in a cardboard box and blasts off to space or swings a stick around like a magic wand, they are pulling from the area of the brain that makes us human. The Human Brain gives us the ability to think beyond the here and now and to innovate, create, and connect with others on a deep, intellectual level. It allows us to control our more primal instincts and emotions with rational thought and deliberate action.

Disclaimer: This layer does not fully develop until about your mid-twenties (shout out to all the Big Kids with not fully developed brains reading this book)![30]

These three "brains" don't work in isolation—they're constantly interacting. The Reptilian Brain might react first to a perceived threat, but the Mammalian Brain adds an emotional response, and the Human Brain steps in to analyze the situation and make a rational decision and plan for the future.[31]

If we view the brain functionally as a three-story house, we can see how the different floors contribute to the overall running of the house.

I do need to highlight that when the basement and main floor are in "panic mode" due to an emergency or perceived emergency, the door to the upstairs is locked. This means that when we are in a state of fight or flight, we don't really have access to the areas of the brain responsible for critical thinking, sound decision-making, and planning, which can cause chaos in the home. As much as I love the three-story house analogy, it is important to point out that our brains are a constant flow of extremely active neural connections that are like a mini galaxy within the constraints of our head. They are not three distinguished separate areas, but instead an entire intertwined universe of limitless interactions.

The Brain as a 3-Story House
A functional representation of the brain

The Study or Office
This is where your Human Brain functions. It is a place of entellect, imagination, creativity, and critical thinking. This is where we plan for the future, think through and solve problems, assess situations.

The Main Floor
This is where the Mammalian Brain lives. It is where we integrate our senses and emotions. It is where life becomes living. We create meaning, feelings, memories here. It is the main floor of the home where we entertain guests and spend most of our time.

The Basement
This is where our Reptilian Brain (brainstem) lives. This is where we find the things that keep the house functioning at a baseline level. It is where we find the furnace, thermostat, electrical plans, plumbing access, emergency shut offs. For humans it would be breathing, heartrate, temperature regulation, etc.

Figure 4.1 The human brain represented as a 3-story house

Now I want to remind you that as I take you through these early chapters, I am talking only about typical development. I am not talking about circumstances that result in atypical development; we'll touch on that in a bit.

Left vs. Right

We have just broken down development into three distinct but interactive areas of the brain, but I now want to take a minute to discuss laterality of the brain, aka left vs. right brain. Most of us have heard expressions such as, "She is so creative, she must be right-brained" or "He is so logical, he is totally left-brained." While it is true that each hemisphere has a different "personality" or set of skills, no one is truly half brained (at least I hope not)!

If you are familiar with the terms left and right brain, you may be aware that the right brain is credited with being our "big picture" and abstract-thinking side and our left brain is more the detailed, linear, and logical side. Most people have one hemisphere that tends to take the lead. This is called hemispheric dominance, and a slight preference for one side is completely normal. In fact, it's part of what helps us develop unique strengths and learning styles. Your left and right hemispheres interact with each other constantly, helping with communication, language, coordination, motor function, cognitive functions, and even immune function. The interaction of the two hemispheres are extremely important—they balance each other.[32] When one hemisphere is delayed and the other is overactive, the disconnect can be so great that results are serious functional deficits.

Let me share a bit about the characteristics associated with each hemisphere:

Left Brain	Right Brain
Sees the small picture (trees, but not the forest)	Sees the big picture (the forest, but not trees)
Logical or Linear thinking	Understands abstract concepts and ideas
Likes routine, schedules, structure and doesn't like change	Likes new and different things, enjoys change
Mathematical abilities and calculations	Math reasoning
Verbal communication	Nonverbal communication
Fine motor or small muscle control	Gross motor skills and large muscle control
High frequency sounds	Low frequency sounds
Low frequency light	High frequency light
Reading the words (not necessarily the story)	Comprehension (hears the whole story)
Processing information	Interpreting information
Conscious actions	Unconscious actions
Receiving auditory input	Interpreting auditory input
Curious (looking to complete thoughts)	Cautious, safe actions
Impulsive actions	Spatial awareness, interoception
Positive Emotions	Negative Emotions
Immune system activation	Immune system depression, digestion
Pattern recognition	Digestion, sense of taste and smell, social skills

I did not specifically list creativity as a right-sided characteristic for a very important reason. Both "left-brained" and "right-brained" people demonstrate creative ability and creative potential. The left brain is incredible at honing in on the fine details—for example, reading and playing intricate music or drawing beautiful pictures—based on its incredible attention to detail. The right brain is incredible at abstract thinking, bringing forward ideas and thoughts that did not previously exist in reality. Abstract art is a true right brain activity.

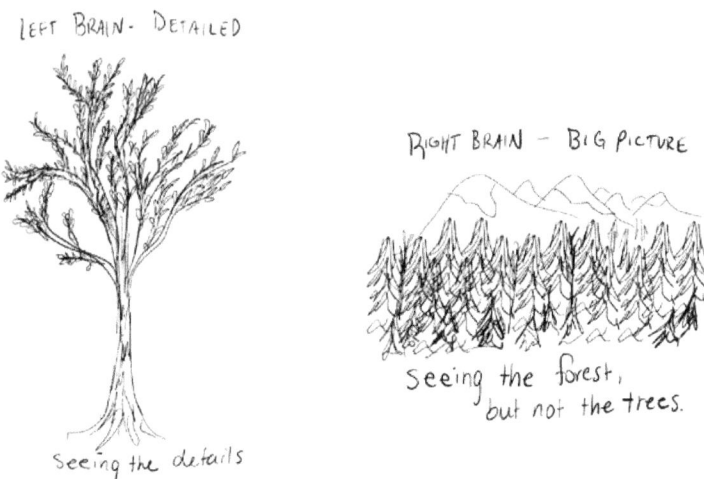

Figure 4.2 The right brain focuses on the big picture, it sees the forest but not the trees. The left brain is more detail oriented.

So, why is all of this important? Well, as I've mentioned before, no one operates with just half a brain—we use both hemispheres. However, when there's a significant dominance on one side of the brain and a corresponding delay or deficiency on the other, it can cause noticeable challenges in childhood. These imbalances can show up in learning, behavior, emotional regulation, and even social development.

One of the leading experts in this area is Dr. Robert Melillo, a world-renowned functional neurologist and pioneer in the field of childhood brain development. He's best known for identifying and explaining what he believes to be the underlying cause of many of the developmental disorders we see today—diagnoses like ADHD, ADD, dyslexia, autism, OCD, ODD, and more. According to Dr. Melillo, these are not separate conditions, but rather different manifestations of one central issue: a condition he calls functional disconnection syndrome (FDS).[33]

In his groundbreaking book, *Disconnected Kids*, Dr. Melillo lays out the concept of FDS in great detail. He explains that rather than being caused by localized brain damage or structural abnormalities, these disorders often stem from a breakdown in communication between the left and right hemispheres of the brain. One side becomes overactive, while the other lags behind. And because the two hemispheres are supposed to work together—like dance partners—this imbalance can disrupt everything from focus and impulse control to emotional processing and academic performance.

A key point Dr. Melillo emphasizes is that the right hemisphere develops first, beginning in the womb and continuing to dominate through early infancy. It's the part of the brain responsible for nonverbal communication, sensory processing, emotional understanding, spatial awareness, and social connection—all of which are foundational in the early stages of development. The left hemisphere doesn't really start to take the lead until around age two, when language, logic, and sequential thinking begin to emerge more strongly. So if something interferes with development in those early right-brain-dominant years—whether it's environmental, neurological, or sensory—it can set the stage for long-term imbalances.

This may help explain why, according to Dr. Melillo, we often see more right hemisphere deficiencies than left. For example, common diagnoses associated with right hemispheric delays are autism spectrum disorder (ASD), attention-deficit/hyperactivity disorder or ADHD (most types), sensory processing disorder, oppositional defiant disorder, and Tourette's, to name a few. As for left hemispheric delays, we see diagnoses such as dyslexia, reading disorders, speech delays, dysgraphia, some forms of learning disorder, and a different form of ADHD. And that's why understanding this early development is so crucial. If we can recognize the signs of hemispheric imbalance early on, we can begin to support the brain in reestablishing balance—through addressing primitive reflexes, targeted movement, sensory engagement, and specific activities that stimulate the weaker side.

We'll dive deeper into this concept later, especially when we talk about what happens when development doesn't follow a "typical" path. But for now, if you're new to this topic or just curious to learn more, do yourself a favor and check out Dr. Robert Melillo's work. *Disconnected Kids* is one of the most helpful and accessible resources out there for understanding the brain, behavior, and how to support children who may be struggling in unseen ways.

In addition to using the left and the right hemispheres to identify imbalances that can affect learning and development, we can also use the left and right hemispheres to identify different learning styles. In her book, *The Dominance Factor: How Knowing Your Dominant Eye, Ear, Brain, Hand & Foot Can Improve Your Learning*, Dr. Carla Hannaford[34] uses brain dominance to help identify thirty-two different dominance profiles, which she describes as the key factor to understanding how we respond and think. By identifying your unique dominance profile, you can better understand the ways in which you think, learn, and respond to different situations. It is a way to help you become the best version of you by gaining an understanding of yourself that helps you perform at your highest level.

Having a better understanding of the interactions between the three main areas of your brain as well as how the left and the right hemispheres interact are foundational in identifying typical and atypical development and can give you insight into what is normal and abnormal and when and where to seek support for your students and children. Let's use this as the foundation for the "A" in M.A.G.I.C., Assess Developmental Needs.

Identify and Address

This is a great time to highlight that development doesn't always go according to plan. Remember when we were chatting about numbers? At the time of writing this book, one in six children are diagnosed with a developmental disability. This means you are pretty much guaranteed to encounter a child who used to struggle or is currently struggling with interruptions or delays in typical development. It may also be an everyday part of your reality, impacting your home, your classroom, your group, your team, etc.

Our "M" is all about meeting the child where they are and celebrating their differences, their individuality, their unique abilities, and their magic. It's about recognizing that each child brings something irreplaceable to the table—whether that's their sense of humor, creativity, problem-solving skills, or other talents that might be waiting to shine. Our "A" section, on the other hand, is about identifying their challenges and struggles as they relate to delays or difficulties in achieving developmental milestones. There seems to be this discussion that we need to either celebrate differences and neurodiversity OR "fix it." In my opinion, that's where we have gone wrong for our children. It is not one or the other; it is and always has been BOTH. We need to celebrate them in addition to identifying their challenges so we can help guide them to be the very best version of themselves. Celebrating a child doesn't mean ignoring the ways they might be struggling, just as recognizing challenges doesn't mean we overlook their gifts and strengths.

Imagine if we viewed every child as a whole, dynamic person, rather than a checklist of strengths and weaknesses. By seeing them as they are—embracing their uniqueness while also addressing areas where they need help—we're not just providing them with support. We're showing them that growth and acceptance can exist together, and that they can be celebrated for exactly who they are while still working toward skills that will empower them.

This balance between celebration and support is at the heart of a truly nurturing environment. It teaches children they don't have to be perfect to be loved or valued. Instead, they see they are worth investing in because every part of them—strengths, quirks, and challenges alike—matters. And for children, this dual focus can be incredibly freeing. They learn they are allowed to be themselves and still aspire to grow. They see they are more than any single diagnosis, any missed milestone, or any particular skill set.

In honoring each child's magic while recognizing areas that may need support, we're actually building resilience. We're creating spaces where children feel safe to try, to fail, to succeed, and to try again, knowing they're supported every step of the way. This approach isn't just good for kids who have developmental challenges; it's good for all children, for every classroom, and for every community. Embracing both celebration and support is how we build an inclusive world that doesn't just tolerate differences but actively values them and builds on them. Ultimately, it's about seeing that every child deserves the chance to be seen, celebrated, and supported in becoming their best selves.

It is important to note that these children are very well aware they are struggling; they just may not know why. Kids are also incredibly good at noticing when grown-ups are not being honest or sincere. Telling them they are perfect and ignoring their struggles can often cause more stress and anxiety than simply telling them they are loved and that you can address their challenges and struggles together.

So, now it is only a matter of what and how.

The Ripple Effect

When I speak of the what and the how, I'm referring to two critical steps in supporting a child's development: what are their delays or struggles and how we can address them. Identifying the "what" is about observation— seeing the areas where a child may not be meeting expectations or is facing challenges. Addressing the "how" is about action—determining what tools, strategies, or interventions can support their progress and when it is time to seek outside help.

Understanding both the "what" and the "how" is so essential. When we know what to look for, we can take action to support the child effectively. Missing milestones is our first clue that a child is out of sync. Early recognition is the first step toward early intervention, which has the potential to change the trajectory of a child's development in profound ways. By addressing these foundational needs, we're not just solving immediate challenges; we're building the framework for long-term growth, resilience, and success.

To guide you in this process, I've included a chart of developmental milestones[35] at the end of this book. This chart should be used as a reference for understanding what "typical" development looks like at different stages. It should serve as a helpful map to set realistic expectations and identify when something might be "off track." It can also shed light on potential gaps in curriculum design that may not align with where children are developmentally, allowing you to better adapt to their needs.

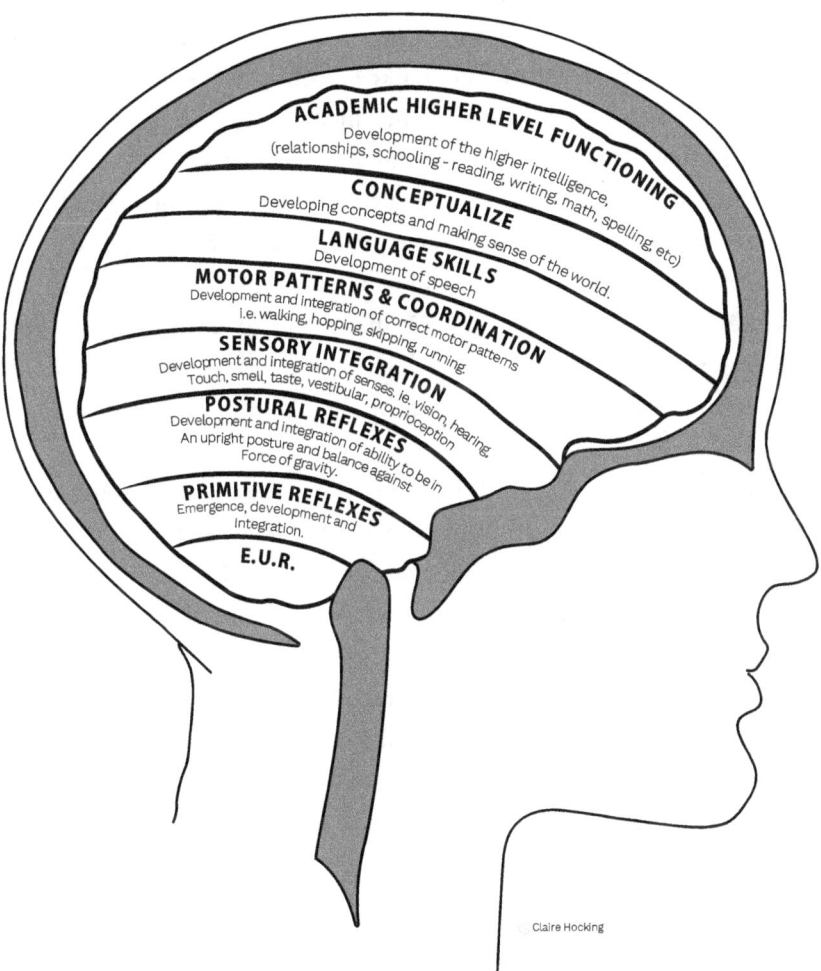

Figure 4.3 This illustration represents the hierarchical system of human development, beginning before birth with in-utero reflexes and continuing into adulthood. Each stage builds upon the foundations of primitive and postural reflexes; if these foundations are unstable or incomplete, higher levels—such as motor skills, perception, speech, and academic functioning—can also be undermined (Image adapted from Claire Hocking.)[36]

When missed developmental milestones go unrecognized, they create a ripple effect that greatly impacts the child across many different areas—physically, academically, behaviorally, socially, emotionally, and beyond.[37] A delay in one area often sets off a chain reaction with other areas, extending beyond the original deficit. But what does this mean and what does it look like in our classrooms? Let's use the example of missing a developmental milestone like crawling. You will see this show up as deficits in bilateral coordination, which affects reading, writing, and problem solving later on. Developmental milestones are building blocks for higher level skills like cognitive development, emotional regulation, and executive function. Similarly, retained primitive reflexes[38] may make sitting still nearly impossible, leading to fidgeting, missed instruction, and the perception that the child is inattentive or disruptive. The root challenge is developmental or neurological; however, as it shows up in the classroom, it may be mislabeled as laziness, defiance, disruptive behavior, or lack of ability.

Furthermore, brain hemisphere imbalances create additional ripple effects. A child with a left hemisphere delay may have difficulty with challenges like dyslexia, dysgraphia, certain types of ADHD, and speech or language disorders. In the classroom, this can look like difficulty decoding words, slow or inaccurate reading, weak spelling, and trouble memorizing math facts or following multi-step directions. These students may avoid reading aloud, fall behind in subjects that require heavy text processing, or rely heavily on pictures and hands-on activities to learn. Without support, they can appear inattentive or to be "not trying," when in fact they're working much harder than their peers just to keep up.

A right hemisphere delay is often linked with nonverbal learning disorder (NVLD), autism spectrum disorder (ASD), most types of ADHD, and social-emotional regulation challenges. These students may struggle to read facial expressions, understand sarcasm or tone, organize their work on a page, or interpret graphs and charts. In group settings, they might misinterpret social rules, appear "off topic" in conversations, or become overwhelmed in noisy environments. Academically, they may excel at rote memorization or verbal recall but falter when a task requires visual-spatial reasoning, problem solving, or flexible thinking.

When a hemisphere delay goes unrecognized, the child's uneven skill profile can lead to misunderstanding. Adults may overestimate them in some areas and underestimate them in others, missing the underlying developmental gap that's driving both the strengths and the struggles. Our current methods of intervention for these children attempt to address the symptoms and never the root cause. This furthers the delay and the divide and can often lead to the child feeling "broken" or frustrated. And with the number of children diagnosed with developmental delays at an all-time high (as mentioned earlier), this greatly effects every single child in the classroom and beyond.[39]

As you explore the milestone chart, keep in mind that it's more than a checklist. It's a tool to help you see the bigger picture, connect the dots, and support children in becoming their best selves, as well as getting them the support they need when they are off track. The wonderful thing is there are people who are educated in ways to help these kids get back on track and restore the balance. There are ways to address these childhood issues, not just by medicating kids so they can sit through class, but by changing their actual brain so they can reach their fullest potential.

The connection between the body and mind has been studied since, well, forever. Study after study confirms that the brain and body are a team—they don't just coexist; they rely on each other to function. Honestly, isn't it kind of common sense? We're not just working with a brain or a body—we're working with a whole child.[40] Missing milestones is our first clue that a child is out of sync. We are seeing this in both developmental disability as well as mental health diagnosis. Our standard "plan of action" for our children both at home and in schools is not working. We need more and we need better. Research, like the groundbreaking work of Dr. Melillo, shows us that evidence-based approaches can truly help children (and even grown-ups) get back on track.

One of the most profound and urgent areas of study today is the connection between brain asymmetry and mental health. As we grapple with one of the most significant mental health crises affecting children in history, this is not something we can afford to ignore. It's a wake-up call—a reminder that understanding and addressing developmental needs isn't just important; it's critical. This is why the "A" in M.A.G.I.C.—Assess Developmental Needs—is so vital. Yet, it's often where we see the least understanding, the fewest resources, and the greatest gaps. But here's the truth: This is foundational. It's the bedrock for every intervention, every curriculum, and every expectation we place on childhood. Without it, we're building a house with no solid ground. Our children deserve better. I am not asking that you all become doctors or experts in neurology. In my opinion, however, you should, at the very least, familiarize yourself with developmental milestones. You should understand when your kids or students are off track and know where to look for support. Again, if you are working with or have your own children, you must know basic child development, which is why it will be included as a resource in this book for you to take with you. OK, I am getting off my soap box and I will leave that right there.

The Plastic Mind

So now we've covered the very basics of how the brain is formed—but what happens as a child learns, grows, and navigates the world? You've heard me mention it before, but now's the time to dig in a little deeper. Let us revisit neuroplasticity.

This term has gotten more buzz lately (thankfully), but it's more than a trendy neuroscience word—it's the miracle behind how kids learn and why development is possible at all. In simple terms, neuroplasticity is the brain's ability to change its structure and function in response to experience. And in childhood? That ability is supercharged. Children have more synaptic plasticity—more potential connections available, more opportunities to strengthen or prune them, and a heightened sensitivity to input. This is why childhood is such a critical window for learning, skill-building, and even recovery from setbacks or delays.

Kids' brains are constantly building, tweaking, strengthening, and sometimes even re-routing the connections between neurons based on what they do, feel, and experience. Every time a child practices a skill—whether it's tying their shoes, solving a math puzzle, or making a friend—the brain fires specific neural pathways. With repetition, those pathways strengthen. And, liked we talked about at the beginning of this book, that dirt trail eventually gets paved and widened into a superhighway, making these neural connections faster, more efficient, and more automatic over time.

This idea is summed up in one of my favorite neuroscience phrases: **"Neurons that fire together, wire together."**[41]

And that's not just a catchy line—it's a core principle of how kids build everything from reading fluency to emotional regulation. The brain physically adapts to the demands placed on it. In the medical world, we often say, "Form follows function." Muscles grow in response to use, and the same is true of the brain. Functional demand drives growth. When a child uses a particular skill or engages in a certain type of thinking often enough, the brain literally reshapes itself to support that function more effectively.

But neuroplasticity isn't just about becoming faster or smarter—it's also the brain's built-in plan B. If something's not working—whether it's due to developmental differences, trauma, injury, or a missed milestone—the brain can often find a workaround. It may recruit different regions, re-route tasks, or build entirely new pathways. That's how kids with language delays, for example, can develop alternate strategies to communicate. Or how children who are blind often show enhanced development in other senses, as their brains shift resources to adapt.

This is also why early intervention is so powerful. If a child shows signs of struggle—socially, emotionally, academically—the earlier we understand and respond, the more likely the brain is to respond with growth. The longer we wait, the more those inefficient or disconnected patterns get reinforced. But when we meet a child's needs early—whether through movement, multisensory activities, connection, or developmental support—we activate the brain's natural ability to grow and adapt. In other words, the brain is not a fixed, static system. It's alive, responsive, and waiting for input. And that is what makes the next part of our journey so exciting.

Now that we've explored how the brain wires itself through experience, we're going to shift gears into how we can guide that wiring process in the most developmentally appropriate way: through the body. Because when it comes to childhood learning and development, movement isn't optional—it's essential.

5

Guide Using Whole Body Strategies

"Tell me and I forget. Teach me and I may remember.
Involve me and I learn."

—Benjamin Franklin

Y ou have met the child where they are and have begun to assess them developmentally—now things heat up a bit. Before we get deep into our "G"—Guide Using Whole Body Strategies—I think it is a good time to share my story. I am a doctor of physical therapy by trade and profession. I began my career in professional athletics, working with a women's professional soccer team in Italy (an incredible experience with a team who went undefeated; ask me about it when you see me). I continued my work with athletes when I came home to the States, working with professional athletes, child athletes, and even your weekend warrior. I also did some work with adapted sports, hospitals, a children's hospital, Broadway (not as an actress, but rather treating the actors and actresses backstage... super cool, I know!), private concierge care, etc. It wasn't until I was pregnant with my second child that I decided to make the switch into the schools. I have always loved working with kids. It could be a birth order thing—as the oldest of five children, I was always the go-to babysitter both at home and in my neighborhood. Or it could be that I see eye to eye with kids (it's a short joke) or, perhaps, it's because of my youthful personality and limitless energy. I always said, "I am just a kid in a grown-up body"— well, until my spicy middle child pointed out, "Mommy, you don't really have a grown-up body." Either way, I landed where I was meant to be. I have spent over a decade working in more than twelve different school districts. I have worked with many teachers, kids, related service providers, parents, and administrations. It was this part of my life that led to this book.

You see, I am not a "regular" physical therapist. I never focus solely on physical deficits, but rather the whole child. Despite what many school staff believed, I did not just do push-ups, sit-ups, and stairs with my students. Right from the start, I would ask each student's teacher and parents, "What are their challenges and struggles?" I mostly got answers like, "They walk into walls and fall out of their chair... they have no body control... they bump into people and objects... they can't keep up with their peers." Those are all very important things to work on, of course, but they are not the whole picture.

I then began to inquire, "What are their academic, behavioral, social, emotional deficits?" At that inquiry, I was met with confusion, as if to say, "Why do you care?" I even had one elementary school principal who had just brought in a brand new Applied Behavioral ABA class, filled with four- and five-year-old children with severe needs, ask me if I can work in a stairwell with these kids. When I asked for a space to treat the students, he stated, "Don't you just do stairs with them, anyway?" There seemed to be a disconnect, larger than I could have imagined, between the importance of the body in academics. There was an incredible lack of understanding of the holistic nature of being a kid. It was as if teachers were responsible for the brain and I was responsible for the body, like they were two separate and distinct entities. (For those of you who have not heard the term *ABA*, it stands for applied behavioral analysis and is a subset of a special education classroom made up of children who often have the greatest developmental needs, typically autism. They have a low student-to-teacher ratio and contain extra support staff to assist in close behavioral support, additional structure, and data collection.)

So, naturally, I did things my way. I learned about the kids and designed programs that targeted the areas of the body and the brain responsible for their systemic deficits. I referred kids for visual assessments and other assessments based upon looking at them as a whole child. We did things like hop scotch math, sight word push-ups, focused work on movement, but also worked on stillness and postural control, and on areas that targeted self-regulation and executive function.

What did I notice? Well, my students weren't just improving physically—they were improving academically, behaviorally, socially, and emotionally. They were more self-confident. Took more of an interest in their program, developed a better sense of agency. These were kids who struggled with movement, and yet they loved coming to PT and doing their program, even the hard stuff. You see, I am pretty fun—I mean, I'm right up there with gym and recess fun.

It was then that teachers began asking me to come into their classroom to see what I was doing. I was asked to "take a look" at some of their "typical" kids or help them rework their classroom set up. I was asked my opinion on activities they could do to incorporate some of these strategies for their whole class and when to use which tools. You see, good teachers are always looking for resources to help their students, but, often, it is hard to know how to use them. Many of these teachers had acquired activities from Teachers Pay Teachers (TpT), Pinterest, Instagram, etc.; however, they were having challenges with implementation.

I began to pool together my resources, explanations, and activities to create something I could share with other teachers. When I brought this to our local elementary school principal, he looked at me and said, "You wrote a curriculum!" I was like, "I did?!" And **How To Be A Kid**™ was born. It has been an absolute joy and pleasure teaching professional development, running workshops, and speaking with teachers, parents, kids, and administrators. I love working with and for kids. When I help one kid, it touches my heart to know I am changing that one life. When I work with one teacher or administrator, I know I am helping many kids now and into the future.

Why do I share this with you? I wanted to give you the full picture of what I mean when I say Guide Using Whole Body Strategies. You see, sometimes—no, most times—the only way to access the brain is through the body. Movement is the foundation of brain development. Once again, we are dealing with whole children, who have been artificially broken down into parts. Let's bring them back together. And what better way to start the process of guiding them than to understand how kids ACTUALLY learn. I sense a great start to this next part (haha).

Making Sense of our Senses

"Learning is experience. Everything else is just information."
—Albert Einstein

All right, it is time to make sense of our senses! Let's start by testing our knowledge: How many senses do we have? HINT: The answer is

NOT five. We've all been taught about our five senses—sight, hearing, taste, smell, and touch. But did you know there's a whole sensory universe beyond this classic line-up? Yes, our sensory world is far more complex and intriguing than just the fab five!

While those are the big players, there are actually a bunch more senses that shape our experiences and help us navigate the world. Scientists can't quite agree on the exact number, but let's explore some of the most commonly recognized ones.

Sight (Vision): Detects light, color, and movement to help us interpret the world around us.

Hearing (Audition): Processes sound waves to recognize speech, music, and environmental noises.

Taste (Gustation): Senses flavors through taste buds, detecting sweet, salty, sour, bitter, and umami (savory).

Smell (Olfaction): Identifies odors through chemical signals, influencing taste and memory.

Light Touch (Tactile Discrimination): Detects gentle contact, textures, and fine details on the skin.

Deep Pressure: Senses firm touch, compression, and body weight, contributing to comfort and grounding.

Nociception (Pain Perception): Alerts the body to potential harm by detecting painful stimuli.

Proprioception (Body Awareness): Provides feedback on body position, movement, and force by detecting stretch and pressure in muscles and joints, allowing coordinated movement without visual input or guidance.

Vibration: Detects oscillating or pulsating stimuli, aiding in touch sensitivity and texture recognition.

Vestibular (Balance and Spatial Orientation): Located in the inner ear, this system detects head movement, acceleration, and gravity to help maintain balance, posture, and coordination.

Thermoception (Temperature Sensation): Detects heat and cold, helping regulate body temperature responses.

Interoception (Internal Body Awareness): Senses internal signals like hunger, thirst, heartbeat, and emotional states, helping regulate bodily functions.

With these additional senses, you could say the human body has at least twelve senses, and some researchers think there could be even more as we learn more about how our body and brain interact.

OK, I'm going to quickly get a little neuroscience nerdy, but just for second. Our sensory organs take in sensory input, which is then converted into electrical signals that get transmitted via sensory nerves to the brain. Most sensory information heads straight to the thalamus, which is like our switchboard for incoming sensory input. The thalamus organizes and relays that input to specific areas of the brain for further processing. There is one sense that bypasses processing in the thalamus and heads straight for our memory and emotional centers—any guess on which one? SMELL! This direct pathway is why certain smells can instantly trigger vivid memories and strong emotional reactions.[42]

So why are these senses so important? First and foremost, our senses act as our personal safety system, alerting us to danger. The smell of smoke or a sudden loud noise can be a lifesaver. Even though pain isn't exactly pleasant, it's a crucial alert system that tells us when something's wrong. In addition to protecting us, they are the windows through which we view and interact with the world. From the moment we're born, our senses are busy gathering information and helping us make "sense" of our surroundings. Did you ever notice you remember a place better when multiple senses are engaged?[43] For example, recalling a beautiful sunny day at the beach is easier when you hear the sound of waves and smell the ocean (or sunscreen).

Our senses are also key players in developing motor skills. Balance and spatial awareness depend on vision, proprioception, and the vestibular system—basically, your brain's internal GPS.[44] These senses help with coordination and fine-tuning those gross and fine motor skills. Let's take walking, for instance: When you walk into the kitchen to grab food, you don't actively plan every single step. Instead, your senses perceive your environment and relay that information to the brain, which then causes a motor response faster than you can decide what you're eating for lunch. This seamless coordination between sensory input and motor output allows us to navigate our world.

In addition to motor skills and coordination, our senses are also crucial for cognitive development. Kids learn by touching, tasting, and exploring their world. For instance, some of our very first learning occurs when we discover that touching something hot means "ouch" or that banging on different objects creates different sounds. This hands-on learning teaches kids about cause and effect and helps develop problem-solving skills.[45] Learning happens differently and more effectively when multiple senses are engaged. In an increasingly digital world, kids are often learning through screens, which primarily engage vision and hearing. Real-world experiences, however, involve all the senses, making learning richer and more impactful. For example, when kids prepare a meal and eat the food in real life, they engage their senses, emotions, and problem-solving skills, which helps form deeper, more meaningful memories and experiences. This active participation makes the experience more memorable and allows them to learn through hands-on interaction. In contrast, watching a video of someone preparing a meal only provides passive observation, limiting their ability to connect and retain the learning experience. It is also not as fun and delicious.

I also want to take a moment to highlight that our senses are vital for social and emotional learning as well. Familiar sensory experiences, like a parent's soothing voice or comforting touch, are key to forming emotional bonds and attachments. We also use our senses to pick up on social cues like facial expressions and tone of voice.

Sensory input is also incredibly helpful with self-regulation. Have you ever found that deep pressure can be calming (just ask Olaf, who can cure anything with warm hugs)? The calming effects of deep pressure are your sensory system at work. Plus, there's a growing interest in the relationship between social emotional learning and interoception.[46] Research suggests that being more aware of our internal states can help us understand others better and is tied to the development of empathy.

I also cannot finish this section without highlighting one of my absolute favorite roles of our sensory system—creativity and imagination! Engaging in multi-sensory experiences can lead to innovative thinking and fresh ideas. Exploration and exposure to different textures, sounds, and sights can inspire new solutions to problems or creative projects.

Senses aren't just a part of learning—they are learning! They shape how children engage with their world, how they process information, and how they develop into well-rounded individuals. Our senses are far from passive recipients of information—they're active participants in our learning and development. A life rich in multi-sensory learning helps kids to fully understand the world around them, build deep and lasting connections, and reach their fullest potential.

How Memory Actually Works: Real Learning vs. Memorization

With a better understanding of the role that our senses play in, well, everything, we can now take the next step in understanding how memory works. Memories in kids are woven together through experiences, senses, emotions, and context, like intricate tapestries. I want to make it clear that the retrieval process is not like pulling from a file cabinet, but rather reconstructing the memory from bits and pieces.[47] When kids learn something new, it's not just about storing a dry fact somewhere in their minds. Instead, it's a rich, multi-sensory process, where each sight, sound, smell, taste, and touch—along with the emotions and context in which the experience happens[48]—gets layered together to form the memory. This process creates neural connections that bring meaning to the experience, making it easier to remember and even enjoyable to recall.[49]

For example, let's say a child learns about plants by planting a seed. They dig in the soil (sense of touch), smell the earth, see the tiny seed and the vibrant green of leaves, feel excitement and curiosity, and get to work outdoors rather than sitting in a classroom. Later, when they recall how plants grow, they're likely to remember much more than "plants need sunlight and water." The sights, smells, sounds, and even their emotions associated with planting that seed add to their understanding.

That knowledge becomes "alive" for them, anchored in real, personal experiences.[50] I love this gardening example because, not only is it practical, but it is one I have used in my own life. My own children have helped their grandfather in the garden. They have even harvested tomatoes and fresh spices, processed them, and made a fresh sauce (that is our Italian heritage coming out).

In addition to my own children, it has been an incredibly useful method of learning for my middle school and high school life-skills kids. The occupational therapist and I would work with the students in the garden, weeding, cleaning up, and planting. The OT even had the students plant their own seeds in a cup of soil and begin the process before helping them place the whole plant in the garden. Watching these kids thrive outside the classroom was heart-warming and incredibly memorable. Both my children and my students remember their experiences and ask to repeat them come spring.

Memories begin with encoding, which is how the brain processes incoming information. It is dependent upon engagement as our senses collect the details. The hippocampus (which is located in the brain's temporal lobe) plays a crucial role in deciding which information is worth remembering. The more sensory-rich or emotionally charged the experience, the stronger the memory is likely to be, as such events activate multiple areas of the brain and create multiple anchors.

To further understand memory storage, let's look at short-term vs. long-term memory. Short-term memory is held briefly in the prefrontal cortex. If a memory is deemed important enough for long-term storage, it is consolidated and moved to other brain regions, like the hippocampus and the cortex. It is then divided further into declarative memory (facts and events), which lives in the temporal lobe, and procedural memory (skills and habits, like riding a bike), which is stored in areas like the cerebellum and basal ganglia. Our synapses, or connections between our neurons, strengthen based on the importance of this information.

Now, here's the difference between true learning and simple memorization. Memorization is like having a fact on a flashcard in your mind: You can pull it up in response to a specific prompt (like recalling a date for a test) without really understanding its meaning or connection to other knowledge. It's temporary and often fades if it's not reinforced. True learning, on the other hand, is about comprehension and connection. When a child learns something deeply, they see how it fits into the bigger picture and why it matters. They understand it well enough to apply it to new situations. For example, if a child truly learns about the growth process in plants, they could apply that knowledge to understand other life cycles, the importance of nature, or even concepts like patience and nurturing. True learning sticks with them because it's connected to other meaningful experiences and is less likely to be forgotten. This is the reason that we learn better through teaching others; we have to problem solve and creatively apply learned concepts across situations and context to help others fully understand.[51]

Memories tied to strong emotions or multi-sensory inputs are often easier to recall because they have more anchor points in the brain. Our memories aren't perfect due to the fact that they are dynamic and subject to "updating" or reinterpreting each time they are recalled and are influenced by current experiences and emotions. When learning is rich and connected, it leads to genuine understanding rather than just isolated facts. True learning is resilient, adaptable, and lasting, while simple memorization is fleeting and limited in scope.

Mr. Homunculus

I would like to take a moment to introduce you to my friend, Mr. Homunculus. While he may appear a little silly looking, he is, in fact, the way our brain "sees" our body through the primary sensory and motor cortices. Mr. Homunculus is a visual representation of which areas of our body get the most "real estate" in those brain regions. He highlights the importance of a sensory-rich learning experience and how we are actually wired to learn through our senses.

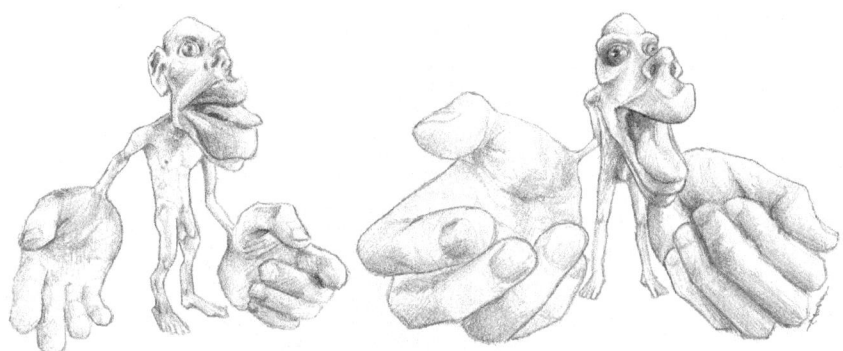

Figure 5.1 This illustration of Mr. Homunculus, also known as the cortical man, was created by neurosurgeon Dr. Wilder Penfield to illustrate how the brain perceives the body. The distorted proportions show how much brain area is devoted to sensation and movement in each region. The sensory cortex is represented in the left image and the motor cortex is represented in the image to the right. (Illustration by Eszter Czap-Tóth, adapted from Dr. Wilder Penfield's cortical man).

Mr. Homunculus shows that certain body parts—especially the hands, lips, and tongue—are given extra space in these brain maps.[52] When kids actively participate in learning by using their hands to manipulate, their mouths to speak or sing, and their bodies to move, they engage multiple sensory and motor areas at once.[53] This overlap creates stronger, more interconnected neural pathways, which improves understanding, memory, and retention. Hands-on activities reinforce learning because the hands have such a large representation in the sensory and motor cortices.[54] Kids are hardwired to learn through doing. Speaking and explaining further activate the brain, since forming and expressing ideas recruits both motor and language networks. Listening is important, but when done passively, it's less powerful than when it's paired with action, discussion, or other sensory engagement.

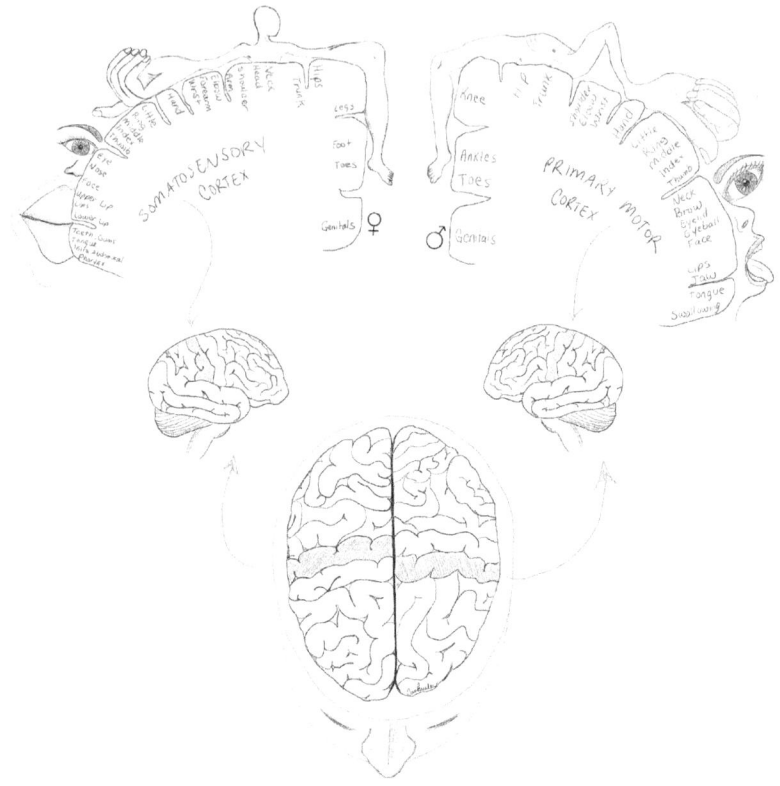

Figure 5.2 This cortical map, based on the work of Dr. Wilder Penfield, illustrates the somatosensory (left) and motor (right) cortices of the brain. The image shows neurological representation devoted to different body regions, with areas requiring fine motor control or heightened sensation—such as the hands, lips, and tongue—occupying disproportionately large portions of the cortex.

Mr. Homunculus reminds us that our sensory and motor systems help shape how the brain functions. Activities like singing, speaking, and moving light up the hands, mouth, and body—areas with significant cortical representation—while also engaging the prefrontal cortex, where executive functions like focus, planning, and self-regulation live. Multisensory experiences strengthen neural connections, helping children organize thoughts, regulate emotions, and sustain attention. By combining these elements, we not only support sensory integration and communication, but also enhance executive function, giving children tools to think critically, collaborate effectively, and learn deeply.

When I said kids need to move to think, I wasn't kidding. Thank you, Mr. Homunculus, for just being you.

Communication, Music, and the Brain

We often talk about the importance of good communication, but I want to take a moment to highlight the speaking part here, especially as it ties into our use of the multisensory and motor approach (and highlights a lot of what we learned from Mr. Homunculus). This is where oracy comes in (a word that, up until relatively recently, I didn't even know existed). *Oracy* is the ability to express thoughts clearly, listen actively, and engage in meaningful conversation. Just as numeracy is to math and literacy is to reading, oracy is to the spoken language. It's more than just talking; it's about thinking, expressing ideas, challenging thoughts, and engaging with others in meaningful ways. Too often, discussions in the classroom are limited to subjects like reading or science, while areas like math are treated as quiet, individual learning experiences. But when kids are encouraged to talk through their reasoning, defend their ideas, and listen to others' perspectives, their learning deepens across all subjects. It is the bridge between thinking and understanding. Oracy is more than just speaking—it's giving kids a voice and empowering them to think, collaborate, be heard, connect more meaningfully with others, and make sense of the world around them.[55]

A school in London, known as School 21, has made oracy a cornerstone of its education.[56] In every subject, students are not just encouraged but expected to engage in thoughtful discussion. They learn how to articulate their ideas, respectfully challenge different viewpoints, and invite others into the conversation—especially those who may not feel comfortable speaking up on their own. They also develop the skill of active listening, learning that a conversation is more than just waiting for their turn to talk. When oracy is woven into education deliberately, kids develop not just academic confidence, but real-world confidence—the ability to engage in discussions, navigate disagreements, and communicate effectively in any situation.

School 21 shares some of the many different methods they use, including collaborating with the kids on setting rules for engagement, utilizing oracy in every subject, including math and language, and using different formats of speaking, including large group, different arrays of smaller groups, and lining up face to face to speak. And, yes, I love the part where they are getting up and moving around to engage in conversation, discussion, and debate.

Encouraging kids to speak out loud not only improves communication skills and self-confidence, but it activates multiple different areas of the brain simultaneously, including Broca's Area in the frontal lobe (responsible for speech production and articulation), Wernicke's Area in the temporal lobe (responsible for understanding language and making meaning of what is heard or read), the prefrontal cortex, which governs higher order thinking, decision making, and self-regulation (it's where executive function lives), the motor cortex, which is in the frontal lobe (controls the physical act of speaking, including movement of the lips, tongue, and jaw), the auditory cortex, which is in the temporal lobe (processes spoken language, both what the child hears and their own speech), the hippocampus, which is part of the limbic system (supports memory formation and retrieval—speaking helps consolidate learned concepts into long-term memory), the amygdala, which is also part of the limbic system (responsible for processing and managing emotions—speaking helps add meaning and context to learning), and the cerebellum, which coordinates speech-related motor activity and supports timing and fluency.

That was a long and detailed way of saying that speaking and debating are not just communication activities—they are whole-brain exercises that develop critical skills like reasoning, memory, and emotional regulation. Oracy is another way to engage multiple regions of the brain and turn passive consumption into active, meaningful experiences, which can prepare kids to think deeply, communicate effectively, and facilitate real learning.[57]

This may also be a good time to bring music into the mix. Although I could write a book on the amazing benefits of music alone, I thought this may be a wonderful place to incorporate the impact music has on learning and development. Music, oracy, and movement are deeply connected and together create powerful, multisensory learning experiences for children (take a moment to think about kids learning all fifty states—did they learn the song, or did they memorize a list? Which is more effective?). Music develops rhythm, vocabulary, listening, and storytelling skills that align with the fundamentals of oracy, enhancing fluency, comprehension, and creative expression.[58] When paired with movement—such as clapping, dancing, or acting out lyrics—music engages multiple brain areas, strengthening memory, focus, and coordination.[59] These multisensory approaches activate the whole brain and create emotional connections, turning passive learning into active, meaningful participation. By integrating music, oracy, and movement into lessons, children not only retain knowledge more effectively but also build essential communication and social-emotional skills, aligning with natural neurodevelopment for deeper, more impactful learning.

Think about it: Music is present in every culture and in every language across the globe. No matter what you listen to, play, or sing in the shower, most people have a connection to music in one way or another. But how does it impact our mind and body as it relates to learning? Music can act as a bridge between physiological regulation, emotional balance, and cognitive performance. By creating a state of harmony between the body and brain, music can set the stage (see what I did there) for more effective and meaningful educational experiences. Music enhances memory by activating both hemispheres of the brain, combining language and creativity, making information easier to encode and recall. The rhythm that is brought about by music influences brainwaves (for example, slow and calm music helps produce alpha waves, which are linked to relaxation and focus, while upbeat tempos can stimulate beta waves, which enhance alertness and problem solving). Rhythmic music can also help by creating a steady heart rate variability, which is associated with reduced stress and improved emotional regulation.[60] Music can also trigger the release of neurotransmitters like dopamine and serotonin.

So why did I put all this great stuff about music here? By activating key areas of the brain involved in speech production, comprehension, and emotional processing, music strengthens neural pathways for effective communication. It goes back to me saying that the arts aren't the "extra" but rather foundational. Group music activities foster connection and collaboration, while music in general enhances communication by engaging in both verbal and nonverbal expression.

Join the Movement

"Real learning—the kind that establishes meaningful connections for the brain—starts with movement."

—Dr. Carla Hannaford[61]

It all—brain development, emotional regulation, learning, everything—begins with movement. Movement is the first language of the brain—the spark that builds the pathways for everything else to follow.

I want to take a tiny step back, just a few chapters, to revisit brain science. Let's focus on that third layer, the neocortex, aka the human brain. The human brain is where our most complex networks of neurons are created. It is the area that gives us imagination, creativity, higher-level thinking, self-regulation, and basically everything that makes us human. The human brain (specifically the prefrontal cortex) is where executive function lives. It is also the area that is under construction until our mid-twenties. Why is this so important? Well, because we are literally creating our executive function branch throughout childhood. One of the biggest reasons I asked you to "join the movement" is because it is movement that has one of the greatest impacts on the effective development of our human brain and thus, executive function.

During childhood, the development of executive function is a slow and steady process, shaped by experiences that challenge the brain to focus, adapt, and regulate. Movement plays a crucial role in this process, helping to stimulate and organize the neural networks in the prefrontal cortex where executive function resides. Activities that require coordination, rhythm, or balance—like running, dancing, and crawling (remember crawling, that milestone that was removed from the CDC Developmental Milestone list... yet still remains one of the most important developmental milestones?)—directly support skills like attention, self-regulation, and problem solving.[62] These moments of physical engagement aren't just about energy release; they're building the very cognitive tools children will rely on to navigate the complexities of learning and life.

The relationship between movement and executive function is rooted in how the human brain evolved. Long before classrooms and cubicles, our ancestors relied on constant motion (according to Dr. John Medina in his book, *Brain Rules*, about twelve miles a day)—tracking prey, gathering food, and navigating unfamiliar terrain—to survive.[63] This required not just physical strength but also sharp cognitive skills: planning ahead, adapting strategies, and maintaining focus under pressure. These early challenges shaped the neocortex, tying movement and executive function together in ways we still see today. Modern research confirms that activities like walking, running, or engaging in complex physical tasks stimulate the prefrontal cortex, sharpening skills like working memory, attention, and emotional regulation.[64] In other words, movement primes the brain not just for survival, but for success in our increasingly complex world.

Before we move on, I want to highlight one very important piece of information. This area of the brain does not fully develop until our mid-twenties. Oh, wait, did I say that already? Good. It is that important! I highlight this because there seems to be an expectation of very young children to "behave" or "control themselves," whether in school or at home. And while yes, I do demand this of my own children and students, I am also very well aware that this is a developing skill and that I bear some of the responsibility of helping it develop. And yet, in many schools, we've made this the gold standard of behavior. The quietest class earns more dojo points. The most motionless kids are labeled "well-behaved." Self-control and composure absolutely have their place—stillness has its own kind of power (and we'll explore that in a later section)—but we've taken it too far. We've built classrooms around silence and compliance instead of curiosity and engagement. And everything we know from neuroscience tells us we've got it backward. Because motion doesn't get in the way of learning—it opens the door to it.

Movement primes the brain. It boosts cognitive function, sharpens attention, improves memory, and regulates emotional responses. It increases circulation, delivering the oxygen and glucose that fuel the brain. Even objective measures like brain scans show significantly more activity in children who take a walk before a test than those who sit quietly. Movement isn't a break from learning—it's what makes learning possible. And engaging with the world around us isn't a distraction from education—it is education.

So if this is so well documented—if the research has been clear for decades—then why in the h… ippocampus do we keep forcing kids to sit still in their chairs? (Science nerd joke: If you "remember," the hippocampus is the brain's memory center… and yes, it lights up with movement.)

We've designed classrooms to manage behavior rather than to maximize learning. We've misunderstood motion as misbehavior and dismissed movement as purely physical. But in doing so, we have been cutting kids off from the very thing that enables their brains to grow.

For many students, the only protected space where movement is still encouraged is physical education. And we need to pause and recognize our physical education teachers—because they've held the line. They are often the only adults in a child's day who truly understand that movement isn't just a "special"—it's essential. They know what the research has been screaming for years: Kids are built to move. Their default position is movement. These teachers deserve our gratitude, our resources, and our support. But they cannot—and should not—be expected to carry this alone. Movement isn't the job of one teacher. It's the responsibility of everyone who works with children.

If you're still not sure, just ask a kid what their favorite part of school is. They will most likely answer, "gym and recess." It's not just because they "get to run around." It's because during those moments, their bodies and brains are in sync. They're engaged. Alert. Alive. They're learning in the way they were designed to learn—through motion, play, and connection.

I'll never forget the day I went to pick up a middle schooler—we'll call him Teddy—for his PT session. I went to grab him from the band room during third period. From the moment I saw him, I knew something was wrong. By the time he reached the hallway, he was hyperventilating and overwhelmed, teetering on the edge of a full-blown panic attack. I gently asked if he wanted to go to the nurse. He shook his head and led me wordlessly to the room where we usually held our sessions. Inside, he tried to speak. "I didn't mean to…" and "It's all my fault…" were all he could get out. I asked him to take three deep breaths. He couldn't. So I gave him a different task: "Jump on the elliptical and go as hard as you can for three minutes. Go." He didn't hesitate.

Three minutes later, Teddy stepped off, steadied his breath, used a few calming techniques we'd practiced before, and looked at me: "I'm ready to talk now." And then he spoke. He told me everything—the traumatic situation that had just unfolded, the panic that followed. I then escorted him to the nurse and notified his counselor.

It was a bit unsettling to me that he had made it through three class periods in that state and no one had noticed or taken any action. Even if they had, the standard protocol would have been to ask him to talk, possibly to "breathe" or "calm down." But he was in too much of a state of fight or flight to access any area of the brain that involves actual thinking. Who would have utilized movement to break the cycle, even taken him for a walk? And yet it was movement—not words—that helped him come back online.

That day, movement wasn't just an intervention. It was the access point. It was the only thing that worked. And that's the lesson. We can't lecture a child out of stress. We can't worksheet them out of anxiety. We can't teach emotional regulation by telling them to sit down, calm down, and hold it together. Sometimes—actually, often—the only way to reach a child's mind is through their body.

Movement sends oxygen-rich blood to the brain, circulates glucose for energy, and activates regions responsible for focus, memory, and executive function. Dr. John Ratey's book *Spark* details how schools that increased physical activity—not academic time—saw radical improvements in test scores and emotional resilience. One public school in Naperville, Illinois, jumped to first in the world in science and sixth in math after revamping their physical activity program. The secret? Not more academic time, but movement. The greatest part is that the success of Naperville has been repeated in other districts across the country. We are not talking about only the wealthy elite private schools but public schools with diverse populations and people living below the poverty line.[65] Giving our children the ability to follow their biology and move costs nothing, but the benefits are priceless.

Dr. Robert Melillo's work in developmental neuroscience goes even deeper, showing how movement is what builds the brain. From developmental milestones, such as rolling and crawling patterns, to cross-lateral movement and balance integration, every layer of motor development helps wire the brain for higher-order thinking, social regulation, and emotional control. Movement strengthens the bridge between hemispheres, enhances neural connectivity, and repairs developmental delays. If we don't stimulate our brain cells, they will die! And that's kind of a big deal in growing young kids. "Use it or lose it" isn't just a saying—it's neuroscience.

Are you familiar with Steve Jobs? He was a pretty smart guy, so I hear. Steve Jobs was known to have walking meetings with his employees, partners, or potential collaborators. Yes, meetings while walking! It looks like this pretty smart guy was onto something.

Movement isn't something we tack on after the "real work." It is the real work. It's the gateway to brain development, academic success, and emotional well-being. We are not giving them "Brain Breaks"—we are giving them an opportunity to make sure their brain is awake. And with how little kids move outside of school today, what happens during the school day matters more than ever.

We don't need to wait for curriculum reform to begin. We can integrate movement into what we're already doing—today, right where we are. You'll find guidance, ideas, and space to make it your own in the "I" section of this book. But the shift doesn't start with strategy—it starts with belief.

The brain builds through the body.

If we want better learners, we start by letting them move.

Pay Attention

Now for a shift in focus. One of our greatest challenges with kids is to get them to "pay attention." Quite frankly, all neuroscience and research aside, I am pretty sure that writing this book alone has made me an expert on focus and attention. The battle for focus is a constant, a challenge withstanding the test of time. The difference for our kids today, however, is that they are competing against the highly stimulating environment that surrounds them and is everpresent everywhere they turn, including in pockets and on wrists. That is right—overstimulating distractions are literally attached to our children (and adults). There are entire Pinterest boards, Instagram reels, and TikTok videos dedicated to the multitude of strategies that claim to have activities to get kids to focus better. But honestly, if we don't understand what attention actually is and the science behind it, we quite frankly can't compete.

In order to truly understand what it means to "pay attention," I would like to break it down into parts and systems. First of all, we tend to use focus and attention interchangeably, but there is a fundamental and foundational difference. **Attention** is not just one thing, but rather a whole system of skills working together, helping filter information, shifting focus as needed, and filtering distraction. **Focus** is a type of attention; it is a bit more specific. It involves actively maintaining concentration on a single task or thought while filtering out competing stimuli.

Before we break down the deeper science and components of attention, I want to take a brief moment to share the difference between covert and overt attention. Covert attention is when your focus shifts without moving your eyes or body. It's your discrete, secret, and sometimes deceptive-looking attention. It's when you are looking at one thing or person, but your actual attention is elsewhere (like my kids pretending to read, while secretly eavesdropping on my conversation, or my students looking at me, but listening to the drama on the other side of the room). Overt attention, on the other hand, is when your eyes or body are locked in, physically oriented toward what you are focusing on (like following a hockey puck down the ice during a breakaway and watching it go into the net for a goal—let's go, Islanders!).

OK, now the science stuff. Let's start with the attentional network theory.[66] Michael Posner and Steven Peterson (1990) described the attentional network theory by breaking it down into three distinct but interconnected brain networks:

1. **The Alerting Network (Reticular Activation System or RAS):** The RAS, which is located in the brainstem, is the alertness regulator. This system governs basic arousal and wakefulness and helps determine what gets through the brain's attention filter, deciding when the brain is ready to focus on incoming information. It helps us stay vigilant and prepared to respond to a stimulus.

2. **Orienting Network (Posterior Attentional System or PAS):** The PAS is our orientation system. It is responsible for visual attention, orienting, and focusing on a specific stimulus and helps us with selective attention and divided attention. The orienting network helps guide us on where to direct our attention.

3. **Executive Control Network (Anterior Attentional System or AAS):** The AAS is the executive attention center. It is located in the prefrontal cortex and addresses areas of executive function, such as impulse control, decision-making, and sustained focus. The executive attention center helps us manage distractions, regulate impulses, and stay

focused on goal-directed tasks. This theory is important because it highlights that attention isn't a single skill but a combination of systems working together. It can give us grown-ups a better understanding to support our children in strengthening the different aspects of attention, particularly with learning and self-regulation.

With the basic understanding that we have different areas in the brain contributing to our overall attention network, we can then begin to highlight the key aspects or components of attention: sustained attention, selective attention, shifting attention (also referred to as alternating attention or task switching), divided attention, and goal-directed attention. Being able to effectively pay attention requires a balance of these key components as they work together to help us stay on task, process relevant information, weed out distractions, and work to achieve our goals. The ability to develop and strengthen these aspects of attention relies on practice, mindfulness, and healthy executive function. Let's take a closer look at each of the five components.

1. **Sustained attention** is the ability to maintain focus on a task or activity over an extended period of time. It allows us to stay engaged and resist fatigue or boredom, even when the task is repetitive or lacks immediate rewards. This skill is essential for completing long-term projects or studying effectively. It requires not only cognitive control from the prefrontal cortex but also motivation and energy. Weak sustained attention often results in starting tasks but struggling to finish them or having a difficult time paying attention to the teacher during a lesson.

2. **Selective attention** is the ability to focus on a specific task or stimulus while ignoring or filtering out irrelevant distractions. It relies heavily on the prefrontal cortex to filter out competing information and prioritize what matters. For example, a child focusing on a teacher's instructions despite classroom noise demonstrates selective attention. Without it, managing competing demands becomes overwhelming,

leading to scattered effort and reduced productivity. A child who struggles with selective attention may become overwhelmed by irrelevant stimuli, making it harder to concentrate on the task at hand. Deficits may manifest in difficulty filtering out distractions, like being unable to focus on a conversation in a crowded room or on the teacher giving a lesson or during a group activity.

3. **Shifting attention**, also called alternating attention or task shifting, is the ability to transition focus between different tasks or mental states. This skill is critical in dynamic environments where flexibility is needed, like alternating between responding to emails and attending meetings without losing productivity or coherence. A child transitioning from math to reading needs to shift their attention between subjects. If the child has difficulty in task-switching they may struggle when asked to switch between the activities, leading to frustration or difficulty staying organized. This may also be visible when a child has to shift from recess back to classroom work or if you are trying to get a child ready to go and they can't seem to shift their attention from what they are doing (not like I have personal experience here... like every single day #momlife).

4. **Divided attention** is the ability to focus on multiple tasks or stimuli simultaneously. For example, a child might need to listen to the teacher's instructions while taking notes or follow a group discussion while keeping track of their own contributions. If a child struggles with divided attention, they may have difficulty juggling multiple demands, such as paying attention to what the teacher is saying while organizing their materials or completing a classroom activity. This can lead to missed information, incomplete tasks, or feeling overwhelmed in busy environments like group projects or classrooms with many simultaneous activities.

5. **Goal-directed attention** helps us focus on tasks that align with our intentions and objectives. This purposeful attention ensures we stay on track, filtering distractions that are irrelevant to our desired outcomes,

like sticking to a project deadline. A child who struggles with goal-directed behavior may become sidetracked by distractions and not complete their homework assignment or task. Although goal-directed attention is closely linked to sustained attention, the key difference lies in motivation. Goal-directed attention is about choosing to focus on a specific goal, whereas sustained attention is about maintaining focus over time regardless of motivation or whether it is interesting or not. For example, goal-directed may be seen in a hockey player skating toward the goal, keeping laser-focus on maneuvering the puck past defenders to take the shot. He will have to actively ignore distractions (crowd noise, opposing players trying to check him, etc.) because the goal is clear—score! A distraction may lead to not achieving the goal (may as well keep the hockey examples coming). With sustained attention, you may see a student sitting through a forty-five-minute lesson maintaining focus on the teacher, even if the lesson is not particularly engaging. It is more about persistent attention over time, ignoring distractions such as classmates fidgeting, hallway noise, and boredom.

Back to Executive Function

Let's go back to executive function for a sec. Executive function serves as the "manager" of attention, essentially helping the brain decide where to focus, managing distractions, maintaining mental effort, and determining when to shift focus to adapt to new priorities. Maintaining attention and resisting distractions are core components of executive functioning, which are governed primarily by the prefrontal cortex. They enable us to control and direct our mental resources, including focus.

Impulse control refers to the ability to suppress immediate reactions or distractions to maintain focus on a task. This self-regulatory skill prevents us from acting on urges, like checking social media during work (or school), and supports sustained productivity. For example, a child may feel the urge to speak out of turn during a lesson. If they successfully resist, they are demonstrating impulse control.

Working memory is the mental workspace where we temporarily

hold and manipulate information for short periods of time. It allows us to remember instructions, solve problems, and link ideas in real-time, making it an essential component of focus and complex thought. For instance, a child may need to remember a set of directions like "take out your math book, open to page twelve, and complete the first three problems." Deficits in working memory lead to the child becoming confused when they make mistakes, forgetting parts of the instructions, and having to ask for help repeatedly. Now, if they struggle with both working memory and impulse control, you may see them interrupting each time they have a question or thought, despite being asked to wait until the end. They are aware they cannot hold onto the thought or question until the end—they won't remember it. And if they try to write it down, they will miss the next step, all leading to the cycle of anxiety and stress, which in and of itself will inhibit attention and learning.

Now let's add cognitive flexibility, which is the ability to adapt our thinking and attention in response to changing demands, rules, or perspectives. It allows us to switch strategies or viewpoints, which is essential for problem solving and navigating unfamiliar or complex situations. For example, if a child is building or doing a puzzle and realizes a piece doesn't fit, cognitive flexibility helps them try a different piece or approach. Difficulty with cognitive flexibility will result in the child becoming frustrated or upset when something doesn't work out or if they have to change tasks or strategies, leading to difficulties in problem solving or adjusting to new situations.

The Truth About Multi-Tasking

We have covered the five main components of attention and the executive function skills that support it, but there is another component I deliberately left out, and it is a cause of some heated debate: multi-tasking. There is much research that quite frankly states that multi-tasking doesn't exist. Yup, they say both Bigfoot and multi-tasking are just myths. A key study by the American Psychological Association (APA) found that multi-tasking can reduce productivity by up to 40 percent due to the "switch costs," basically the time and mental energy lost in shifting attention.[67] The rationale was that each switch requires the brain to reset and refocus, which takes up time and depletes cognitive resources. The studies on multi-tasking support that the brain struggles to perform more than one task at a time, especially when both require cognitive effort, and therefore divides attention between the tasks. This leads to decreased attention on both tasks. It is the main argument when it comes to the safety of texting and driving.

Stanford University researchers found that multi-taskers also performed worse on memory tasks and are more easily distracted than those who focus on one task at a time (making it counterproductive to focus, which is why it was kicked off the components list).[68] The truth is there is no actual "multi-tasking," meaning doing multiple tasks that require cognitive resources simultaneous. Nope, multi-tasking is actually just ineffective divided attention (trying to do too many effortful tasks at once) or inefficient shifting attention (constantly jumping between tasks before finishing them). As someone who has always prided myself on being great at multi-tasking, this came as a bit of a slap in the face. After a little bit of digging (as a result of harsh denial), I did discover a few exceptions or rather, other factors.

First off, it is no question that many people are overconfident in their multi-tasking abilities (not me, of course). Second, there is a dopamine release associated with task shifting, leading to a feeling of accomplishment and positive reward with each shift (whether we completed the task before the shift or not). For those with high sensation-seeking tendencies, the novelty or challenge of managing multiple inputs boosts dopamine release, interpreting the switch as "progress" and reinforcing the behavior even if it's inefficient.

But let's take a look at something that changes the equation—autopilot. When we engage in more automatic tasks, such as walking and chewing gum, which involve familiar motor functions largely controlled by the brainstem and cerebellum, or cooking a familiar meal, which involves well-rehearsed motor and procedural memory (managed in areas like the basal ganglia), this leaves the prefrontal cortex and executive function free for other activities. Since one task is running on "autopilot," it creates the illusion of successful multi-tasking (or actually, effective divided attention), even though you are actually only focusing on one activity at a time, which helps avoid mental fatigue and cognitive overload.

Hemispheric Processing and Attention

If you think that is a lot of information to focus on, just wait, there is more! Now that we have explored the networks and executive systems that make attention possible, it is useful to consider natural functional variations that influence how we process information. There is a lot of information out there about learning styles, cognitive types, and how children process information.[69] While these frameworks do help us to recognize different learning styles and give us helpful insight to individualize education, it is important to understand the foundational neuroscience first. Using the basic information we covered regarding attention and executive function, we can now see how these individual differences in processing emerge from the way our brains are wired. This understanding sets the stage for looking at how right and left hemispheric tendencies shape the way we think, focus, and learn. Each of us use both our right and left hemisphere (I don't believe I have any half-brains reading this book), but individuals often have natural strengths in one area over the other. These strengths are not signs of dysfunction; rather, they reflect preferred processing tendencies that shape how we approach tasks, solve problems, and sustain attention. By understanding these functional differences, we can better appreciate why some learners naturally excel at seeing the big picture, while others thrive when focusing on details.[70] It is also important to remember that movement, sensory experiences, and coordinated activities also play a crucial role in building the connections between the hemispheres, supporting more balanced processing and effective attention.[71]

Right Hemisphere – Global Processing

The right hemisphere supports big-picture, integrative, and holistic thinking. It helps us see patterns, connect ideas across contexts, and process spatial, social, and emotional information. Learners with right-hemisphere strengths may naturally approach tasks by considering the overall goals first and then attending to details as needed. When applied to attention, these learners often excel at tasks requiring integration of multiple ideas or contexts, such as synthesizing information across subjects, brainstorming, or creative problem solving. Understanding and leveraging this strength allows them to maintain focus when weaving together ideas and navigating complex or open-ended tasks. Even without any neurological delay or imbalance, a learner with a right-hemisphere preference may find sustained attention on repetitive, detail-heavy tasks more challenging, simply because their brain is naturally oriented toward the big picture. Again, we are not referring to a deficit, but rather a natural processing style that can be supported with appropriate strategies.[72]

Left Hemisphere – Local/Analytic Processing

The left hemisphere supports detail-oriented, sequential, and analytic thinking, including language, logic, and step-by-step problem solving. Learners with left hemisphere strengths may approach tasks by focusing on specifics first and building toward the larger understanding. Left hemisphere learners excel at tasks that require precision, structure, and sequential reasoning, such as following multi-step instructions, organizing information, or completing detail-oriented assignments. When applied to attention, they may sustain focus on structured, linear tasks more easily than on tasks that require synthesis of multiple ideas. When a task requires integration or creativity, a left hemisphere learner can develop strategies to engage their right hemisphere strengths, just as a right hemisphere learner can strengthen their attention to detail. The key is to recognize and balance these tendencies and distinguish them from hemispheric imbalances and dysfunction.[73]

Balancing Hemispheric Processing

Most learners use both hemispheres, but the strength and preference for each can influence how they naturally process information. In kids, this process is even more dynamic, as their brains are still developing. When hemispheric processing is relatively balanced, a child may show a dominant tendency, such as a preference for global, big-picture thinking or for detail-oriented, analytic thinking. They can, however, still flexibly engage the other hemisphere as their brain continues to develop and mature. In contrast, a child with a hemispheric delay or deficiency will begin to show signs of struggle and dysfunction and may present with missed milestones or behavioral concerns. It is important to identify these kids and help them get the support they need.

Environmental Factors

Let's move on from the science to the environment. There are some rules of focus that are just global kid rules (probably grown-up rules also). In his book *Brain Rules*, John Medina blatantly states everything we already know but tend to overlook in children with his statement, "We don't pay attention to boring stuff." Bam! And there you have it! Sometimes the things we are asking kids to pay attention to are just, well, boring! Our kids are looking for things to stimulate their senses, engage them, and create emotional experiences and social connection, and boring curriculum is just not going to cut it. This little fact has always been true, however, the difference for kids today is that their outside world is SOOOO stimulating that the discrepancy is much higher and more difficult to overcome.

Now, let's add in factors like sleep, nutrition, stress, health, physical activity, outdoor time, hydration, emotional well-being, etc.—all of which play a crucial role in brain function and all of which have become more than a problem with our children. We are in a bit of childhood crisis. Sleep allows the brain to recharge and consolidate memories, while sleep deprivation impairs attention, working memory, and impulse control. Chronic stress floods the brain with cortisol, disrupting the prefrontal cortex and making self-regulation and adaptability difficult.[74] Nutrition provides the fuel the brain needs; a diet rich in essential nutrients like omega-3s supports sustained attention, while sugary, processed foods can cause energy crashes (we aren't even talking about major toxins such as food dyes and high fructose corn syrup, which are a major part of most kids' diets). Physical activity boosts focus by increasing blood flow, oxygen, and dopamine, which enhance cognitive function and impulse control. Even mild dehydration can reduce processing speed and attention span, while emotional well-being is critical, as anxiety or depression can create mental fog and distract from learning.[75] Supporting these areas holistically ensures children have the foundation needed to focus and succeed in both academic and personal tasks.

The Digital Debate

One more quick thing that needs to be addressed. I have heard so many times from parents, "My kid can hyper-focus when it comes to video games... so maybe we should practice that." It's important to understand that while hyper-focus is a form of intense attention, it doesn't necessarily translate into the ability to stay focused on tasks that don't offer the same kind of immediate stimulation. This type of hyper-focus is a common experience for children with ADHD—it is not a lack of focus but a shift in how and where their attention is directed. Many of these kids are drawn to certain activities like video games; this happens because video games often provide immediate rewards, stimulation, and high levels of engagement, which can draw their attention intensely. The difference is that while they can become intensely focused on something stimulating, they may struggle with tasks that are less stimulating, like schoolwork or chores. The key here is that video games provide a constant stream of rewards, which aligns with how their brains respond to immediate feedback.

Video games are designed to provide quick and frequent feedback (points, levels, achievements), which stimulate the brain's reward system and create a cycle of dopamine release. This trains the brain to seek instant gratification, which, quite frankly, does not come from chores and schoolwork or even the feeling of working hard toward achieving a long-term goal (goal-directed focus). Helping them transfer that ability to focus into other areas often involves creating environments or activities that also offer clear, consistent feedback or finding ways to make other tasks more engaging.

The part we don't talk about is that educational companies are using the same tactics. They have taken a similar approach, using gamification in learning apps and platforms. For example, apps like Duolingo, Khan Academy, Kahoot!, iReady, and various others provide instant feedback, rewards, and levels to encourage continued learning. While this can be motivating and engaging for children, it also encourages them to seek immediate gratification and can make it harder for them to focus on less stimulating academic tasks, such as reading a long chapter or working on an open-ended project that doesn't provide instant feedback. While there is a claim that using gamification can "motivate" learning, we can't ignore the fact that they may be missing out on developing the ability to focus on tasks that require prolonged effort without immediate reward. This may inhibit internal motivation and affect the development of true attention skills that extend beyond instant gratification.

The use of gamification, smartboards, and personal devices also lends itself to another very important question: What counts as screen time? A recent survey demonstrated that American children spend five to eight hours in front of electronic screens each day. This is in stark contrast to the four to seven minutes they spend engaged in unstructured outdoor play (despite a recommendation of at least three hours of outdoor time per day). When I first read the results, my reaction was, "How is it possible for kids to spend five to eight hours on screens daily when they are at school most of the day? There isn't enough time left!" It was my brilliant eight-year-old who said, "Mommy, we are on screens at school." Oh, yeah!!

So, again, what actually counts as screen time: gamified school programs, smartboard activities, personal laptop homework, YouTube, video games, Zoom calls, FaceTime, fantasy leagues, family movie night? Long story short, I don't have an answer for you, and even if I did, the digital world is changing so fast that my answer may be different by the time you read this book. The fact remains that screen time is affecting kids in many ways and we as the adults need to stay diligent. We need to understand the effects on the brain, body, and development, understand how to counteract the negative effects (for example, with movement, outdoor time, hard work, and even boredom), and embrace the positives.

So What Now?

As this section demonstrates, a lot goes into the simple question, "Why can't kids pay attention?" But what can we do about it? The answer is, a lot! First and foremost, recognizing and understanding these factors is paramount. Simply stating and complaining that "kids today can't pay attention" is not going to do anything but further the divide. Today's kids have a disadvantage in development of these areas and, yet, because the developing human brain is so amazing, they can still be salvaged. We need to set realistic expectations based on your starting point (whether it is your children or this year's students). Make time for simple games that can enhance skills, such as working memory, impulse control, cognitive flexibility, and different components of attention. I have included my favorites in the workbook section under the integration or "I" chapter.

Stillness is an Active Process, NOT a Passive Process

I did mention we would revisit the importance of stillness, so here it is. As we transition from movement to focus to stillness, it's important to understand the profound role the neocortex plays in this process—and specifically, the prefrontal cortex. The neocortex (aka human brain), the brain's most advanced layer, is responsible for higher-order thinking, creativity, imagination, and emotional regulation. Within it, the prefrontal cortex acts as the control center for executive function, governing skills like self-regulation, focus, and impulse control.[76] Stillness, often viewed as a passive state, actually requires significant mental effort, engaging the prefrontal cortex to suppress distractions, regulate emotions, and maintain composure. While it is movement that helps develop these abilities, stillness is where they are actively practiced and refined.

This is where the challenge arises, particularly for children. In schools, we often expect them to sit still, remain quiet, and manage their behavior for extended periods. While these expectations might seem reasonable to adults, they demand a level of self-control and emotional regulation that children are still developing. Young children are biologically wired for movement and struggle with prolonged stillness. When we expect them to consistently demonstrate skills they haven't yet cultivated, the result is often frustration, stress, anxiety, restlessness, or behavioral challenges—not because they are unwilling, but because they are unable. We must remember that if a child does not have enough movement in their early years, the area of the brain required for stillness does not have the opportunity to fully develop.

It's important to recalibrate our expectations to align with normal developmental timelines. Instead of expecting young children to instantly master stillness, we can help them develop these skills gradually. Movement and sensory activities provide the foundation, as they strengthen the neural pathways in the prefrontal cortex.[77] Once this groundwork is laid, we can introduce practices like mindfulness, breathing exercises, or short periods of guided stillness to build their capacity for self-control. Activities that require focused attention, such as yoga or structured play, also provide opportunities to practice emotional regulation and intentional pauses.[78]

Rather than demanding stillness as a prerequisite for learning, we should view it as a skill that develops over time, much like reading or math. By offering children opportunities to practice self-regulation in supportive, age-appropriate ways, we create an environment where they can succeed—not just in sitting still, but in managing their emotions, focusing their attention, and navigating the complex demands of life.

One thing we haven't addressed yet is, why does it seem that some children are better able to achieve stillness and self-control at younger ages than others? Seeing as sitting still, self-control, and emotional regulation are all representative of appropriate brain development, the fact that one in six children are diagnosed with a developmental disability will definitely have a visible impact here.

And then there is the fact that not all kids are the same. The prefrontal cortex, which manages self-regulation and impulse control, develops gradually and at different rates for each child, meaning some may naturally be more ready for stillness than others. For example, it is no secret that this area develops more quickly for girls than boys, which explains why my best friends with girls were able to sit down with their girls and enjoy craft time, creating and coloring, while my boys ate the crayons, threw the crafts, and destroyed, well, everything they built.[79] Temperament also plays a role—some children are naturally more adaptable and calm, while others are more active or impulsive, making stillness more challenging. Environmental factors, such as consistent routines and opportunities to practice self-regulation, can further influence a child's ability to meet these expectations.

The important thing to note is that self-control is an important skill to develop. While we can recognize that all children are different, come from different backgrounds, and have different skill sets, we must also acknowledge that early development of skills, such as self-control, are extremely important and help to predict long-term outcomes of success. Have you ever heard of the Marshmallow Study from the 1970s? In the famous Stanford Marshmallow Study, young children were given a simple yet revealing choice: Eat one marshmallow now, or wait fifteen minutes and get two. The study, led by psychologist Walter Mischel, aimed to explore delayed gratification and self-control. What researchers found was striking—children who were able to wait longer tended to have better life outcomes in areas such as academic performance, health, and emotional regulation. But what's often missed in retellings of this study is that the ability to wait wasn't magical—it was supported by strategy. Children who succeeded weren't just born with stronger willpower; they distracted themselves, sang songs, covered their eyes, or turned away. In other words, they learned how to manage their impulses by regulating their environment and behavior.[80]

Stillness is no different. It's not simply the absence of motion—it's the presence of self-regulation, the skill of managing our internal states. And just like movement, it must be taught, modeled, and supported. Stillness is powerful. It is where reflection, mindfulness, and focused attention take root. But it should never be confused with compliance or used as a benchmark for "good" behavior. Just as we must honor the body's need to move, we must also nurture a child's ability to be still—when they are ready, and with the right tools. Movement may be the ignition switch, but stillness is the space where deep learning, creativity, and resilience take hold. Both matter. And both can be learned.

Mindfulness in a Noisy World

What better place to wiggle in our section on mindfulness than following our discussion on stillness? Before we can truly understand mindfulness, we have to first recognize the value of slowing down. In a world that constantly demands our attention—buzzing, flashing, and pulling us in every direction—stillness has become a lost art. But stillness alone isn't enough. It is one thing to pause, to sit in the quiet; it's another to be fully present in that moment. That is where mindfulness comes in.

Now, I have no intention of turning you all into meditating yogis. There are entire books, courses, and podcasts dedicated to mindfulness, but my goal here is simply to make the case for why it matters—why it plays such a vital role in a child's development and why, in today's world, it is more necessary than ever.

Let us start with a workable definition. Despite popular belief, mindfulness is not just deep breathing and yoga poses. *Mindfulness* is the fundamental human ability to be fully present, aware of where we are and what we are doing, and not overly reactive or overwhelmed by what is happening around us. It sharpens mental clarity, helps regulate emotions, and creates the kind of internal safety that is essential for learning.[81] Because, let's not forget—learning cannot take place in a state of fight or flight.

So why is this so important for kids today? For one, they are growing up in a world that bombards them with stimulation—constant notifications, flashing screens, and packed schedules that leave little room for simply being. As a result, the skills required to tune into their surroundings, to listen to their bodies, and to experience the world without judgment are not just underdeveloped; they are actively being pushed aside.

At the same time, we have to be mindful (pun intended) that in our attempts to enrich children's experiences, we don't unintentionally overwhelm them. Sensory overload is real, and when a child is bombarded with too much—too much noise, too much movement, too much expectation—their nervous system shifts into overdrive. What we often interpret as misbehavior or inattention is sometimes just a child who is drowning in input. Mindfulness offers a way to counteract this. It teaches children how to slow down, to process their emotions, and to find a sense of calm and quiet amidst the noise.[82]

Incorporating mindfulness doesn't mean forcing kids into silent meditation for thirty minutes a day. It can be as simple as taking a deep breath before responding to frustration, feeling the ground beneath their feet before starting a lesson, or noticing the rhythm of their own heartbeat after running across the playground. The goal is not perfection—it is practice. And with that practice comes a gift: the ability to be present in a world that constantly pulls us away.

There are many simple and fun ways to weave mindfulness into a child's day, as long as we understand what it is and why it matters. The workbook pages in the "I" chapter will help give you some ideas, as well as give you space to include your own. At its core, mindfulness is about tuning into our senses and cultivating awareness—of ourselves, our surroundings, and our emotions. Its importance goes far beyond just being still; it plays a crucial role in self-awareness, self-regulation, focus, attention, emotional control, and overall mental and physical well-being. When we intentionally create moments for mindfulness, we are not just helping kids find calm—we are teaching them that when the world around us is filled with chaos, we can create space inside.

Self-Regulation

I know that self-regulation has come up multiple times throughout this book—talking about stillness, attention, executive function, movement, etc. But I would like to circle back around and take a minute to directly focus on what it means to have self-control. The ability to self-regulate and maintain self-control is a skill, one that is a challenge for many children today, and, quite honestly, many adults!

Self-regulation isn't just about managing emotions—it's about controlling impulses, adapting to challenges, staying focused, and responding to stress in a productive way. It's what allows a child to wait their turn, handle frustration without a meltdown, or shift gears when plans change. But here's the thing: Self-regulation is not something kids just know how to do. It's a skill that requires a strong neurodevelopmental foundation and needs to be learned, whether through explicit instruction or modeling (remember, kids learn what they live).

The ability to self-regulate is strongly tied to the prefrontal cortex, the part of the brain responsible for impulse control, problem-solving, and decision-making.[83] It works in balance with the limbic system, the one that processes emotions, and the brainstem, which controls automatic survival responses. When these areas are well-developed and working together, kids can handle frustration, navigate transitions, and respond to challenges without completely losing control. But when something interferes—whether it's stress, sensory overload, anxiety, or frustration—the limbic system and brainstem take over, triggering a fight, flight, or freeze response. When this happens, the prefrontal cortex (the thinking brain) essentially shuts down, making it impossible for the child to self-regulate in that moment.

This is well-known brain science, and yet, when do we most often see adults trying to address or teach self-regulation to kids? Right in the heat of a meltdown. Self-regulation cannot be learned during dysregulation (actually, nothing new can be learned during this state). If a child is mid-meltdown, they are not in a state to process logic, listen to reason, or apply strategies. This is why telling a child to "calm down" or "make good choices" in the middle of an outburst rarely works—it's like asking someone to solve a math problem while they're being chased by a bear. The brain is in survival mode, and learning is not happening.

So how do we actually teach self-regulation? First, we have to stop treating behavior challenges as something to be controlled and start addressing them as something to be understood. For decades, schools have relied on behavior management systems—behavior charts, color-coded warnings, and behavioral techniques designed to reinforce "good" behavior and punish "bad" behavior. But behavior charts don't fix developmental challenges. They don't teach skills, they don't provide tools for self-regulation, they are not working to change the brain, and therefore, they don't create lasting change.

Instead, we need to strengthen the neurodevelopmental foundations that support self-regulation. Movement and sensory input play a critical role in helping kids regulate their nervous systems. Deep pressure and heavy work (like pushing a weighted cart, wall push-ups, or carrying a backpack) provide proprioceptive input, helping the brain organize and process sensory information more effectively. Even simple actions like an Achilles stretch can have a powerful calming effect on the nervous system. Rhythmic and repetitive movement, like rocking, swinging, or marching to a beat, can also help synchronize brain activity and improve focus. Breathwork and mindfulness techniques give kids an internal tool kit to manage stress before it escalates. The purpose of teaching these techniques is to avoid a meltdown. They are taught during periods of reflection (like after discussing the aftermath and what to do for next time) or during periods of calm. Even gentle reminders at the early phases, where they are becoming stressed or overwhelmed, but haven't quite flipped their lid are helpful.

Once again, these are tools and techniques that can be taught to help manage the systems responsible for self-regulation and self-control. You can ONLY teach these techniques when the child is in a calm state, with the intention that they will use them when they begin to feel like they are losing control. You CANNOT teach them mid-meltdown and, to be honest, once a child is in a full-swing meltdown, they may not be able to fully utilize them. At that point, going outside, walking, or doing something to break the fight-or-flight cycle is your only answer.

The other very important piece to this is that self-regulation and self-control rely on executive function skills, which are part of the prefrontal cortex (in the human brain). First off, we know this area is "under construction" in children. Second, we are now very well aware that when there is interruption to development, it directly affects these higher-level skills. And just as a reminder, we as a society have greatly interfered with typical development—one in six kids have a developmental disability.

Most importantly, we need to recognize that self-regulation looks different for every child. Some kids need movement breaks, while others need deep pressure. Some need space and quiet, while others need social support and reassurance. Many kids have underlying developmental challenges and need to be referred to a knowledgeable specialist. Our job is to help them discover what they need and what works for them, rather than forcing a one-size-fits-all approach.

And, finally, we need to rethink our approach to discipline and intervention. If a child struggles with self-regulation due to developmental delays, sensory processing differences, ADHD, or another underlying challenge, we need to recognize that and provide meaningful, developmentally appropriate support. Our interventions should be rooted in neurodevelopment, focusing not just on managing behavior but on strengthening the brain systems responsible for self-regulation.[84] This means identifying and addressing underlying delays rather than simply modifying outward behavior.

Too often, the focus is on managing symptoms rather than truly supporting development. While some interventions, including medication, may have a place, they should never be the only solution. Behavior charts or medication alone do not teach self-regulation, build coping skills, or address the root causes of a child's struggles. To make a real difference, we must focus on the brain itself—how it develops, how it functions, and how we can strengthen it.[85] Experts like Dr. Robert Melillo have dedicated their careers to understanding these connections, providing invaluable insight into how we can help children reach their full potential. By shifting our focus from symptom management to true developmental support, we empower kids with the skills they need—not just to get through the day, but to thrive for a lifetime.

The Truth About Social-Emotional Learning

I want to start by saying I am a huge advocate of social-emotional learning (commonly referred to as SEL). I have sat on the district-wide social-emotional learning committee as well as the elementary and grade-school committees in my home district since 2020. Social-emotional learning is essential. These are life skills that follow us forever. I would be willing to say they are more important than academic skills; however, this isn't the entire truth. In actuality, academic success is rooted in proper development of these skills.[86]

The term *social-emotional learning (SEL)* is often thrown around and has become quite the buzz word, particularly following the COVID-19 pandemic. I hear the term often and there is a general agreement that it should be a priority, but I have noticed that many do not know exactly what it means. Most have a general idea and recognize that it seems to make sense, but they lack the depth of understanding that helps us make a true change and lasting impact.

For those who are not familiar with the term, *social-emotional learning (or SEL)* is the process of helping children—and adults—develop the skills to understand and manage their emotions, build healthy relationships, make responsible decisions, and navigate challenges in positive ways. It's about more than "being nice" or controlling behavior; SEL teaches self-awareness, self-regulation, empathy, communication, and problem-solving, so individuals can thrive socially and emotionally as well as academically. Think of it as giving people the emotional "toolkit" they need to handle life's ups and downs, work well with others, and grow into resilient, compassionate, and capable human beings.

To fully understand what I am about to share, I want to take you back to where the term *social-emotional learning (SEL)* was developed. The Collaborative for Academic, Social, and Emotional Learning (CASEL) is a leading organization that shaped the field of SEL since its founding in 1994. CASEL was established by a group of educators, researchers, and practitioners, including Dr. Daniel Goleman, psychologist and author of *Emotional Intelligence*. They recognized the need to address students' social and emotional skills in addition to academics and defined SEL as a critical component of education. CASEL developed their first comprehensive framework for implementing SEL in schools in 1997.[87]

Throughout the period of 2000 through 2010, CASEL emphasized research and worked to develop an evidence-based approach to SEL. In 2013, CASEL published its well-known SEL Framework, which outlines the five core competencies:

1. **Self-awareness**
2. **Self-management**
3. **Social awareness**
4. **Relationship skills**
5. **Responsible decision-making**

Take a look at those five core competencies—do they look familiar? You may recognize them from our recent discussion on executive function. All five SEL competencies are influenced by the neocortex and the prefrontal cortex, as these areas are responsible for higher-order thinking, emotional regulation, and social cognition. Additionally, executive functions like impulse control, emotional regulation, cognitive flexibility, and decision-making play a significant role in enabling the development and expression of these competencies. I won't bore you with all of the brain science; I just want to highlight that it is, well, brain science.

That being said, cookie-cutter, box-checking SEL programs are just not enough to make a real impact. These are neurodevelopmental principles that affect that "under construction" area of a child's brain and, as such, must address neurodevelopment.

In addition, while I do believe SEL should be explicitly taught, it will not be effective if it is not embedded into the curriculum, culture, and even the community. When we are working on the SEL framework skills, we have to include collaboration with home, school, and even clubs and athletics. The home education component is absolutely essential, as the parents and care-givers are ultimately the gatekeepers.

While SEL was already gaining popularity, the COVID-19 pandemic and aftermath really pushed the movement forward and exposed a lot of shortcomings that our kids were already experiencing. If we are truly looking to make an impact and not check the SEL box, it is essential we understand this from every angle. We discussed the challenges our kids are up against, including rates of developmental disability and a mental health crisis. Then there is the change in childhood and increase in the impact of technology. If we do not address how these issues impact the development of SEL core competencies, we are setting our kids up for failure and, honestly, could potentially make a challenging situation worse.

So, how do we start to build a program that embodies the core principles of SEL? We start with making sure we are first addressing the area of the brain that is responsible for learning and processing these skills. Making sure we are addressing neurodevelopmental principles and identifying children who are struggling or delayed in development will help us set realistic expectations. Second, it is essential that we as the grown-ups actually demonstrate it. If children hear you say, "Be kind," and then hear you talking badly about another staff member or student, or if they hear you say, "Manage yourself," but you struggle managing you own emotions, well, that can be a bit of an issue. True story. Have you ever heard the famous poem, *Children Learn What They Live* by Dorothy Law Nolte? She wrote it in 1954 as part of her weekly column on creative family living for a local newspaper in southern California.

"Children do learn what they live then they grow up to live what they've learned."—Dorothy Law Nolte

Children Learn What They Live
By Dorothy Law Nolte

If children live with criticism, they learn to condemn.

If children live with hostility, they learn to fight.

If children live with fear, they learn to be apprehensive.

If children live with pity, they learn to feel sorry for themselves.

If children live with ridicule, they learn to feel shy.

If children live with jealousy, they learn to feel envy.

If children live with shame, they learn to feel guilty.

If children live with encouragement, they learn confidence.

If children live with tolerance, they learn patience.

If children live with praise, they learn appreciation.

If children live with acceptance, they learn to love.

If children live with approval, they learn to like themselves.

If children live with recognition, they learn it is good to have a goal.

If children live with sharing, they learn generosity.

If children live with honesty, they learn truthfulness.

If children live with fairness, they learn justice.

If children live with kindness and consideration, they learn respect.

If children live with security, they learn to have faith in themselves and in those about them.

If children live with friendliness, they learn the world is a nice place to live.

Figure 5.3 This poem, Children Learn What They Live, was written by Dorothy Law Notte

My dad gave me this poem to hang on my wall when my oldest child was born, and it has been there ever since. This seems like a good place to start—what do you think?

To sum it up, social-emotional learning (SEL) is not something we do—it's something that happens when we create the right conditions for it. When we focus on neurodevelopment, building a healthy and supportive culture, reducing screen overuse, and prioritizing human connection, essential SEL skills emerge naturally. Children don't learn self-regulation from a worksheet or empathy from a scripted lesson; they develop these skills through lived experiences, meaningful relationships, and environments that allow them to practice and refine them in real time. If we try to teach SEL without first addressing the deeper issues that impact a child's ability to develop these competencies, we're missing the point—and setting kids up for frustration. The truth is, when we get everything else right, SEL doesn't need to be a separate curriculum, because it becomes woven into the fabric of a child's everyday life.

6

Incorporate into Child's Program (or Existing Curriculum)

"If a child can't learn the way we teach,
maybe we should teach the way they learn."

—Ignacio Estrada

I pretty much set myself up for the world's greatest chapter transition! We have moved onto the "I" in M.A.G.I.C., which is to Incorporate Strategies into the Child's Program Based on Individual Needs. There is a lot of chatter about the cost of individualizing education and how it is "not practical." I am here to tell you there is no merit to the argument "we can't afford it." On the contrary, when it comes to individualizing education, we can't afford NOT to!

I guess I have another "I" here: individualize education. Wow, I even impress myself! But here is the thing: Individualizing education doesn't necessarily mean every single kid needs a one-on-one teacher with a new and innovative curriculum tailored to them. And it is not some lofty goal that must wait for legislative changes and system overhauls. Nope, this is something we can do starting tomorrow (or Monday morning, if it is a weekend for you). We can achieve it simply by Meeting the Child Where They Are, Assessing Their Developmental Needs, Guiding Them Using Whole Body Strategies, Incorporating These Strategies into their Program Based upon their Individual Needs, and Creating a Nurturing Environment that highlights the magic in each child.

Yes, we individualize education for each child by finding and highlighting the *Magic* (see what I did there)! So, back to the original "I": let us work on Incorporating these whole body strategies into each child's program so we can Individualize their education, set up an Ideal environment for success in all areas, spark their brilliant Imagination, promote Independence, positively Impact their whole life and... Identify their favorite Ice cream flavor. OK, I digress, but that was fun. Back to the point before you become Impatient with me.

The reason I am so proud of the transition into this chapter is that Dorothy Law Nolte's poem transcends into this section as well. The first step for an adult (whether teacher, parent, grandparent, caregiver) for incorporating strategies into a child's life or program is to be a good model. Kids are constantly learning from our actions. The "do as I say, not as I do" mentality does not work in real life. They are watching you, always (kinda creepy, but kind of awesome). My kids are aware of their teacher's favorite colors, their favorite sports teams, their morning routines, what makes them smile, and what triggers them. They are also annoyingly aware of my idiosyncrasies: the way I hug my coffee mug with my hands, how I clean up after myself when I cook, but also how I take absolutely forever to put away the Christmas decorations (seriously, it's almost February).

I bring this concept of modeling first mainly because it is not just what strategies you incorporate into their program and life, but how you go about doing it. If you are coming from a place where you have met the child, connected with them, have truly assessed their challenges, struggles, and strengths, and understand and are able to guide them using their whole body, then you will be able to seamlessly work these strategies in creating an individual experience even in a group setting. If you rush this part and push your strategies and become frustrated when they don't work as expected, you will not achieve your desired outcome. Again, it is more about the how than the what.

"To be or not to be, isn't the question… the question is how to be or how not to be."—Abraham Joshua Heschel

The Workbook

I am hoping that by now you are feeling the *Magic* and understand the importance of using it as your model and guide. You know how to meet the child where they are, assess their developmental needs, guide them using whole body strategies and now, we can work together to incorporate these strategies into their every day.

The rest of this section is interactive. It is where I get to help guide you through creating your own program for your kids and students. This section should be a great resource for you. It can and should grow and change over time. This is your space to explore, experiment, and create a personalized approach that fits your kids' and students' needs while matching your own individual style. In each section, I will share with you some of my favorite go-tos, along with my most valued resources.

I will also leave room to fill in with your own ideas, observations, and adaptations. It will be your own personal toolkit, one you can keep adding to as you discover what works best for you, your kids, and your students.

This will be broken down into areas including movement, attention and focus, self-regulation, stillness, mindfulness, ChiLL™ Time (Child-Led Learning), outdoor learning, multi-sensory learning, and collaboration. Each section will have a brief summary followed by my favorite activities and resources and finally an open area for you to add your own magic. The goal is that you will not only have a deeper understanding, but also a personalized plan in place that you can use to make a real difference in a child's life.

Grab a pen (or pencil or multicolored gel pen) and open your mind... Let's start incorporating strategies that truly support and empower Kid Magic!

Movement

We have talked a lot about movement and how foundational it is to child development. Movement is not just about healthy bodies, but also fundamental to cognitive development, emotional intelligence, social emotional learning, self-regulation, awareness, control, and more. Movement opportunites should be abundantly available to children as it is how they learn, grow, and develop. In this interactive section, I will share with you different areas in which you can incorporate movement, I will share my favorite ideas and resources and I will leave space for you to add your own. Please photocopy, sticky note, and write all over these pages. They are your plan to keep, cherish, change, and do whatever you need to help make you the best you!

Brain Breaks

Brain Breaks are probably the most well known way to incorporate some movement into the school day. Many teachers use resources such as go noodle, games and activities to give kids' brain a break by adding some form of fun movement activity. It is also a great play to work in cross midline movement patterns to engage both the left and right side of the brain:

- Dancing games such as freeze dance or online activities such as "Go Noodle"
- Human Knot
- High Five Chain
- Mirror Movements (done as class, pairs or small groups)
- Themed Yoga
- Brain Gym (Paul and Gail Dennison)

Transitions

Transitions are one of the easiest ways to experiment with bringing movement into your day. It is that in between time when you are transitioning between activities, subjects, or segments of the day (like special, lunch and recess).

- Have the kids help choose how they transition...let them be creative!
- Animal walks
- Jumping, bouncing, snapping, anything really
- Can use music and/or dance

Movement Enhanced Learning

Using movement and the whole body to enhance the learning process. Movement becomes relevant to the lesson. For example measuring angles in the classroom or creating them with your arms and legs.

- Hopscotch math
- Snowball game (using cotton balls, dip them in A cup of water and throw them at a relevant target, for example a math problem or site word, questions, etc)
- ABC Push-ups (Letters, sight words, phrases, partner work)
- Alphabet Dance (adapted from Ball-A-Vis-X)
- Brain Gym (Paul and Gail Dennison)
- S'cool Moves
- Pink Oatmeal
- Simple toolkit using dice, bean bags, color spots, etc.

Movement

Some room for more movement ideas:

Thoughts and Resources:

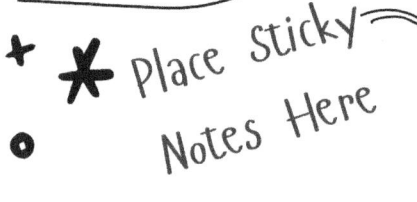

Place Sticky Notes Here

Movement

Some room for more movement ideas:

Thoughts and Resources:

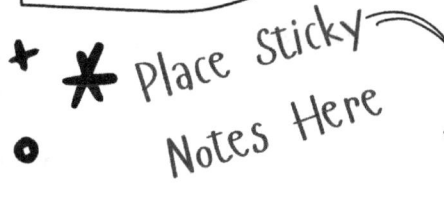

Place Sticky Notes Here

Attention

I have a secret to tell you, one that no one wants you to know. Are you ready? Paying attention? Good. Do you see what I did there...I played on your emotions. Emotionally charged events or statements tend to grab more of your focus and attention. That is one of the reasons that storytelling can be such an effective method of teaching. Remember, if your goal is to gain a kid's attention, you need to remember a bit about what attention is and how it works. It is not about using fancy programs, but more about a solid knowledge of the foundations and being about to use them to everyone's advantage. I say everyone because it benefits the adults to be able to earn a kid's attention and the knowledge shared benefits the kid. Win-win!

Types of Attention

Do you remember the different types of attention?

Covert vs. Overt

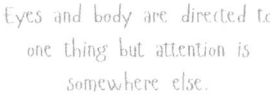

Eyes and body are directed to one thing but attention is somewhere else.

Eyes and body are directed towards the area of focus or attention.

- Sustained Attention
  - Maintain focus on single task over extended period of time
- Selective Attention
  - Maintain focus on single task while filtering out competing stimulus
- Divided Attention
  - Focus on multiple tasks simultaneously
- Shifting Attention
  - Transition focus between tasks or mental states
- Goal-Directed Attention
  - Prioritize focus on tasks aligned with our intentions or objective

Factors to Consider

Attention is not all about what is happening here and now. There are a lot of other factors that go into a child's ability to focus and pay attention. Be aware of the many factors.

- Did they get enough sleep
- Proper nutrition
- Hydration
- Stress levels
- Outside worries or anxieties
- Illness (upcoming or getting over)
- Disability (visible or invisible)

Games to Enhance Attention

- Story Telling and Re-telling
  - Instead of asking what a kid did over the weekend, have them share with a partner and the partner shares with all.
- Going to the Moon/Going on a Picnic
  - Age-old game of memory and add on. Starts with one person, "I'm going on a picnic and I'm bringing apples." Everyone adds on repeating all previous, "I'm going on a picnic and I am bringing, apples, bananas, cupcakes, donuts…"
- Listen and Draw
  - Play either a song or nature sounds. Have kids choose one thing and draw, write, poem, etc. focusing on one component and filtering out the rest.
- Game Time
  - Games like Spot It, Story Cubes, Monster Face Race, Edison Deck, Memory, Fluxx

Attention

Some room for more attention ideas:

Thoughts and Resources:

✱ Place Sticky
Notes Here

Attention

Some room for more attention ideas:

Thoughts and Resources:

Place Sticky
Notes Here

Self-Regulation

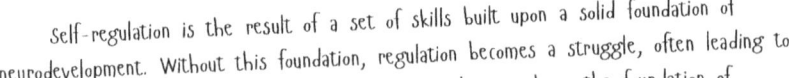

Self-regulation is the result of a set of skills built upon a solid foundation of neurodevelopment. Without this foundation, regulation becomes a struggle, often leading to frustration, outbursts, or meltdowns. We need to work on the foundation of neurodevelopment for this system to fully function. I am going to share a few strategies, resources, and tools that can help strengthen these skills as they are developing. They are designed to support the nervous system and keep kids out of fight-or-flight mode. They are simple things that can be taught when a child is calm and encouraged to use when they begin to feel like they are losing control. These best time to use these strategies is before a full blown meltdown. If we get to meltdown mode, your only options are to find a way out of fight or flight (walking, getting outdoors, etc.). Having this toolset and teaching kids about how to stay in control of their emotions and actions is empowering and gives them a sense of agency.

Calming Corner

There are many different ways to create a calming corner or calming cave. Create a space that can be used as a reset or break for when a kid is feeling overwhelmed or overstimulated. Teach them how to use the space BEFORE they need it. In my experience, kids who are taught how to use this space truly benefit from it - as does the entire class or group, including the adults.

- Get inspiration from online - Pinterest, TpT, Instagram, Google...
- Create a space that is calming and utilizes tools that are known to have calming effects
    - Breathing activities, Silly Putty, sensory stickers and toys, beanbag chair or cushions, weighted toys, warm/cold
- Include positive affirmations and some guidance
- Keep it judgement-free and safe

Factors to Consider

You may have seen this before in previous sections (like literally a few pages ago), but that is because it is important. There are always other factors to consider as we are dealing with a WHOLE child:

- Amount and quality of sleep
- Proper nutrition
- Hydration
- Stress levels
- Outside worries or anxieties
- Illness (upcoming or getting over)
- Disability (visible or invisible)

Calming the Nervous System

- Sensory Lessons
  - Teach them about their bodies. The Calm Book is a good start.
  - Sensory Telephone (just like the original, but can use other senses, like eyes closed how many hand squeezes or draw on palm)
  - Heart-rate Lesson (take it at rest, have them exercise, and take HR again, breathing activity then take HR again).
- Hand Clocks (imagine a clock on palm and use the other hand to push really hard at each number around the clock - both hands)
- Pretzel (cross legs and arms, squeeze tight, and breathe)
- Heavy Work (have student carry heavy box to another teacher or have the class try to "move the wall" or rearrange furniture)
- Exercise (jumping jacks, jog in place, to the ground and up, etc.)
- Outdoors (Take them outside, let them play, nature walk, scavenger hunt)
- Sensory Stickers (keep them on their desk, notebook, etc.)
- Co-Regulation (remember heart math - your calm affects them)
- For kids who struggle - secret signaling (like coin on desk)
- Rocking or Rhythmic Initiation

Self-Regulation

Some room for more Self-Regulation ideas:

Thoughts and Resources:

Place Sticky Notes Here

Self-Regulation

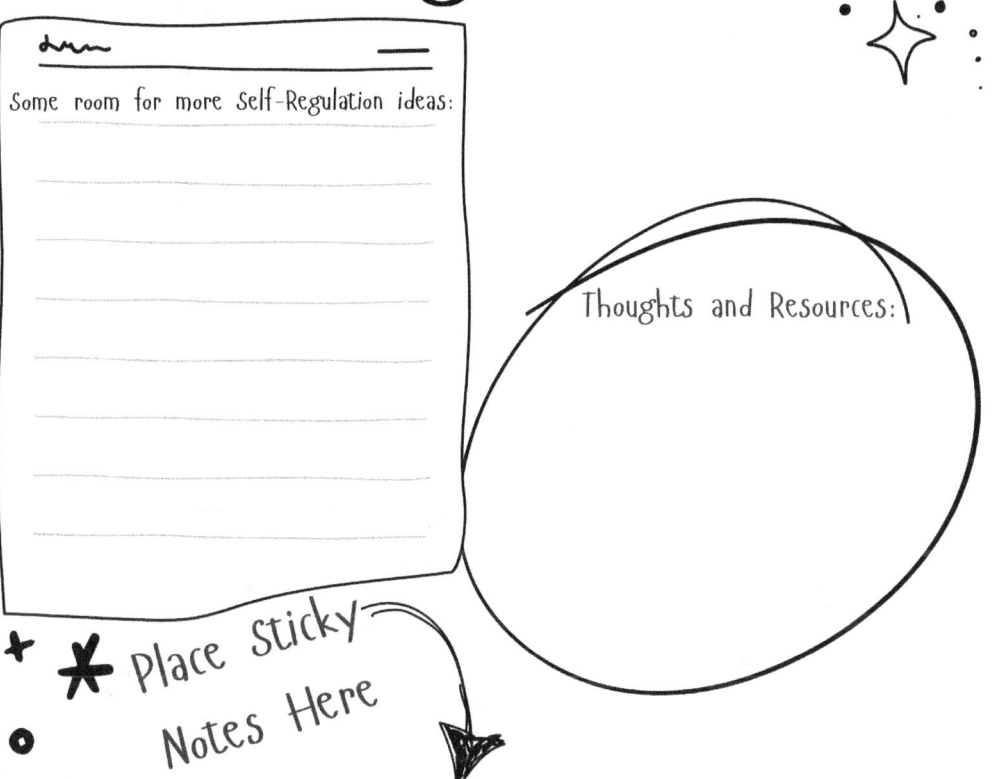

Some room for more Self-Regulation ideas:

Thoughts and Resources:

Place Sticky Notes Here

Mindfulness

Mindfulness is about being fully present and aware of where we are and what we are doing. It allows us to tune into our surroundings, thoughts, and emotions without becoming overwhelmed or overstimulated. In a world that constantly demands our attention—filled with noise, distractions, and stress—mindfulness helps us find balance, offering a sense of control over how we respond to what's happening around us. The practice of mindfulness is just that - practice! There are a few things that you can do to work this practice into your every day. The practice of mindfulness teaches us that even when the world around us is full of chaos, we can create space inside.

Breathing Activities

Studies show that those who breathe live longer than those who don't - trust me, I know, I'm a doctor. All joking aside, learning how to breathe is incredibly important.

- Regulates the Nervous System
  - Deep breathing shifts the body from fight-or-flight to a calm, regulated state, improving emotional control and focus.
- Engages the Diaphragm
  - Diaphragmatic breathing optimizes oxygen flow, reduces stress, engages your core, and enhances brain-body function.
- Creates Heart & Brain Coherence
  - Rhythmic breathing improves heart coherence, which enhances brain function, emotional regulation, and decision-making.
- Empowers Kids
  - Teaching controlled breathing gives children a simple tool to reduce anxiety, improve attention, and support learning. It is something they can control and do on their own, giving them agency

Factors to Consider

Attention is not all about what is happening here and now. There are a lot of other factors that go into a child's ability to focus and pay attention. Be aware of the many factors.

- Developmental Stage - Tailor mindfulness to the age and attention span of the children.
- Active Engagement - Mindfulness doesn't mean stillness - Move/Breathe/Interact
- Sensory Sensitivities - Be mindful of kids who are overwhelmed by certain techniques
- Environment & Atmosphere - Create a calm, welcoming space - minimizing distractions
- Consistency & Routine - Make mindfulness a regular part of the day
- Non-Judgmental Approach - Allow kids to engage at their comfort level
- Connection to Real Life - Help students understand how mindfulness can help with focus, emotional regulation, and stress in their daily lives
- Teacher Participation - Model mindfulness yourself! Kids are more likely to engage when they see adults practicing alongside them.

Mindfulness Activities

- Relax Kids
  - Guided Meditation Books
- Chocolate Meditation
  - Using all the senses to heighten awareness and experience
- Breathing Activities
  - 5 Finger Breathing
  - Breathing Ladder
  - Tracing Shapes Breathing
- Glitter Jar Analogy
  - Show them the clear calm jar, seeing through and thinking clearly
  - Shake the jar to represent chaos, can't think clearly
  - Everyone breathes calmly until jar is settled and can see clearly again
- Sensory Exploration
  - Find something you can see, hear, smell... feel heartbeat
- Seasonal Yoga Poses (I use Pink Oatmeal)
- Visualization
- Use Nature

Mindfulness

Some room for more Mindfulness ideas:

Thoughts and Resources:

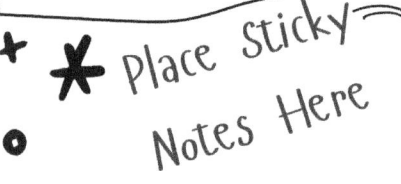
Place Sticky Notes Here

Mindfulness

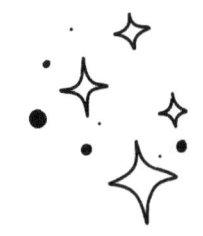

Some room for more Mindfulness ideas:

Thoughts and Resources:

Place Sticky
Notes Here

ChiLL™ Time

ChiLL™ Time (Child-Led Learning) is a way to create space for kids to take ownership of their education. Much like play, child-led learning fosters problem solving, critical thinking, cognitive development, social-emotional growth, and intrinsic motivation. When children are actively involved in their learning, they don't just absorb information—they own it. They develop a sense of agency, which builds confidence and deepens engagement. There are many simple ways to allow our kids to be more involved in the learning process. Start small and as you get more comfortable, it will open your eyes to what they are actually capable of. It's one thing to ace a test, it's another thing to actually learn!

Finding Kid Magic

Do you remember when I talked to you about Kid Magic? How every kid is born with a special magic and that it is their responsibility to discover it and help them grow? I want to revisit that because part of finding Kid Magic is having opportunities to discover it. Kids are often so busy being told what to do and what to learn that they don't often have time or exposure to the thing that may bring their magic out. Many kids going to college have absolutely no idea what they want to do with their life. Unless they were lucky enough to be exposed to that thing that combines their talents and their passions, they may not even start the process of looking until after they graduate! Giving them opportunities young to push their boundaries, explore their passions, totally mess up, and find their own limits is essential in helping them find their Kid Magic!

Maker's Space

The idea of a Maker's Space, where kids are free to create and explore using all different mediums and tools, is absolutely brilliant! I have seen the success of this firsthand with set-ups as simple as just a few sections with different materials, to advisors who set up weekly creative and innovative challenges that are optional for the kids.

I even have a good friend who runs a Cardboard Shed, in which adults and kids from all over come and just create the most amazing things! The heartwarming stories that come from the Cardboard Shed transcend paper play and often create life-altering changes. For inspiration check it out:
https://www.clairegillespie.co.uk/thecardboardshed

Ways to Incorporate ChiLL™ Time

- Personalized Space
- Alternative or Self-Selected Seating
- Kid-Run Lessons
- Project-Based Learning
- Kid-Chosen Transitions between activities or subjects
- Choice Board (i.e. - Mon - pick writing tool, Tues - pick seat, etc.)
- Soft Start
- Maker's Space
- Give Opportunities for Kids to share or "teach" their interests
- Journaling
- Let Grow (look into the challenges and organization)
- Allow Opportunities for Kids to identify a challenge or problem in their school or environment, then find and implement a solution
- Utilize principles of Oracy

♡ ChiLL™ Time ✦

Some room for more ChiLL™ Time ideas:

Thoughts and Resources:

✱ Place Sticky
Notes Here

♡ ChiLL™ Time ✦

Some room for more ChiLL™ Time ideas:

Thoughts and Resources:

Place Sticky
Notes Here

Outside

Getting kids outdoors for learning isn't just a break from the classroom—it's a powerful way to engage the senses, enhance development, and improve overall well-being. Time in nature provides rich sensory input, helping to regulate the nervous system, sharpen focus, and reduce stress. It encourages movement, curiosity, and hands-on exploration, making lessons more meaningful and memorable. Outdoor learning also counteracts the negative effects of excessive screen time, supporting mental health and cognitive function. Whether through structured lessons or free play, taking learning outside taps into the way kids naturally absorb information—through movement, discovery, and full-body engagement with the world around them.

Inspiration and Resources

There are so many programs and resources that share information and help to encourage the movement to get outside. Here are some of my favorite:

- Let Grow
  - An organization the supports childhood independence and free play, encourages kids to get out of the digital world and into the real world.
  - letgrow.org
- 1000 Hours Outside
  - Created by Ginny Yurich (Until the Streetlights Come On)
  - Encourages kids to strive to be outside for 1000 hours
- Find and Create Opportunities to spend more time outside or in nature around your home/school/community
  - Gardens, Eco Projects, Nature Spaces, Nature Walks

Factors to Consider

Outdoor time is an important way to counteract the negative impacts that screens have had on our children. It provides sensory rich input and provides countless benefits including:

- Reducing overactivity in the prefrontal cortex, reducing mental fatigue
- Improving ability of PFC to plan, focus, and regulate emotions
- Stimulates neurogenesis, which enhances learning and memory
- Nature calms the Amygdala resulting in decreased stress and improved emotional regulation
- Nature helps enhance focus, manage attention, stimulate problem solving and critical thinking, regulate behavior

Take Learning Outside

- Just about all subjects can make use of the great outdoors, although science pretty much lends itself to Nature's Playground
- Reading Outside
  - As a group or individually
- Presentations or Group Activities outdoors
- Hopscotch Math
  - Work your way through hopscotch by equations
- Utilizing the space outdoors provides for demonstrations and multi-sensory lessons
- Inspiration for writing activities
- Class discussions
- Mindfulness activities

Outside

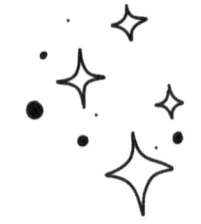

Some room for more Outside ideas:

Thoughts and Resources:

Place Sticky Notes Here

Outside

Some room for more Outside ideas:

Thoughts and Resources:

✱ Place Sticky Notes Here

Collaboration

Collaboration should not be an afterthought or a bonus. It is essential and foundational for fostering growth, learning, and a strong sense of community. When children of different ages work together, younger kids benefit from mentorship while older kids develop leadership and empathy. Likewise, meaningful collaboration between teachers, staff, and parents ensures that children receive consistent support both at school and at home. When educators and caregivers work as a team, children feel more secure, understood, and motivated to learn. A connected, cooperative environment—where ideas, responsibilities, and learning experiences are shared—creates a culture of support that benefits everyone involved, strengthening both academic and social-emotional development.

Parent-Teacher Collaboration

Parent-teacher collaboration is a shared responsibility that creates a stronger support system for children. Open communication, regular check-ins, and classroom involvement ensure that both parents and teachers stay informed and engaged in a child's growth. When parents reinforce learning at home and teachers create a welcoming environment for collaboration, it builds trust and consistency. By working together as partners—sharing insights, addressing challenges, and celebrating progress—parents and educators create the foundation for a child's success both in and out of the classroom.

We Need Each Other

Collaboration amongst us grown-ups is crucial to the success of our kids, but also for us. We seriously need each other. It helps us feel a sense of support and shared responsibility. When teachers, aides, administrators, and parents collaborate, we not only share ideas and strategies but also create a community where everyone feels valued and backed. That network that we create helps us to create the foundations needed to support our students, our kids, and our community. More than that, we need to look for opportunities to include our kids. It is going to take all of us to Unlock Kid Magic.

Collaboration Across All Boundaries

- Buddy Project
  - Organize a collaborative project between two different classes (for example, 1st and 6th graders). Have them meet monthly or quarterly.
- Reading Partners
  - Create opportunities for different classes to read together; even better if younger kids read to older kids and vice versa.
- Give older students a larger role in new student orientations
  - Give the older students opportunities to talk to incoming kids
- Create opportunities for staff and student collaboration, teacher and parent collaboration, and common areas where interaction is fostered.
- Make it a point to include students with special needs
  - Have "typical" students sit with them at lunch, participate in physical education classes, come into their classrooms for lessons or activities, participate in other specials together. It benefits all!

Collaboration

Some room for more Collaboration ideas:

Thoughts and Resources:

+ * Place Sticky
o   Notes Here

Collaboration

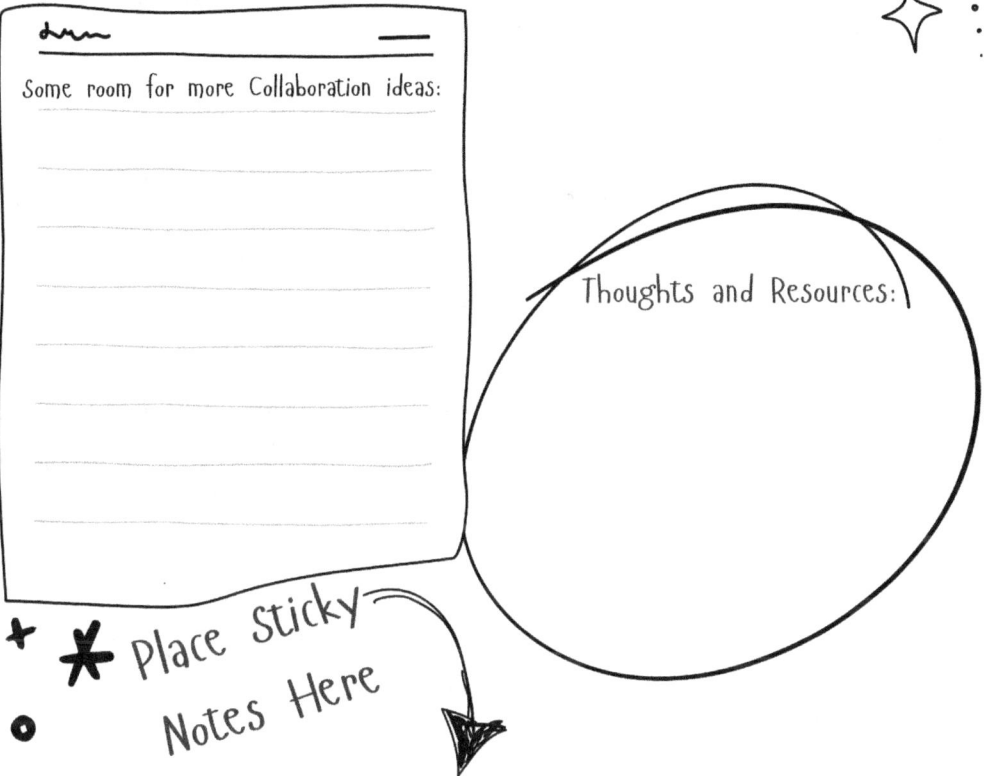

Some room for more Collaboration ideas:

Thoughts and Resources:

Place Sticky Notes Here

Multi-Sensory

Pop quiz: Do you remember how many senses we have? The answer is not five! We have at least twelve different senses. If you have learned nothing else (which would be ridiculous because you are so smart), I hope that it is clear that real learning ONLY happens through our interaction with the world around us. We interact with the world around us through our senses. Our brain (specifically starting with our thalamus - the sensory switchboard for all senses except for smell) then processes this input and responds accordingly. So multi-sensory learning is in fact just MORE EFFECTIVE learning! But here it is, in writing with it's own section, literally so that I can say once again, the more senses involved in the learning process, the stronger the connections and learning will be!

Stimulating the Senses

Think about all the ways that you can stimulate the senses and then make it a point to try to include as many senses as you possibly can with each activity you do. I have included an image with the senses on it for a guide. Some things you can do will give you more bang for your buck:

- Use nature and outdoor learning. It's like a sensory stimulating superhighway.
- Movement gives opportunity to engage multiple senses.
- Include the arts, all of them. Learning through playwriting, acting out, singing songs, creating visuals engage not only many senses, but also our emotions.
- Create a dynamic learning environment and take advantage of oracy.

Our Senses

Multi-Sensory

Some room for more Multi-Sensory ideas:

Thoughts and Resources:

Place Sticky Notes Here

♡ Multi-Sensory

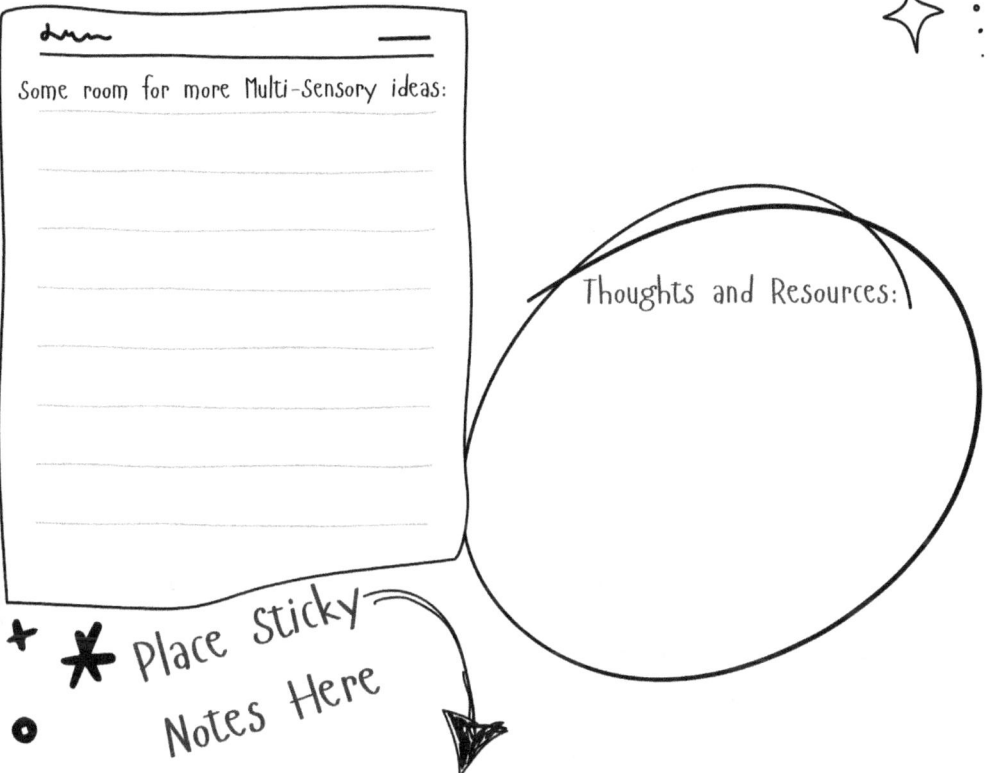

Some room for more Multi-Sensory ideas:

Thoughts and Resources:

Place Sticky Notes Here

The 5 Stress Responses

Of the

Automatic Nervous System

and what that may look like in a kid

Fight

Aggressive, Hitting, Biting, Kicking
Defensive, Blaming, Deflecting
Self-preservation top priority
Oppositional, Defiant
Yelling, Screaming

Flight

Wanting to escape or run away
Unfocused, Hard to pay attention
Restlessness, Fidgeting
Procrastinating, Avoiding
Anxious, Panicked

Fawn

Self-Abandons and Appeases
Overly helpful, People pleaser
Avoids conflict, Flatters
Can't say No
Co-dependent

Freeze

Spaced out, "I don't know"
Shutting Down, Mind goes blank
Gets stuck, Hides, Isolates
Zones out, Overwhelmed
Fearful, helpless

Flop

Hopelessness
Total Submission, Exhausted
Resignation or Apathy
Completely shutting down, May faint
Physically and Mentally Unresponsive

Chronic stress can lead to heightened responses to perceived threats.

Extra Thoughts Here

Really Good

Take Notes

Name.

Date.

Doodle Here

Scribble Here

Sign Here (if you want)

Extra Thoughts Here

Really Good

Take Notes

Name.

Date.

Doodle Here

Scribble Here

Sign Here (if you want)

Extra Thoughts Here

Really Good

Take Notes

Name.

Date.

Doodle Here

Scribble Here

Sign Here (if you want)

7

Create a Nurturing Environment

"To assist a child we must provide him with an environment
which will enable him to develop freely."

—Maria Montessori

When talking about creating a nurturing environment, we have to start with creating an environment where the child feels safe. While I love discussing how to set up an environment and culture of growing, learning, and creativity, if a child does not feel safe, none of that matters. Today's educators face the delicate balance of maintaining a nurturing environment while being prepared for serious safety concerns. The key is implementing necessary safety protocols without creating an atmosphere of fear. Just as we teach fire safety through calm, practiced routines, we can approach other safety measures with the same measured, reassuring attitude. The goal is to help children feel protected without feeling frightened, maintaining focus on learning and growth while being appropriately prepared.

Physical Safety

When talking about physical safety, we are assessing the environment to assure they do not fall victim to physical harm. For example, we want to make sure all furniture is safe and secure—no wobbly bookshelves or heavy things balanced up high where they can fall and hurt someone. For younger children, this means keeping outlets safe and covered, scissors or other dangerous objects in secure spaces, making sure the classroom environment doesn't have many tripping hazards (like wires or uneven surface changes), etc.

This also ensures there are clear expectations and protocols for emergencies, big and small—for example, well-rehearsed fire drills but also conversations about what to do if a classmate (or adult) falls and becomes injured. Understanding how to call for help and identify exits is also part of staying safe. The area of physical safety is typically the one that most of us are pretty good at as long as you care, and if you're reading this book, well, I can tell that you care.

The one tiny bit of advice I will leave here is to have regular, calm, and open conversations about keeping the environment safe. Make sure your kids know it is everyone's responsibility to keep their space safe. We often don't give kids enough credit, but it is truly amazing what even young children can do when we empower them.

Emotional Safety

Let's move on to something a little less visible: emotional safety. A child's ability to learn and thrive is tied to how they feel in their environment. If they are scared of being embarrassed, harshly criticized, or dismissed when they speak up, they will be in a constant state of fight or flight, which makes them unavailable for learning or engagement. Emotional safety in schools means creating an environment where students feel valued, respected, and supported. Teachers set the tone by modeling kindness, encouraging questions, and responding to mistakes with guidance rather than shame. Modeling a culture of emotional safety in an environment is one of the most impactful and foundational approaches (remember our poem from a few chapters back, *Children Learn What They Live*). A child who knows their emotions matter and that their voice is heard will be more willing to take risks in learning and grow from their experiences.

Psychological Safety

While emotional safety focuses on a child's daily emotional experiences and expressions, psychological safety extends to their deeper sense of security and willingness to take intellectual risks. A psychologically safe environment is one where children don't just feel safe expressing their emotions—they feel secure enough to raise their hand even when unsure of the answer, to try new approaches to solving problems, and to share their unique ideas without fear of judgment. When children feel psychologically safe, they move beyond just managing their emotions to actually thriving in their learning environment. They develop resilience, creativity, and a growth mindset that serves them well beyond their time in our classrooms. They don't fear making mistakes and will take chances with their thinking. This kind of safety runs deeper than day-to-day emotional well-being—it shapes how children view themselves as learners and members of the community. The most powerful tool we have in creating both emotional and psychological safety is relationship-building. When children have strong, trusting relationships with their teachers and peers, they're more likely to speak up when something doesn't feel right—whether it's a personal struggle or a safety concern they've noticed.

This was beautifully illustrated by the Handle with Care system my son's teacher implemented. At open house one year, she handed each parent a small piece of paper, similar to a homework pass. As she drew our attention to it, she explained its purpose. The slip read, "Handle with Care." She told us that if our child was going through something—anything—we could place this note in their folder, which she checked every morning. No questions asked. If we wanted to share details, we could, but it wasn't required. The moment she saw that note, she would do everything in her power to ensure our child felt safe, supported, and nurtured throughout the day.

I personally had to use that special pass. It is incredibly hard to send your child off to school when you know they are struggling—when their eyes are filled with tears, or when their heart is heavy with something they don't yet have the words to express. But knowing my son's teacher saw him as more than just a student—that she cared for him as a whole person, beyond his math scores—put my heart at ease. It allowed me to get through my day, knowing he was in the hands of someone who truly understood the power of human connection.

While we can separate safety into different categories for discussion, in practice, these layers of safety are deeply interconnected. A child who feels emotionally secure is more likely to speak up about physical safety concerns, just as a physically safe environment supports emotional well-being. Each layer reinforces the others, forming a strong foundation for a truly nurturing environment. But perhaps the most profound outcome of a safe, connected community is that it empowers children to take an active role in maintaining that safety. When children understand that their voice matters in creating and maintaining safety, they develop a sense of agency and responsibility that extends far beyond the classroom walls. They learn to recognize and speak up about unsafe situations, to stand up for themselves and others, and to contribute to the well-being of their peers. This transformation—from being protected to becoming protectors—is one of the most powerful gifts we can offer our children.

Creating the Village

At its core, creating a nurturing environment isn't just about meeting a child's physical and emotional needs—it's about surrounding them with people who offer safety, stability, and connection. It is human nature to strive to be part of a "village." We are essentially pack animals, so to speak. We weren't meant to do this alone. Raising, teaching, and nurturing children has never been a solo act—it's a collective effort, a shared responsibility woven into the fabric of every healthy environment. When we build a strong village, we don't just raise safe children; we raise future adults who understand that every child's safety is everyone's responsibility. And the strength of that village begins with us.

As adults, we are not just caretakers—we are protectors, role models, and lifelines. A child's village isn't just their home; it's their school, their neighborhood, and the many people who cross their path each day. And trust me, today's kids need their village. Our responsibility extends beyond our own families and into the broader community. If I see a small child about to run into a busy street, or if I notice a child alone or in distress, I will act—I believe (or at least hope) that most of us would. Not because they are my child, but because they are a child—and that is enough. It is the human thing to do. When children are surrounded by trusted adults who see them, know them, and care about them, they develop a deep sense of safety and belonging that allows them to explore, learn, and grow with confidence.

The connection does more than create a sense of security—it shapes the brain. Human relationships, particularly consistent and positive ones, serve as the foundation for mental, emotional, and psychological well-being.[88] Through connection, children learn how to regulate emotions, navigate social dynamics, and develop resilience. A child who has strong, supportive relationships is far more likely to manage stress, handle challenges, and develop healthy coping mechanisms. Trust is built through these everyday interactions—the teacher who greets them warmly each morning, the neighbor who remembers their favorite game, the coach who encourages them even after a tough loss. These moments may seem small, but they add up to something profound: a child who feels seen, valued, and safe.

This is why when talking about creating a nurturing environment, we must highlight that it is not just the physical environment. It is not limited by your budget and doesn't require anything too fancy (even though some of the fancy stuff is kind of fun). A Pinterest-perfect space does not necessarily equal a nurturing environment. You need the human connection—that creates the village.

I want to share a quick story about how one principal used the power of the village to help a young boy. This young boy was a sweet, caring, and playful first grader who loved school and loved being around his friends. A little ways into the school year, he started telling his mom he did not want to go to school. His mom offered some encouraging words and a hug, which seemed to work just fine to get a smile and get him off to the bus. But by midway through the year, the young boy was becoming a bit withdrawn, cried every morning before school, saying he hated it, and begged his mom to not have to go. When asked about his teacher and friends, he said he liked them all. He did mention he hated recess—that was the major red flag!

The mom had had many conversations with the teacher, who was doing everything she could to help, but at this point, the mom decided to speak with the elementary school principal. The principal observed the child during recess and found there was one boy who was being very aggressive and even kicked the young boy. The principal called the mom and shared his observations and immediately jumped into action, setting up a meeting with the mom, teacher, school psychologist, and himself.

The plan was simple, but very unique. The principal had arranged for the young boy to have a "check in" and "check out" each day with different staff members. He had the security guards, cafeteria workers, or aides check in with him in the morning with a simple, "Good morning, how is your day going?" The principal himself would "check out" with the young boy, telling him jokes and asking him to share any he knew. The plan also included weekly visits with the school psychologist with the ability to visit her whenever he wanted during the week. They talked about strategies, but according to the young boy, they just played and talked. His teacher would welcome him each morning; she even gave him extra math work to do for the week that she would reward him for at the end of the week. I know that sounds kind of silly, but doing extra and being praised for it was just the confidence boost this young boy needed. To round it all out, the mom was in frequent communication with all members of "the village." She even started to give him small missions, like say something kind to three different people or give a compliment to someone you don't know well. The turnaround in this young boy was incredible—and fast! By the second week, the boy came home to the mom and told her he was now friends with the boy who had spent the year hurting him on the playground. The young boy told his mom he gave him a compliment, found out he didn't have very many friends, and then decided they should be friends.

This is a true story; I should know, I'm the mom. The way the village showed up for my son still brings tears to my eyes. Not only was it life changing for him, but he is now a kid who has made it a point to be a part of everyone's village. This story seems complex, but if you break it down to each individual, it didn't take much effort; however, the results were astounding and impacted all involved.

You see, the village doesn't just support the child—it also supports the adults who care for them. When parents, teachers, and caregivers are connected to a strong, supportive community, they are better equipped to show up for the children in their lives. As a human, it feels good to be a part of the village. The support is good for all. In the story, the relationships between all the adults as well as adult to kid and vice versa were all enhanced by those subtle interactions. A stressed, overwhelmed adult cannot create a nurturing environment, just as an unregulated adult cannot regulate an unregulated child. If we want to raise emotionally healthy children, we must first create a village that nurtures the well-being of the adults responsible for them. Connection is not a luxury; it's a necessity—for both children and the grown-ups guiding them.

Heart-Brain Connection

Do you remember the part where I said, "An unregulated adult can NOT regulate an unregulated child"? I'll say it one more time: "An unregulated adult can NOT regulate an unregulated child." Seems simple enough, right? Pretty much common sense. However, this simple yet profound statement carries even more weight when we understand the scientific reality behind it. While we often think of creating nurturing environments in terms of physical spaces and intentional actions, groundbreaking research from the Heart Math Institute reveals we influence our environment in ways that extend beyond our conscious awareness.

We have spent a lot of time talking about our brain, as there is so much rooted in neuroscience and neurodevelopment. Now, I would like to shift focus for a moment to an area that hasn't gotten much attention yet—the heart. We mostly refer to our heart as the organ that pumps blood throughout the body. A very important, yet simple job that, well, keeps us alive. But what I want to focus on today is the other role of the heart that isn't really given much scientific credit.

Across every language, in every culture, and spanning the test of time, there are phrases such as "listen to your heart," "trust your heart," "your heart will guide you," "put your heart into it," "suffering through heartache," so on and so forth. It appears there is a long line of scientific research that stands behind these phrases being more than just metaphors. You see, the heart is an electrical organ with its own complex nervous system, also known as the heart brain. The heart and the brain are in constant communication. The Heart Math Institute shares that, contrary to popular belief, there are more neurological connections or, rather, more communication from the heart to the brain than brain to heart. What this means is that the heart regulates the brain, not the other way around. The communication from the heart heads directly to our amygdala and into our thalamus, which are our emotional systems and systems of processing.

Their research supports that the heart is such a strong electrical organ, in fact, that its rhythmic bioelectricity creates a 360-degree electromagnetic field around the heart that travels through every cell in our body and has been measured to extend out up to three feet in every direction. What this means is that while the brain runs the show inside our body, the heart actually communicates outward. Electromagnetic fields carry information, an electrical form of communication. Simply put, your heart can influence those around you and vice versa.[89]

This becomes even more interesting when we add in the concept of **coherence**. The research from the Heart Math Institute goes into great depth on the impact of coherence. Coherence is a healthy measurable state in which there is alignment of the heart, mind, and emotions. If you try to picture it, think about heart waves or even sound waves. A state of coherence would show nice smooth waves, while incoherence would look very jagged and abrupt, almost like driving while pushing on both the gas and the brakes. Coherence is naturally triggered by positive emotions (love, joy, happiness, peace, etc.), while incoherence is triggered by stress, fear, anger, etc. The Heart Math Institute refers to **psychophysiological coherence** as synchronizing the rhythm of all systems in order to seamlessly work together—respiration, digestion, immune, hormonal, brain function, heart function—to achieve health and high performance with less energy expenditure. When all major functions positively sync up, we have regulation of our autonomic nervous system (which is in charge of all of our major life functions).[90] But why is this important?

Most of us understand intuitively that children can "feel" our emotional state. We've all experienced moments when a child seems to absorb our stress or calm. What's fascinating is that this isn't just a metaphor—it's biological reality. Think about that for a moment. Every time we interact with a child, our heart is literally broadcasting our emotional state into the space around us. The complex nervous system within our hearts—our heart brain—communicates directly with our brain's emotional centers. This heart-brain connection doesn't just affect our own emotional state; it creates a tangible energy that influences the emotional state of the children in our care.

This understanding can transform how we think about being "present" with children. When a teacher enters their classroom feeling stressed or anxious, their heart is sending out that information like a radio signal, even if they're trying to hide it behind a smile. Conversely, when a teacher has achieved genuine emotional regulation, their heart broadcasts a coherent, calming signal that helps create a truly nurturing environment. This is why practices that help us maintain our own regulation—like mindful breathing, emotional awareness, and stress management—aren't just self-care luxuries. They're essential tools for creating the nurturing environments our children need to thrive.[91]

The implications of this research extend beyond individual inter-actions. When we gather children together in a classroom, we're creating a complex web of these heart-generated fields. A regulated adult at the center of this web can help establish a coherent, harmonious environment that supports everyone's emotional and psychological well-being. This biological reality underscores why emotional safety, which we discussed in our previous chapter, is so fundamentally important.

It is important to mention here that this is not too complex to explain to the children themselves. In all honesty, they may actually understand it better than the adults (Kid Magic at work here)! In fact, I included this information in a presentation I gave at a conference at UCLA (University of California, Los Angeles). The audience was adults; however, there was one beautiful five-year-old girl and her baby sister there with her mom and dad. I gave her a few sensory stickers and a smile as she quietly sat through my presentation, kicking her feet innocently in her chair. The next day, I had the opportunity to spend some time with this young lady and her parents at the Getty Museum. As we walked through the halls, her dad said something to the extent of using her mind. I don't quite remember what he said, but I clearly remember the young girl's response, "Daddy, you know that your heart actually controls your brain, right?! Yeah, you have to take care of your heart because it talks to your brain through tiny connections." She went on to school her dad and mom all about what she'd learned. I'd had no idea she was even paying attention!

Understanding the science of heart-brain communication helps explain why certain classrooms just "feel" different when you walk into them. That feeling isn't just about the physical setup or the decorations— it's a literal sensing of information being broadcast through the space. Making the kids part of the process and including them by teaching them will empower you and them. Trust your heart on this one.

A Place for the "Arts"

While we are on the topic of heart, I figure this is a good place to squeeze in the arts. The arts are the one language that is truly human. I want to say that again for the people in the back... **THE ARTS ARE THE ONLY LANGUAGE THAT IS TRULY HUMAN!** The arts carry a universal message of joy, hope, sadness, despair, playfulness, and seriousness and are the only form of communication that can capture the true complexity of human emotion, human thought, and the human experience. The arts influence the heart as they influence our emotions.

When I speak of "the arts," I am referring to all forms of art: drawing, painting, photography, sculpture, music, dance, theatre, poetry, culinary arts... ALL of it! I read the following quote in Ed Catmull's book, *Creativity, Inc.,* and it struck me: "Art isn't about drawing, it's about learning to see. What organization doesn't need this ability?"

I was fresh off a conversation with my oldest son, who had just said to me, "I don't like art." I was like, "Of course you do!" After a bit more conversation, we concluded he did not like the type of drawing projects he had to do in his school art class, which I pointed out to him was VERY different than "not liking art." We discussed the importance of the art all around us, and particularly, in his life. He highlighted the importance of music (both listening to music and playing the drum set) and how it helps him when he is anxious or upset. We also talked about the importance of art in his passion for cooking (you know, the culinary ARTS). He then became very excited and explained to me the importance of plating and presentation, as well as the need to balance color and texture in each meal. He continued on with the discussion of how the decor and environment of a restaurant is so important in how someone experiences their meal. He then asked me why art class was only drawing.

My answer to this was simply to reinforce that the arts are not a separate subject, a special, an elective, but rather the human foundation upon which we experience our world and therefore our education. All those who excel in their trade, whether a neurosurgeon or a local barista, view their work as a form of art. Even my son has so eloquently stated that he will be studying the culinary arts, not "cooking."

Maybe the arts find their way into the "extra" category because their impact is not measurable. Maybe because they are difficult to grade or categorize. Perhaps it is due to the fact that they don't rank high on what Sir Ken Robinson calls the "academic hierarchy."[92] Regardless of why they don't find their way into the role they ought to be in, the fact is we are doing our kids a disservice if we don't fix this.

Not everyone will experience the arts in the same way, and that is the beauty of it. For some, the arts provide an escape—a refuge from the structure and pressures of daily life. For others, they offer an alternative, a different way of seeing and expressing the world when words or numbers fall short. Art has a way of revealing truths about who we are. It gives us permission to explore, to create without limits, and to express what often can't be put into words. It's not just about painting a picture, playing an instrument, or performing on stage; it's about discovering how we process emotions, how we connect with others, and how we make sense of the world around us. Whether through music, movement, visual art, or theater, the arts give us a space to be fully present, to take risks, and to find joy in the process of creating.

Do you remember the story about my performance in sixth grade as part of the children's chorus for *Joseph and the Amazing Technicolor Dreamcoat?* It was during that simple extracurricular activity that I found my voice. With the help of Mr. Kramer (my director) and Ms. Jean (my choreographer), I discovered parts about myself I never knew existed. Parts that became relevant to me in my practice of medicine, parenting, my new career path, and just life in general. If you told ten-year-old me that I would be writing a book and speaking publicly, I am pretty sure she would laugh at you. That same ten-year-old me hated writing and hated the spotlight even more.

I will continue my story with one more little nugget—my college experience. I was accepted to what was called the Delta College program at my school. It was an alternative to the core general education classes required. The unique part of the Delta College program was its emphasis on real-life learning and the arts. In lieu of testing and the typical format of classes, the classes within the program were heavily rooted in conversation, debate, presentation, and the arts. We would have frequent trips to museums and galleries, we would learn through writing plays— music and dancing and acting it out—we had collaborative projects, we had heated debates in which we were taught how to debate (listening to all sides, respectfully disagreeing, etc.), we even made mandalas by the lakeside. We were required to participate in a local, a national, and an international internship before graduation. All of these things, while definitely not easy, made our classes more engaging, enjoyable, and dynamic. It wasn't until beginning my doctoral program post-graduation that I truly appreciated what this unique education did for me. I had an easier time communicating my thoughts as well as presenting my findings than many of my peers. I also noticed that making human connections with my patients came a bit more naturally to me. The arts are not the "electives" or the "specials" or the cherry on top of education, but, instead, are the foundation and should be embedded into our education and lives.

In a world that often prioritizes efficiency and measurable outcomes, the arts remind us that not everything valuable can be tested or quantified. They provide a space for exploration, for self-discovery, and for growth in ways that traditional academics simply can't. Every child deserves the opportunity to find their place in that space—to experience the power of creativity in a way that speaks to them. Because, sometimes, it is through art that we discover our most authentic selves.

The Physical Space

OK, I know I said that physical space isn't the most important thing—but I never said it wasn't important. What I meant is that you don't need a massive budget or the latest trendy furniture to create a space that truly supports learning and growth. Fancy seating, Pinterest-worthy decorations, and expensive materials are nice, but they are not the main thing that makes a space work. What does make a difference is how the space feels—welcoming, flexible, and inviting. And that can be achieved with whatever you have, as long as it is set up with intention.

Whether you're a teacher arranging your classroom before the school year starts or a parent organizing a play area at home, the way a space is designed impacts how we feel and function within it. When we're able to personalize our environment—even in small ways—it fosters a sense of comfort, creativity, and ownership.[93] And if that's true for us as adults, it's even more true for kids. So the real question is: How can we give kids that same sense of agency over their own spaces? How can we help them feel ownership of their learning environment?

One simple but effective way is to allow kids to customize their space. Something as small as creating their own name tags or an "All About Me" poster can give them a sense of belonging and individuality. Beyond just making the space feel personal, these small details also serve as valuable tools for teachers. If little Zachary loves hockey and is struggling with a math problem, a quick glance at his poster can remind the teacher to re-frame the problem in a way that connects to his interests. This use of physical space not only helps with engagement but also strengthens relationships between students and teachers, showing kids they are seen, known, and valued as individuals. This sense of ownership or agency is significantly correlated with learning progress.[94]

This idea of giving kids ownership over their space extends beyond decorations. One powerful addition to any learning environment is a calming corner—a designated area where kids can take responsibility for their own emotional regulation. This is not a punishment zone or a "time-out" spot. Instead, it's a space designed to help them reset, recharge, and use self-regulation strategies when they need them. Imagine a cozy nook with soft lighting, sensory tools, and calming visuals—somewhere a child can retreat to when they're feeling overwhelmed, overstimulated, or just need a moment of stillness. When we teach kids how to recognize their own emotions and give them the tools to manage those feelings independently, we're setting them up for long-term emotional resilience. Teachers who have implemented this in their classrooms and have taught their students how to use the space consistently report that the kids who have learned to use it effectively help their learning.

Even something as simple as allowing flexible seating can significantly impact a child's readiness to learn. It's not just about wobble stools and bean bag chairs—it's about giving kids the freedom to move around their classroom. Whether it's sitting on the floor, by the windowsill, or at different desks and chairs around the room, this flexibility supports both their learning and physical well-being. For example, during independent reading time, allowing children to choose where they sit not only gives them a sense of agency, but also incorporates movement, creating a more dynamic and engaged classroom environment.

Ultimately, the goal is not to create a perfect space—it's to create a space that works for the kids in it. A space where they feel comfortable, empowered, and ready to learn. Because when children feel safe and in control of their environment, they can focus on what truly matters—growing, exploring, and discovering their potential.

Nurture Their Nature

As far back as I can remember, I always wanted to be a mom. I always looked forward to all the wonderful things I would do with my kids and everything I would teach them. As much as I love to say I have and continue to teach my children many things, I believe they have taught me more—starting with my "nurture their nature" revelation. I have had this ongoing debate with myself about what matters more in shaping a person—nurture or nature. We all know we're born different, each with our own strengths, challenges, and quirks. And we also know our environment plays a huge role in shaping us. But I kept wondering—which one is MORE important? Is it the world around us that defines us, or is it how we interact with it?

Then I had kids. And suddenly, it hit me like a ton of blocks, dumped out of a toy bin—we have to nurture THEIR nature. My second son made sure I learned this lesson the hard way. I tried raising him the same way I raised my first. Spoiler alert: It didn't work. And by the time my third came along, I threw out the "one-size-fits-all" approach entirely. Each child is born different. I had to realize that fairness was not giving them each the same tools, but, rather, the ones they need.

I saw an incredible video posted by an elementary school teacher on TikTok (yes, I'm citing TikTok—@heyaimeej). She explained how she taught fairness in her class. She started by asking the students if they had ever scraped their elbows. She then chose one student and asked him to tell everyone how he hurt his elbow. She then placed a Band-Aid on his elbow. Next she asked who had ever bumped their head. More hands went up and she chose one student to tell the story of how he hurt his head. She then said, "I am so sorry you hurt your head—here is a Band-Aid for your elbow" and she placed a Band-Aid on his elbow. The kids were a little confused at this point, but she continued by asking who had ever scraped their knee. More hands went up and she chose one student to tell the story of how he hurt his knee. She then said, "I am so sorry you hurt your knee—here is a Band-Aid for your elbow" and she placed a Band-Aid on his elbow. At this point the kids were super confused. She stopped her lesson and explained that even though she gave everyone the exact same thing in the exact same way, it wasn't helpful to everyone. She stated, "Fair doesn't mean everyone gets the same thing; it means everyone gets what they need." Each kid has their own unique personalities, needs, and ways of learning and engaging with the world. But here's the key: How they are nurtured determines whether they will thrive and become the best version of themselves.

"It is the supreme art of the teacher to awaken joy in creative expression and knowledge."—Albert Einstein

Not all kids flourish in the same environment. Some sink where others swim. This is why individualized education isn't just a nice idea—it is essential. Every child has boundless potential, but a rigid, one-size-fits-all approach to learning stifles that potential instead of nurturing it. And this is not just about academics. We live in a world that is evolving so quickly that we can't predict what skills our kids will need five, ten, or twenty years from now. The only thing we can do is teach them how to learn, how to adapt, and, most importantly, how to know themselves. When kids understand who they are, they're not just preparing for the future—they are shaping it.

And if we want to nurture who they are, we need to pay close attention to where they are. Environment matters. A child's surroundings can either support their development or stifle it. Again, we must **nurture** *their* **nature**!

Not All Classrooms Have Four Walls

"Children across the world are spending less time outdoors today than maximum security prisoners."—*Free the Kids* (2016)

As we explore how to create a nurturing environment for our children to grow and thrive, we simply cannot ignore the importance of the great outdoors. Children are not meant to sit still inside four walls all day. Their brains and bodies crave movement, exploration, and connection with the natural world. Outdoor spaces offer many things that no classroom can fully replicate. They offer kids (and adults) freedom to move, to breathe, to take risks, to wonder. If we truly want to nurture a child's nature, we need to let them experience nature itself.

The recommended outdoor time for children is three to four hours per day, but according to the Kamik Outside Free Play Survey, American children are spending an average of just four to seven minutes per day in unstructured outdoor play. This is in stark contrast to the five to eight hours they spend in front of electronic screens. Even more concerning, 35 percent of children play outside only once a week or less. What's more, about a third of American primary school teachers take lessons outdoors less than once a month—this is by far the least worldwide.[95]

But even beyond the statistics, it's clear: Children should be outside as often as possible. Nature has something magical to offer a developing child. It provides rich sensory input that encourages the activation of multiple senses, which in turn helps reduce stress, improve emotional regulation, and enhance learning, attention, focus, and memory. It is more than just the number of senses that are activated—it is the quality of how they are engaged. For example, of course we are using vision within the classroom. However, when we are outdoors, the depth, diversity, texture, lighting, and the level of complexity of everything we see stimulates our visual system and our visual processing centers to a whole new level.

Incorporating outdoor learning into the school day can be a game-changer. Taking lessons outside, whether for reading, writing, or math, can increase engagement and creativity. Science comes to life when kids study ecosystems, observe weather patterns, or explore plant and animal life firsthand. Hands-on activities like scavenger hunts, outdoor journaling, and group discussions while walking not only reinforce academic concepts but also keep kids physically active and engaged. Moving beyond the four walls of a classroom allows students to connect with their learning in a more dynamic, memorable way.

Perhaps one of the most important roles of outdoor time is counteracting the negative effects of screen time. Excessive screen use overstimulates the brain's reward centers, leading to shortened attention spans, impulsivity, and difficulty with deep focus.[96] Time spent in nature helps reset these neural pathways, improving focus and attention.[97] Unlike the artificial stimulation of screens, nature provides real-world sensory input, allowing kids to engage with varied textures, sounds, and movements that support healthy sensory processing. Outdoor play also fosters social interaction, cooperative play, and communication skills—key areas that often suffer when kids spend too much time on screens.[98]

And let us not forget the benefits of experiencing nature in all seasons. I remember a mother asking me during a Parent University event, "What do we do with our kids in the winter?" My answer? "Put on a jacket." I'm not suggesting we send children outside in a dangerous blizzard, but a little exposure to the elements can have a profound positive impact on their health and well-being. Whether it's the crisp winter air or the warmth of a sunny afternoon, the natural world offers countless opportunities for growth and development—regardless of the temperature.

"In adventurous outdoor play they build not just their heart, lungs, and muscles, but also their courage and resilience."—Dr. Peter Gray

In short, nature is not just a place to play—it is a classroom in its own right. The benefits of outdoor learning span far and wide, including improvements in executive function, attention, self-regulation, and concentration, as well as reduced stress and anxiety. As we work to create nurturing environments that foster learning, creativity, and well-being, we must make room for time outside the classroom within our daily routines.

Part III

Creating a New Story: Re-imagining Childhood

8

Addressing the Threats to the MAGIC

"Sometimes I believe in as many as six
impossible things before breakfast."

—Alice in Wonderland

As we move into the final section of this book, I want to be upfront with you—I know making changes won't be easy. There will be barriers, and there will be challenges. You will face adversity, and, at times, it may feel like you're taking on the world. And honestly? In a way, you are. But here's what I need you to remember: You are not alone. No matter how isolating this journey may feel at times, there are so many of us walking this same path, working toward the same goal. So yes, it will be hard—but it will absolutely be worth it.

Whenever I run workshops or talk with teachers and parents, I always start with the same question: What are your biggest challenges and barriers? Some of the answers are expected—time, money, resources, support. These are the universal struggles, no matter our role. Others go a little deeper—administration, curriculum restrictions, lack of autonomy. But there's one answer I have heard more often than I care to admit, one that's almost embarrassing to put in writing: other teachers.

Yes, you read that right. Some of the biggest resistance doesn't come from outside forces—it comes from within. Many teachers feel judged, ridiculed, or limited by their own colleagues. And it doesn't stop there—parents often feel the same way, sensing silent (or not-so-silent) judgment from other parents. And what's worse? These perceived barriers end up shaping our real decisions. We second-guess ourselves. We hesitate to try something different. We hold back. Not because we can't do something, but because we fear what others will think.

But here's the thing—I also ask this same question at the end of my workshops. And by then, something shifts. Many of us come to realize these barriers aren't as solid as we once thought. They aren't immovable walls; they're just lines drawn in the sand. And the moment we recognize them for what they are, we realize something powerful: We can step right over them. You have more control than you think. The question is—are you ready to take that step?

The Most Important Thing

The most important thing is knowing what the most important thing is.

Honestly, I could stop right there. One sentence. But a whole section with just a single line might look a little ridiculous, so let's break it down.

From the moment we enter the world, we are fed a narrative about what matters most. Get good grades. Get into a good college. Get a good job. Or, if you're a parent or educator, make sure your child is reading at a Level M by second grade, mastering multiplication facts by third, and scoring above the ninetieth percentile by middle school. There is an endless stream of benchmarks, standards, and external pressures telling us what should be at the top of our priority list.

But have we ever stopped to ask why? Why are these the things we're chasing? Why do we let a letter on a report card or a score on a standardized test define success? More importantly, why do we let it define worth?

The truth is, none of those things matter if we don't first focus on the real essentials—mental and emotional well-being, physical health, human connection, curiosity, resilience, creativity, imagination, and a love for learning that lasts beyond the classroom. Academics are important, of course, but they are not the most important thing. The ability to navigate life, to adapt, to self-regulate, to think critically, and to connect with others—that is what ultimately determines success, not just in school, but in life. Many of our most successful people never finished formal schooling—Thomas Edison, Henry Ford, Richard Branson, John D. Rockefeller, Colonel Harland Sanders, Walt Disney, Quentin Tarantino, the Wright Brothers, Agatha Christie, Florence Nightingale, Venus and Serena Williams, Tim Tebow, and Peter Jackson, to name a few. That is not including college dropouts, such as Steve Jobs, Bill Gates, Mark Zuckerberg, and Michael Dell. Let that sink in.

So, I'll say it again—the most important thing is knowing what the most important thing is. We may want to start by figuring out what that is.

Mic Drop.

Outside the Box

What does it really mean to think outside the box? And, more importantly—who decided there should be a box in the first place? Who is trying to lock our brilliantly creative minds inside rigid boundaries, limiting our ability to see beyond what has already been done?

"Children must be taught **how** to think, not **what** to think."—Margaret Mead

One of the greatest advantages of being deeply rooted in critical thinking and creativity is that thinking outside the box has never been a challenge for me—because, honestly, I never even see the box. It's not something I have to step outside of because, in my mind, it simply doesn't exist. I consider this one of my own unique pieces of Kid Magic—that natural, unfiltered ability to question, explore, and imagine without constraints.

The only downside? Sometimes, I have to work extra hard to recognize the box that everyone else is thinking inside of so I can help guide their minds beyond it. It's like being in a room where everyone else sees walls, but I only see open space. I have to pause, step back, and understand why those walls exist in the first place before I can show others that there's a door—or, better yet, that they don't need the walls at all.

It reminds me of *The Matrix*, where Neo is given a choice—take the blue pill and stay in the comfort of the world as he knows it, or take the red pill and wake up to the reality beyond the illusion. Most people are so used to the box, so conditioned by routine, expectations, and the way things have always been done, that they don't even realize there's another way. Thinking outside the box—or realizing the box doesn't exist at all—is like taking the red pill. Once you see beyond the limits imposed by systems, fear, and convention, you can't unsee it. And that is where real creativity, real problem solving, and real change begin. The possibilities are endless. The question is—are you ready to take the red pill?

Imaginocity

"Imagination is the source of all forms of human achievement."—Sir Ken Robinson

Our children's creativity—and, quite frankly, our own—has been hijacked.

Walk through an elementary school or even a preschool, and you'll see colorful artwork proudly displayed on the walls. At first glance, it's beautiful—a showcase of artistic expression. But look closer. More often than not, you'll find twenty nearly identical versions of the same project— black cats with green eyes, each cut and glued in the same way under the teacher's guidance. Beautiful? Sure. But whose creativity is really on display—the child's or the adult's?

Let's be honest—three-year-olds don't produce uniform, polished masterpieces. They create glorious, chaotic, brilliant disasters. They mix all the Play-Doh colors together until they become an unrecognizable shade of brown. They smush together things that "shouldn't" go together. They might color the sky orange or the grass purple. They smear mud across walls, pile up rocks, dirt, sticks, and bugs, and declare it a work of art. And they're right. Because that is what creativity looks like before we place it inside a box.

But how often do we let kids truly explore their creativity? How often do we give them the freedom to let their imaginations run wild before telling them, "Unicorns don't actually exist" or "People can't actually fly"? How often do we let them follow their curiosity without imposing limits, structure, and rules that tell them how things are supposed to be?

I know—letting go of control isn't always easy. It takes a level of openness, a willingness to embrace uncertainty, and, sometimes, a strong stomach. Case in point: I recently ate one of my son's "brilliant" lunch creations—tuna (straight from the can, no mayo, no seasoning), rice, barbecue sauce, fresh cranberries, and Pecorino Romano cheese. Yup. Imagine that. And I did it with a smile. Because, sometimes, fostering creativity means letting go of how things are supposed to be and just going with it.

In trying to define what I believed to be one of the most beautiful, fundamental traits of childhood, I found myself stuck between **curiosity, creativity,** and **imagination**. So, naturally, I did what any adult who hasn't quite grown up would do—I invented my own word (with a little help from a friend):

IMAGINOCITY.

Imaginocity is curiosity that sparks limitless imagination—and that imagination is what leads to true creativity. Creativity isn't just about art. Yes, the arts are a beautiful and powerful expression of creativity, but it's so much bigger than that. We need to create learning environments or a pedagogy that approaches learning through a combination of collaboration and individuality, giving all students, teachers, and participants a sense of agency, which empowers them to have the courage to take ownership of their magical journey of learning through curiosity and sparks of imagination.

"Creativity is as important in education as literacy, and we should treat it with the same status." —Sir Ken Robinson

In his world-famous TED Talk, *Do Schools Kill Creativity?*, Sir Ken Robinson lays out a powerful argument for why creativity isn't just an artistic skill—it's a way of thinking, a way of problem solving, and a way of shaping the future. Creativity is what has led to technological breakthroughs, medical advancements, and entire industries that didn't exist a decade ago. Yet, in education, we treat it as an afterthought. We refer to some people as "creatives," as if creativity is a rare trait rather than an innate human ability.

The reality is all children are born with extraordinary creative potential. And in Robinson's words, "We squander it, pretty ruthlessly." How? By telling them to color the sky blue and the grass green. By giving them step-by-step instructions on how to "properly" complete an art project. By teaching them that there is a right way to do things.

We cannot afford to keep doing this. By stifling creativity, we are limiting not just our children, but our future.

Think about it—kids starting school today will retire around 2073. Let that sink in. Robinson put it bluntly: "Despite all the expertise that's been on parade... nobody has a clue what the world will look like in five years' time. And yet we're meant to be educating them for it."

So, what's the solution?

Imaginocity.

We don't just need to allow curiosity-led imagination—we need to encourage it. We need to celebrate it. We need to build purpose around it. Instead of forcing children to fit into rigid academic structures, we need to design learning environments that align with their natural curiosity and their thirst for exploration.

Because here's the truth—kids will learn, with or without a formal education. Learning is their default setting. The real question is, what are we doing to harness that power, to nurture it, and to use it to prepare them for a future we can't even imagine?

Why not shift to a kid-centered approach to education? Why not embrace imaginocity and let creativity run free?

We hold the key to **unlock their Kid Magic.**

Play

How could I possibly write a book titled *Kid Magic Unlocked* without addressing **PLAY**? I mean, I can't, obviously—so here it is!

Before I jump in, I have a confession to make—I totally messed this one up at first.

For starters, you may or may not know this about me, but I was quite literally the world's greatest parent—before I had kids. It's true. I had it all figured out. I have always been fun, playful, childlike (my size helps), and imaginative. My favorite character has always been Figment—you know, the actual mascot for imagination—a figment of your imagination. Goofy and Stitch are also on my favorites list. So, yeah, I was meant to be a fun mom.

I started off this adventure with the perfect setup for play. I built obstacle courses, sensory bins, world-class crafting opportunities, monster forts that rivaled medieval castles, and imaginative games that would put Pinterest to shame. My kids had no shortage of structured fun. And then… the world shut down.

Suddenly, I had three kids home full time, plus the challenge of virtually taking care of both my students and my patients (yes, virtual physical therapy—because that makes sense). So one day, I asked the kids to go outside and play for an hour while I regrouped. Their response? "What do we do?"

So, being the fun mom that I am, I built them more obstacle courses and set up more games, thinking I was helping. But I quickly realized I was spending more time setting them up to play than they actually spent playing. This went on for days until it finally hit me—I had spent so much time organizing my kids' play that they had never learned to play on their own! I needed to get out of the way.

The transition was not easy. We went cold turkey. I told them they needed to play outside for an hour before lunch. They insisted they couldn't do it without me. So, naturally—I locked them outside. (Relax; it was in our fenced-in backyard, and I could see them through our big kitchen window.) They responded by sitting on the back stoop and crying—for an entire hour.

Day two: same thing. But this time, they only cried for a little while before wandering into the yard and figuring something out. Progress.

By day three, they went running outside on their own. They even invented "Spud"—you read correctly, their invented game was literally almost identical to spud (a game I played as a kid—I have now officially labeled myself as a child of the eighties). By the end of the week, I had to call them inside and bribe them with cookies.

It took me longer than I would like to admit to get here, but I finally realized that by constantly structuring my kids' play, I had robbed them of the chance to develop the essential skills that only free play can teach.

Remember that quote from earlier in this book? The one about it taking four hundred repetitions to create a new synapse, but only ten to twenty repetitions when done through play? That's not just a fun fact—it's neurological proof of how critical play is to child development.

Dr. Peter Gray, developmental psychologist and author of *Free to Learn*, describes play "first and foremost, self-chosen and self-directed. Players choose freely whether or not to play, make and change the rules as they go along, and are always free to quit. Second, play is intrinsically motivated; that is, it is done for its own sake, not for external rewards such as trophies, improved resumes, or praise from parents or other adults. Third, play is guided by mental rules (which provide structure to the activity), but the rules always leave room for creativity. Fourth, play is imaginative; that is, it is seen by the players as in some sense not real, separate from the serious world. And last, play is conducted in an alert, active, but relatively unstressed frame of mind."[99]

Play isn't a luxury—it is a necessity. Despite overwhelming research on the importance of play, we continue to take it away.[100]

A recent study found that American children participate in five to twelve structured activities per week.[101] With fewer kids playing in neighborhoods and on playgrounds, their opportunities for unstructured play are disappearing. Recess time is shrinking, play breaks are replaced by academic instruction, and kindergarten—the once magical land of learning through play—has become the new first grade.

As one veteran kindergarten teacher told me, "There is no more time for play, as academic standards take up most of their time. They don't get to be little kids anymore… it's heartbreaking."

Elementary school teachers across the country have echoed this sentiment, witnessing firsthand the toll that play deprivation is taking—not just on children, but on themselves. When kids aren't given enough time to move, explore, and just be kids, they struggle to focus, regulate their emotions, and engage in learning. And yet, play time—especially recess—is often taken away as punishment for poor behavior, missed assignments, or academic struggles.

This is completely counterproductive. The children who struggle the most—whether emotionally, socially, or academically—are often the ones who need more movement and play, not less. Taking away recess only increases frustration, dysregulation, and behavioral issues, making the very problems we're trying to solve worse.

Free play isn't just beneficial—it's necessary for all ages. And when kids of different ages play together, something truly magical happens. The first thing people asked me when we decided to homeschool our oldest son was, "How are you going to socialize him?" My first response was, "I'm not—I plan to lock him in his room and never let him see another human." Seriously, all joking aside. If you think about it, school is kind of artificial socialization—isn't it? Where else in life are you forced to only spend time with people who are your own age—as if your date of manufacture (as Sir Ken Robinson calls it) is the most important thing about you? Many of the people closest to me in my life are not my age and that is a good thing. Mixed-age play and integration is so important and makes for a healthier and more well-rounded social experience.[102] When kids of different ages play, the older kids naturally step into leadership roles, guiding younger ones, helping them understand rules, and modeling problem-solving skills. Younger kids, in turn, learn by observing and imitating their older peers, pushing themselves to try new things and take healthy risks.

In mixed-age play, something fascinating occurs: The rules of the game adjust to accommodate everyone. If the game is too hard, the younger kids won't want to play. If it's too easy, the older kids will get bored. This natural self-regulation encourages cooperation, inclusivity, and empathy—not because an adult enforces it, but because the kids themselves want the game to continue.

There's an unspoken rule in free play: If someone gets upset and quits, the game is over. And no one wants that. So kids learn to navigate conflict, compromise, and adapt—all on their own.

If we want our children to reap the full benefits of play, we need to stop over-structuring it. We need to let them be bored. We need to stop filling every moment of their day with scheduled activities. We need to resist the urge to micromanage how they play and instead give them the space, time, and freedom to figure it out for themselves.

Play isn't something kids need to earn. It isn't a break from learning—it is learning. It is where they develop social skills, emotional regulation, leadership, and creativity. It is where they take risks, solve problems, and build resilience. It is where they become who they are meant to be.

The trick to helping kids learn and grow through play is simple—**get out of the way!**

ChiLL Time™

I hope I've made my stance on play crystal clear. That being said, I want to acknowledge a middle ground. Of course, kids can't play all day—there are lessons to be taught, concepts to be introduced, and skills that require explicit instruction. But here's the key: If we truly want learning to happen, kids need to play a bigger role in the process.

I have always asked my students, "What could we do to make school better?" I have gotten some incredible answers, but none stands out more than one spicy answer from a middle school girl: "Well, we could make it more relevant." I asked her to elaborate. "OK, for example, a math problem says, 'Suzy has 20 candy bars, she eats 15, what does she have?' DIABETES! Or 'Johnny has 15 bottles of soap...' Stop right there! It's not like Johnny is doing the dishes! What we learn just doesn't relate to anything in our life." Wow! #truthbomb. Aside from causing me to laugh uncontrollably, it solidified my theory—we need to give our kids a bigger role in their own learning and make it relevant to them.

That's why I came up with the term **ChiLL™ Time**, which stands for Child-Led Learning, as a way to create space for kids to take ownership of their education. Much like play, child-led learning fosters problem-solving, critical thinking, cognitive development, social-emotional growth, and intrinsic motivation. When children are actively involved in their learning, they don't just absorb information—they own it. They develop a sense of agency, which builds confidence and deepens engagement.

But here's the problem: In today's world of helicopter supervision, we've stripped kids of these valuable learning experiences. We underestimate their capabilities, often without even realizing it. And in doing so, we're not protecting them—we're interfering with their development. Mistakes, missteps, and even minor injuries aren't just unavoidable parts of childhood; they're essential learning opportunities. Of course, we want to shield them from real dangers (the life or death kind of dangers), but bumps, bruises, hurt feelings, and failure? That's where growth happens.

One of the biggest realizations I had as a parent was just how much I automatically did for my kids. I had no idea how much independence I was unintentionally taking away from them. When the world shut down in 2020, I asked my kids, "What's one thing you want to learn while we're home?" My eight-year-old (at the time) didn't hesitate—"I want to learn how to flip an egg." Easy enough, right? That is, until I realized I would be trusting an eight-year-old to climb onto a stool, turn on the stove, crack an egg, and flip it—without setting the house on fire. Needless to say, it wasn't long before he got it. But the best part? We sent a video to his second-grade teacher, who was so impressed that she called to chat with him. For the rest of the school year, the two of them exchanged recipes, sharing pictures and stories. Fast forward to today—my son is now twelve, an aspiring chef who cooks full meals for family and friends, works part-time on a food truck, and has even started his own hot sauce company.

At its core, child-led learning isn't about letting go of structure entirely—it's about loosening it just enough to let kids step up and take the lead. Some teachers I work with have implemented a "soft start" to the school day, where, instead of jumping straight into structured lessons, kids begin with self-led, unstructured activities like LEGO building, free drawing, domino stacking, or simple creative play. One elementary school assistant principal stated, "even older students can benefit from the self-led and unstructured, collaborative time that soft start provides." She shared that in her experience as a K-6 STEAM teacher, she initially only used it with younger students but was surprised by how much her older students thrived when this approach was added to their program as well.

Another example is Maker Spaces—dedicated areas where kids are free to explore, design, and create. Some Maker Spaces are stocked with open-ended materials for kids to build and tinker with as they please. Others provide weekly challenges, like "figure out how to get this ball onto that platform without touching it," allowing students to engage in hands-on problem solving. One Maker Space leader I spoke with assigns a different task each week, making the space available before and after school, during recess, and during free periods.

Just as children need the opportunity to take the lead in their learning, they also need the chance to take the lead in their voice. Too often, child-led conversation and discussion are undervalued and underutilized in classrooms. Remember when we explored oracy and its application at School 21 in London? Their model shows us that when children are given space to speak, to experiment with language, and to express themselves without fear of "messing up," they develop a deeper sense of agency and ownership in their learning.

Voice and learning are inseparable. When children learn not only to use their own voices but also to respectfully listen to and honor the voices of others, they are practicing the very skills that make learning meaningful, collaborative, and enduring. In this way, child-led conversation doesn't just enrich academics—it also nurtures psychological safety, strengthens relationships, and adds depth and authenticity to the learning experience.

Beyond conversation, kids also need the freedom to take real action in their learning. Another area of ChiLL™ Time I am sure most of you have at least heard of and many of you probably already do to an extent is project-based learning (PBL). PBL is such a powerful tool in education. Instead of simply memorizing facts, kids engage in long-term, hands-on projects that require them to ask questions, experiment, collaborate, and problem solve.[103] In PBL, failure isn't something to be avoided—it's a necessary part of the learning process. Kids must adapt, adjust, and try again. They learn to manage uncertainty, develop resilience, and take ownership of their learning in ways that traditional worksheets simply can't provide. And just like in free play, the most meaningful learning happens when kids feel invested in what they're doing. When they are given the chance to design, build, and explore ideas on their own terms, they develop confidence in their abilities—not because an adult told them they were capable but because they proved it to themselves. It is important to note here that in project-based learning, the project should be done by the kids—not the adults. No matter how powerful the urge to help, it is their project, their learning, not yours. Or, perhaps, letting them learn is your learning.

If you're looking for even more ways to support ChiLL™ Time and the movement toward childhood independence, I highly recommend checking out **Let Grow**—an organization founded by Dr. Peter Gray (*Free to Learn*), Lenore Skenazy (*Free-Range Kids*), Jonathan Haidt (*The Anxious Generation* and *The Coddling of the American Mind*), and Daniel Shuchman (former chairman of FIRE, the Foundation for Individual Rights and Expression). Let Grow is leading the movement to give kids more independence, resilience, and confidence—something today's children desperately need. They are actively involved in helping schools and parents work toward encouraging more independence and child-led learning. For example, they host an annual independence challenge, encouraging kids to do something they have never done before on their own—that is totally **ChiLL**!

As you can clearly see, this isn't just an idea—it is a movement. So maybe we should get moving—or move over. Maybe we should all take a little **ChiLL™ Time**.

Technology: the Good vs. the Evil

As we continue this conversation about child-led learning and agency, we have to address the elephant in the room—technology. It is one of the greatest tools for fostering independence, yet at the same time, one of the biggest barriers to it. It has changed the landscape of childhood in ways we are only beginning to understand, and whether we like it or not, it's here to stay. It's also one of the most emotionally charged topics in parenting and education, sparking strong opinions in both directions.

While we've become more protective of kids in the real world, we've done the exact opposite in the virtual world—offering them almost unlimited freedom.[104] Games, YouTube, social media, and gamified learning apps provide a space where kids feel independent and in control. The virtual world is designed to be stimulating and immersive, and provides an addictive reward loop (remember dopamine?). It offers an instant escape from boredom and an endless supply of stimulation and entertainment. It's no accident that kids are glued to their screens—these platforms are engineered to keep them there.

So the big question is: Is this good or bad? Or is it both?

This section is not about giving a definitive answer because, frankly, I don't have one. Technology is evolving literally faster than I can type. Instead of drawing a hard line, I want to share my own experiences—the struggles, the choices, and the moments that have made me stop and think. I hope this isn't the end of the discussion but the start of one.

I am going to hit the ground running and dive right in with what is likely the most controversial and hottest topic in the technology debate—the smartphone. When our oldest son started sixth grade, he asked for a phone because clearly it was normal and he needed one. According to him, he was one of the only kids in his grade without one. Our answer was simple—nope. Why? That is a great question—obviously because we are the worst parents ever!

Seriously, though, I will share my thought process on why we feel strongly against the phone. First, we knew that once we handed him that phone, there was no going back (for him or his younger brothers). My second reason is a bit more complicated. I had spent the last five years working in middle and high schools, watching the impact of this phone-based childhood and the very real toll it is taking on our kids (and adults)—how they seemed to be tethered to these devices, unable to go a minute or two without checking them, how social interactions had changed and not for the better, how focus and attention had started slipping away. The hallways are filled with zombies. Lunch, recess, study hall, and even PE—yes, physical education classes—were filled with kids' faces in their phones. The culture shift in schools is kinda eerie—from loud and alive with chatter and laughter to a sea of blank faces, lost in the glow of screens with the occasionally laughing to one's self or sharing of a video.

I also couldn't think of an actual good reason for him to have one. I asked him why he needed one, and he couldn't give me a real answer. He tried, but it all boiled down to one thing—everyone else had one. After going through this for the entirety of sixth grade, he finally came to a profound conclusion—"Mom, I don't think I really want a phone. I just don't want my friends to have one. They aren't fun anymore. They're always on YouTube or social media, and they don't know how to play or do anything."

Wow! Holy Truth Bomb!

His statement left me with such mixed emotions. I mean, I was really proud of myself for sticking to my guns and not caving in. By the end of the year, he was, in fact, the only kid (to my knowledge) in his grade without a phone. But as validating as it was, it also struck me as a bit heartbreaking. At eleven and twelve years old, boys should be outside running around, playing hockey in the street, riding bikes, climbing trees, and even (I can't believe I am saying this) playing video games **together**. Instead, I watched a group of boys sitting in my backyard, each glued to a screen, barely interacting. Of course, I don't want to socially isolate my son, but I am not willing to surrender his childhood without a fight.

That being said, at this age, they can easily be redirected—because their true nature is still in there. When the large group of kids come over, I can simply bring out snacks and tell them to put their phones away. After they grudgingly tuck their phones away, they naturally begin to drag the hockey nets into the streets or pile onto the trampoline. The hardest part is that real-world play, something that should occur naturally, now requires additional effort. It shouldn't, but it does. And when the effort is put in, it's like watching childhood come back to life.

What's even more challenging is that this movement to push kids indoors is coming in hot and heavy from what feels like everywhere. About a month ago, a group of kids in our town organized a huge pond hockey game. They had been enjoying the few weeks of freezing temperatures (aka, the greatest winter ever). Every time they went out, an adult checked the ice to make sure it was safe. It was barely a foot deep, but we still took precautions. It felt like the kind of thing childhood is supposed to be made of—kids, fresh air, winter fun, and absolutely no screens in sight. Then, after weeks of playing, the village mayor sent code enforcement to kick the kids off the ice, citing safety concerns and liability.

I respectfully called the mayor to explain that the adults had been monitoring the ice and that these kids were outside, off digital devices, being active and social, playing a game they loved. Her response—she told me I was selfish for putting the tax-payers at risk of paying in the case of an incident. She stated that, despite not being a parent, she was responsible for taking care of the children and she knew best. I shared that pond hockey was a multi-generational pastime enjoyed in the village for decades. After a few more unkind words thrown my way, I kindly reminded her there was no actual rule against it. After hanging up the phone on and berating a few more parents who called to voice concerns, she responded by hanging up a "no skating" sign.

This is what we're up against. We make it harder and harder for kids to play in the real world, and then we wonder why they disappear into the virtual one. I am assuming she is one of the many not educated that the real dangers lie in this very change.

In his bestselling book, *The Anxious Generation*, Jonathan Haidt explains what he calls "the great rewiring of childhood" and how it is causing an epidemic of mental illness. He breaks down the facts that show the direct correlation between early and excessive screen time with our ever-growing mental health crisis, rapidly growing child suicide rates, increase in depression and anxiety, substance abuse, declining academic achievement, and so on and so on![105] We need to take a close look at what this is doing to our children and what it means to keep them safe while giving them the greatest chances for success.

Haidt shares the terrifying statistics regarding the effects of social media on our kids (in particular, girls) and the access that personal devices give to our kids (like pornography, which he states has a profound negative impact on young boys). In his book, he lays out the statistics, theories, and some real-life solutions. It is worth investigating, at the very least.

I get it: As a parent, we are constantly pulled in so many directions. All I'm saying is, while it may be nice to have a moment of quiet as our kids are on devices, or it may feel like they are safely sitting on the couch instead of biking around the neighborhood out of sight and at risk of being hit by a car, are they really safer?

That being said, I don't believe technology is all bad. My kids have Apple Watches and iPads, and we've worked hard to find a balance that makes sense. I love that they use FaceTime to stay connected with their cousins in other states and friends overseas. I love that they've discovered apps that teach them how to play piano or create digital art. And while I have a love-hate (probably more of the latter) relationship with video games, I even love watching all the boys (including the biggest, my husband) gathered around the TV playing *Madden* or *Mario Kart*, yelling at the screen and laughing so loud it echoes through the house.

And while I think there is too much screen reliance in school with smart boards and gamified curriculum, I do see some incredible value in the use of technology. In second grade, our middle son discovered PowerPoint and made a fifty-slide presentation on the New York Islanders (we are die-hard Isles fans in this house). Our youngest son (inspired by his older brother) used PowerPoint to create chapter summaries for his favorite book and create a "dream" presentation. I am even using Canva with our oldest son for his homeschooling. He has used it for everything from science presentations to creating a logo and labeling for the hot sauce business he created. Our oldest has also used programs to manage his sales from his business.

We are even having conversations about what it looks like to use AI. I will be completely honest, I was terrified of AI at first (visions of *The Terminator*—anyone else?). However, despite my reservations, instead of resisting it, I am choosing to learn alongside my kids and students. They've taught me things I never would have figured out on my own (like how to make the actual coolest images on Bing AI).

Throughout my experience speaking and studying education, I have had the opportunity to tour and explore some of the most amazing schools and methods of education. Some are tech-free zones where hands-on learning is the only approach. I have seen green schools, creative schools, schools that allow kindergarteners to use power tools (with help), and even schools that integrate technology like complex software and 3D printing to help create a flower for pollination after studying pollination and the flowers outdoors (such a great combination of nature and technology).

My point is, when it comes to the role that technology will play in our kids' future, the real answer is no one knows! But we, as the grown-ups, have a responsibility to figure out how to guide them through it. We can't afford to throw our hands up and let them figure it out alone, but we also can't cling to the idea that banning screens entirely is the answer. We need to educate ourselves and them. We need to recognize the difference between screen time that fosters creativity and connection versus screen time that isolates and numbs. We need to find a balance between protecting their childhood and preparing them for a world we don't yet understand.

There is no easy answer, but we have to keep asking the right questions. And most importantly, we have to stay vigilant and keep paying attention—because the stakes are too high to look away.

The Thing About Mistakes

The thing about mistakes is, well, we all hate making them. Who actually enjoys being wrong? No one. It's uncomfortable. Embarrassing. Sometimes even painful. But if we're being honest, mistakes are how we learn. And the biggest mistake—the one that actually matters—is not allowing kids to make them. If you remember from earlier chapters, one of the greatest influences on learning and memory is emotionally charged events. And what elicits stronger emotions that those that come from the consequences of our own mistakes?

Sir Ken Robinson put it best: "If you're not prepared to be wrong, then you won't come up with anything original." Think about that. If we spend our lives terrified of messing up, we'll never take risks, never try something new, never create anything that didn't already exist. We'll play it safe, stick to the script, and miss out on the magic that happens when we push past what we think we know. Of course, that doesn't mean we should strive to be wrong, but without taking the chance, how can we push the boundaries and grow?

Ed Catmull, co-founder of Pixar, takes it a step further: "Mistakes aren't a necessary evil. They aren't evil at all. They are an inevitable consequence of doing something new." He should know—Pixar built an empire by embracing failure. Every great story they've told, every beloved character they've created started as a rough draft full of bad ideas and missteps. Without the willingness to be wrong, there would be no Buzz Lightyear, no Nemo, no Pixar at all.

Mistakes in childhood are supposed to happen. They're supposed to be frustrating, annoying, and sometimes even a little painful. Because those are the moments that teach kids how to problem-solve, how to take responsibility, and how to pick themselves up and try again. A kid who forgets their homework learns to double-check their backpack. A teen who spends their entire allowance on day one learns to budget before they have rent and bills. These small, low-stakes mistakes are the necessary steps for handling life's bigger challenges.

And yet, we've built a culture—especially in education—where mistakes are treated like failure instead of what they really are: stepping stones to success. We stigmatize mistakes, as if they are the worst thing you can do in school. We are quick to correct kids before they even have a chance to think for themselves. We expect them to follow the right formula, fill in the right bubble, and get it all right on the first try. But where's the learning in that?

Childhood is the time to make mistakes. It's when the price of being wrong is still low, when the lessons are still fixable.[106] It's when kids learn to be humble, to trust their gut, to recover when things don't go as planned. A toddler spilling juice on the couch? No big deal. A surgeon slipping up in the operating room? That's a whole different story. In childhood, mistakes come with manageable consequences—spilled milk, a broken toy, a scraped knee. But in medicine, engineering, aviation, or any field where lives are on the line, mistakes can't be shrugged off as a learning experience. If kids never experience the discomfort of a bad decision, they'll have no idea how to handle one when it actually matters. They need to be encouraged to push their boundaries, find different ways to succeed and fail, explore their creativity and boundless potential, and figure out what to do when it doesn't go as expected.

So let them mess up. Let them fall, fail, and figure it out. Because the goal isn't to raise kids who never make mistakes—it's to raise kids who know what to do after they make them. We want to raise the kids who are willing to put themselves out there, come up with original ideas, and help shape a better future for all of us.

9

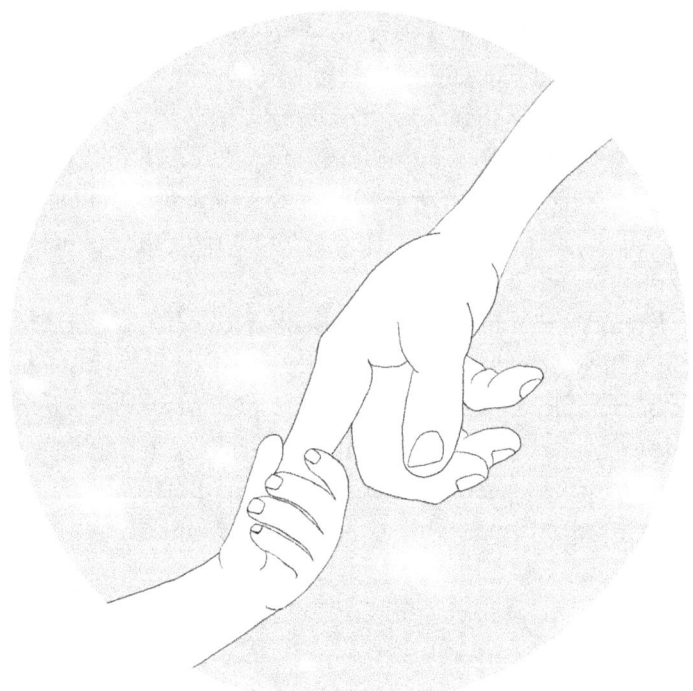

Trusting in the MAGIC

"Children see magic because they look for it."

—Christopher Moore

We've come a long way together. I hope this journey has challenged you, validated you, frustrated you, and inspired you. We've explored how childhood has changed, how our kids are facing challenges at unprecedented levels, and how our education system has barely budged to keep up. We know that one in six children is diagnosed with a developmental disability. We know the mental health crisis is taking a toll on kids in ways we can no longer ignore. We know the world is changing faster than I can type, while education is still clinging to outdated models that may as well have been designed in the Ice Age (OK, maybe a slight exaggeration, but you get my point).

Through this process, I hope you've had moments where your thinking was stretched, where gut feelings you've had about childhood and education were confirmed, and where new ideas lit a fire in you. But more than anything, I hope you feel motivated, hopeful, and ready to be part of the change.

We've reflected on what kids truly need to thrive—connection, movement, independence, opportunities to explore and create. We've looked at what's missing, what's holding them back, and what we can do to restore the magic of childhood. Along the way, we explored the M.A.G.I.C. Model—not as a checklist or a scripted program, but as a way of seeing and understanding childhood in a way that makes sense.

The M.A.G.I.C. Model

M
Meet the Child Where They Are.

This is where it all begins. Before anything else, we have to take a step back and truly see the child in front of us—who they are, what they love, what excites them, what shuts them down. We need to understand their emotional, physical, and developmental state, without judgment, before we can begin to guide them. This connection is an essential first step.

I want to take a minute to say this connection does not mean that everything is on you. In fact, sometimes, meeting a child where they are will show us that not every lesson can come from us. There will be times when another voice, another perspective, another relationship is what makes the difference. Maybe it's a coach, a counselor, a teacher, a security guard, or another staff member who greets them every morning. Maybe it's another student, a sibling, or an older peer. I've had students who needed to hear something from my friend, the male school counselor, for it to sink in. I've had students who learned more from a classmate than they did from me. Even in my own family, there are things my brother can say to my son that carry more weight than if I said them myself. Meeting the child where they are means knowing them well enough to recognize when they need someone else's voice, and embracing that.

A
Assess Developmental Needs.

If you work with kids—or have kids of your own—understanding child development is not optional. It's not extra credit. It's not something to brush off as someone else's job. It is your responsibility.

No, you don't have to be a doctor, a psychologist, or a developmental specialist. But you do need to have a working knowledge of what is typical and what isn't. You do need to know the basic milestones that shape childhood. Because if we don't understand what's expected, how can we recognize when something is off? And if we can't recognize when something is off, how can we help?

Too often, we rely on labels and systems to tell us when a child is struggling, but the truth is, we are on the front lines. Teachers, parents, caregivers—we are the ones who see the little things. The subtle delays, the minor struggles, the moments when something just doesn't seem right. And those moments matter. Because early recognition leads to early support, and early support changes everything.

I've included a guide at the end of this book with key developmental milestones—not as a test, but as a tool. Use it. Keep it as a reference. Keep pushing yourself to learn, to notice, to ask questions. Knowing when to be concerned and when to be patient isn't just helpful—it's essential. The more we understand, the better we can meet kids where they are and give them what they actually need.

G
Guide Using Whole Body Strategies.

If we don't understand how learning actually happens, how can we possibly teach? Kids don't just learn with their eyes and ears—they learn with their entire bodies. Movement, play, hands-on experiences, sensory engagement—all of it matters. If we want kids to be engaged, we have to engage their whole selves.

If we don't break free from rigid, outdated teaching models, we are failing kids before they even get a chance to succeed. Standardized testing, grade-based assessments, and "I do, we do, you do" methods aren't enough. Learning isn't a step-by-step, one-size-fits-all process. It's messy, dynamic, and deeply personal. And so is teaching. This is where you come in. You are an educated, capable, creative human being. You have your own strengths, your own ideas, your own magic. Stop trying to think outside the box— once you truly understand how learning works, there is no box.

I
Incorporate Strategies Into Everyday Learning.

This isn't about adding more to your plate. It's about shifting the way we approach learning so it happens more naturally, more effectively, and with more joy. Kids need movement. They need mindfulness. They need to play. They need ChiLL™ Time (Child-Led Learning). They need opportunities for collaboration and connection. And they need adults who see them, support them, and create an environment where they feel safe enough to take risks, make mistakes, and grow.

This book was designed to be more than something you read once and put on a shelf. It is a working model, a workbook—a space to brainstorm, take notes, and add your own resources. Use it. Let it evolve as you grow in your understanding and as you apply what you've learned. I expect you to scribble, doodle, highlight, take notes, and write all over this book—make it your own!

C
Create a Nurturing Environment that Highlights the Magic in Every Child.

A nurturing environment is safe, welcoming, and built on connection. It's a space where kids (and adults) want to be—where learning is alive, where mistakes are embraced, where curiosity is celebrated. It's not about perfection. It's about creating a space where kids feel free to explore, fail, try again, and become the best version of themselves.

A thriving environment isn't just one where kids are supported—it's one where they take ownership of their learning, their growth, and their connections. When kids feel safe, valued, and understood, everything else falls into place.

We have explored so much together—what has changed in childhood, the struggles kids are facing, the barriers we need to break down. We've questioned outdated systems, looked at what's missing, and challenged assumptions. We've talked about movement, connection, creativity, independence, and what it truly means to create a learning environment that supports kids as whole human beings.

This has been a journey of reflection. A deep dive into the problems we face, the solutions we can create, and the magic that happens when we trust what we know about childhood and learning. But reflection is only one part of the process.

The next step is action.

Because unlocking the magic in childhood starts with us unlocking our own.

Assemble Your Tribe

If we are going to take on the world, we are going to need a tribe—

and if you've made it this far, you are my people!

Finding your people means discovering the folks who light you up and lift you higher. In my life, I have different tribes for different parts of the journey. My core circle—my kids, my family, and my closest friends—keeps me grounded and reminds me where I come from. For parenting, I lean on a community of like-minded parents who support each other wholeheartedly. We show up for one another, share our wins and struggles, pick up each other's kids, drive them to sports, and give a warm hug when they fall and scrape their knee.

Then there's my circle of creative revolutionaries, my tribe for changing the world. This is a group of individuals from all over—yes, the world—who are working together to revolutionize education. We come from different backgrounds, cultures, and childhoods; we are of various ages, races, and genders. Yet, we meet regularly to tackle one of the world's biggest challenges. We listen deeply, support each other's projects and personal missions, and, even when disagreements arise, we remain respectful and focused on our common goal. I learned, sometimes the hard way, that true success isn't about competition—it's about collaboration. Without my creative revolutionaries, this book wouldn't exist.

A word of warning: There will always be people trying to hold you back, telling you you're wrong, or urging you to stop because you're making them look bad. There will be jealousy and naysayers. Hint: These are *not* your people!

So, surround yourself with those who believe in the vision, who celebrate differences, and who work together from the bottom up to create real change. Your tribe is out there, and when you find them, you'll have the support to unlock not only your own magic but the magic of every child you touch.

Creating a New Story

You now have everything you need to start your Once Upon a Time...

Thank you for sticking with me and joining me on this journey. From here on out, you are a revolutionary. We are on the same team, working together from today forward to make a better now and a brighter future for our kids.

Remember, despite the narrative we have been fed for years, our goal is not to create hundreds of straight-A, honor roll students, but, rather, to help each individual child unlock their Kid Magic, reach their greatest potential, and be ready to take on their future! Success is not measured by high test scores, perfect compliance, a sky-high GPA, or an acceptance letter to an elite university—it never has been. Our responsibility is to help each child discover who they truly are—what excites them, what challenges them, and what makes them come alive. Some kids will become artists, others engineers; some will build businesses while others build communities. Some will solve problems we don't even know exist yet. Some will change the world in ways we can't yet imagine.

But none of that will happen if we keep forcing kids to fit into a system that was never designed for them in the first place. We have to change the story.

This is your moment to write a new one—to step outside the outdated script that tells us kids must all learn the same way, at the same pace, with the same goals. Your Once Upon a Time begins the moment you choose to do things differently—to prioritize connection over compliance, movement over memorization, and curiosity over control.

The revolution doesn't happen in one sweeping motion. True change starts at the grassroots—it starts with us: teachers, parents, and kids. It isn't dictated from above by policy makers; change happens from the bottom up, in the small, everyday choices we make. It happens when we let a child lead their own learning, when we replace a worksheet with a hands-on experience, when we meet a struggling kid with understanding instead of frustration, and when we start asking how to make the system work for them rather than forcing them into it.

The story of childhood has been rewritten before. And now, it's our turn.

So go ahead—pick up the pen. Start your Once Upon a Time... And let's make sure that this time, the ending is one worth telling.

10

DEVELOPMENTAL MILESTONES

"No man stands so tall as when he stoops to help a child."

—Abraham Lincoln

The human brain is the most intricate and beautiful system ever created—an incredible masterpiece that builds itself over time, step by step, according to a highly specific blueprint. Each developmental milestone a child reaches—rolling over, babbling, pointing, walking, speaking—is like a carefully placed brick in the foundation of their future learning, thinking, feeling, and relating to others. These moments aren't just cute achievements—they're essential indicators that the brain is wiring correctly, that systems are connecting, and that development is on track. Missing a milestone isn't a moral failing—but it is a message. It's the brain's quiet way of telling us something might be off track. Yet too often, these signs are dismissed with a wave of the hand and a well-intentioned phrase: "Don't worry, all kids develop at their own pace." While that may soothe anxiety in the moment, it can delay the very action a child needs. Yes, there is a range, but there is also a rhythm. And *timing matters*. As Dr. Robert Melillo explains, brain development is like building your dream home. Imagine being handed the architectural plans for a magnificent, one-of-a-kind house—a beautiful structure with hidden hallways, sweeping arches, and intricate support beams. You wouldn't hand those plans to a builder and say, "Just wing it. Skip a few steps if you want. It's probably fine." Ignoring the blueprint would compromise the very foundation and future integrity of the home. So why do we tolerate that mindset when it comes to children?We must stop brushing off missed milestones and start recognizing them for what they are: early clues. Clues that give us the chance to intervene while the brain is still incredibly adaptable. Clues that allow us to support a child before frustration builds, before school becomes overwhelming, before they start to believe something is wrong with them.This is not about blame. It's about partnership. It's about giving the adults in a child's life—parents, teachers, doctors, caregivers—the knowledge and confidence to notice when something is off rhythm and the tools to respond early and effectively. Because when we recognize and respond to missed milestones, we're not labeling a child. We're unlocking them. We're giving their brain the support it needs to follow its own unique version of that beautiful blueprint. We're giving them the best shot at building a life filled with connection, curiosity, confidence, and capability. ***And that's how we help every child unlock their full magic.***

The next pages hold a comprehensive list of developmental milestones organized by age. They are to serve as a reference for you. Refer to them often and familiarize yourself with them. I have organized each page by motor, communication, cognitive, and social/emotional milestones, followed by a short summary and suggestions for how to play, connect, and support development in meaningful ways.

I also encourage you to explore the transformative work of pioneers and revolutionaries like Dr. Robert Melillo, Sir Ken Robinson, Kate Robinson, Anthony Dunn, Dr. John Ratey, Dr. Carla Hannaford, Dr. Peter Gray, Jonathan Haidt, and the many others fighting to restore childhood, rethink education, maximize human potential, and reignite Kid Magic!

*** The majority of the developmental milestones listed were adapted from Dr. Robert Melillo's book, Reconnected Kids. *I strongly encourage you to read this book and add it to your library, as there is more valuable information that shares a whole-family approach for helping parents navigate these formative years to help children reach their full potential.*

Developmental Milestones: 0–3 months

Gross & Fine Motor	Communication/ Speech	Cognitive	Behavioral/ Emotional
Lifts head while on tummy	Coos and makes gurgling sounds, begins to babble	Follows moving objects with eyes	Begins to smile responsively
Supports upper body with arms while on stomach	Turns head toward sounds	Recognizes caregiver's voice	Shows interest in faces
Moves arms and legs symmetrically	Cries to express needs	Begins to develop a routine	Enjoys being held, cuddled and soothed
Brings hands to mouth	Begins to imitate sounds		Responds to and imitates facial expressions
Opens and closes hands, grasps objects	May smile at the sound of familiar voices		Soothed by rocking
Rolls to side			Dependent on parent for feeding, changing, bathing, etc.

Play with Purpose:

Play at this stage focuses on sensory exploration. They will begin to repeat movements and bodily actions that are satisfying and listen to the sound of their own voice. Talk and sing with your baby often. Use soft voices, gentle touch, and black-and-white or high-contrast images to stimulate their developing vision and hearing. According to Dr. Robert Melillo, this type of play will begin the experience of approach and avoidance behaviors. "Approach, a left brain activity, is displayed as joy, surprise, and interest. Avoidance, a right brain learning, is displayed as distress, frustration, fear, anger and shyness" (***Reconnected Kids***).

Developmental Milestones: 4–6 months

Gross & Fine Motor	Communication/ Speech	Cognitive	Behavioral/ Emotional
Rolls from tummy to back	Babbles with vowel & then consonant sounds (e.g., ba, da)	Looks at nearby objects	Recognizes familiar people
Rolls back to tummy by 5-6 mo.	Responds to name	Mouths objects	Laughs
Pushes up on elbows when lying on tummy	Laughs and squeals	Shows curiosity about toys	Enjoys playing with others
Reaches for and grasps objects	Responds to own name	Tries to get objects that are out of reach	Responds to emotions of others
Will rest with hands open	Stares at novel faces longer than familiar ones	Gestures for "up" or "no"	Begins to develop attachment and "stranger danger"
Hand to feet play on back	Vocalizes at images in mirror	Removes cloth from over face	
May sit with support		Bangs and shakes toys	

Play with Purpose:

Encourage tummy time and safe floor play to strengthen core and arm muscles. Playing on the floor and out of walkers, bouncers, and other baby holders helps develop important movement patterns. Continue to talk and sing, as well as read, together. It is also important to note that frequent, loving touch is so very important! Cuddles, holding, and soft stroking help a baby feel safe. It is also important to help with feeling and awareness of baby's own body. Play and touch as often as possible. Games like peek-a-boo help develop trust and connection. (***Don't forget little Molly Wright's TED Talk***).

Developmental Milestones: 7–9 months

Gross & Fine Motor	Communication/ Speech	Cognitive	Behavioral/ Emotional
Sits without support	Uses voice to express joy and displeasure	Finds partially hidden objects	May show fear of strangers
Transfers objects between hands	Imitates sounds	Looks for dropped objects	Enjoys social play
Begins crawling or scooting	Understands "no"	Explores with hands and mouth	Has favorite toys
Grasps objects with radial palmer grasp	Holds bottle for drinking, begins using sippy cup		Shouts for attention
Transitions in/out of positions	Finger feeding		
Crawling and creeping	Uses top lip to clear food from spoon		
May pull to stand	Uses tongue to lateralize food		

Play with Purpose:

At this point, babies are eager to move, explore, and connect. Purposeful play during this stage includes creating a safe space to crawl, scoot, and climb, which helps build coordination and strengthen left and right brain integration. Offer sensory toys that light up, make noise, or respond to touch and engage in simple social games like peek-a-boo (demonstrating cause and effect). Just as important are the back-and-forth interactions: respond to their babble, mimic their sounds, and use exaggerated facial expressions. Read stories using different voices and facial expressions. These playful exchanges are doing powerful work wiring the brain for future language, emotional regulation, and meaningful human connection.

Developmental Milestones: 10–12 months

Gross & Fine Motor	Communication/ Speech	Cognitive	Behavioral/ Emotional
Pulls to stand and cruises on furniture	Says "mama" and "dada" meaningfully	Looks at correct picture when named	May have separation anxiety
May walk with hands held	Rotary chewing, chews and swallows without choking	Looks for toys in box or under cup (object permanence)	Points to get desired objects
Rises to stand through hands and knees, stands alone briefly	Babbling begins to sound like language	Explores objects in many ways	Tests parental responses
Takes first steps	Says first words, imitates simple words	Follows one-step commands	Seeks attention through sounds or gestures
Lowers self from standing with control	Waves bye-bye	Tracks fast moving objects	Shows objects to parent to share interests
Creeps (crawling) rapidly	Vocalizes to songs	Has 20-word listening vocabulary	Learns trust (self, parent, environment)
Pincer grasp to pick up small objects	Practices inflection	Begins symbolic thinking	Approach (+) and Avoidance (-) Behavior
Throws objects			Cries when other kids cry
Attempts 2-cube tower			Developing sense of humor

Play with Purpose:

At ten to twelve months, babies are on the move and motivated by curiosity. Play during this stage should support emerging skills like pulling to stand, cruising along furniture, and exploring objects with their hands. Provide sturdy push toys, stackable items, and simple cause-and-effect toys to encourage active discovery. Imitation becomes a major learning tool—so talk often, name objects, and model actions. Responding to their gestures, babbles, and early words with enthusiasm helps reinforce communication pathways. This back-and-forth interaction builds the social-emotional foundation for connection, and strengthens the brain circuits essential for language and self-regulation. Use storybooks and songs to foster connection and early language. *The most powerful predictor of future reading success is not early decoding—it's the number of books in the home.*

Developmental Milestones: 12–18 months

Gross & Fine Motor	Communication/ Speech	Cognitive	Behavioral/ Emotional
Walks independently	Begins to parrot parents to speak	Follows simple instructions	Shows strong attachment to caregiver
Crawls up stairs, climbs on low furniture	Has vocabulary of about 5-20 words	Recognizes names of familiar people or objects	Hands you a book when they want to hear a story
Pulls toys while walking	Uses gestures like pointing, waving *bye-bye*, nodding *"yes"*	Explores objects by shaking, banging, throwing	Repeats actions to get attention
Begins to throw ball underhand	Begins to label things with single words (*ball, mama, dog, etc.*)	Understands object permanence (*looks for hidden objects*)	Shows interest in other children, engages in parallel play
Stacks 2-3 blocks	Responds to the word *"no"*	Starts to imitate daily routines in play	Begins to show defiance
Picks up small objects with thumb and forefinger	Uses exclamations like *"uh-oh"*	Looks at correct picture when named in book	Seeks comfort when upset
Feeds self with fingers, starts using spoon			Demonstrates wider range of emotions. Beginning to see the terrible twos
Lowers self from standing with control			Begins showing independence
Gets in and out of hands and knees position			Cooperates by helping put things away

Play with Purpose:

Your little explorer is on the move! Between twelve and eighteen months, children are walking, climbing, and getting into *everything*—this is how they learn. Create a safe space that invites crawling, cruising, climbing, and curiosity. Offer toys they can push, stack, fill, dump, or pretend with, as these support coordination, cause-and-effect understanding, and emerging problem-solving skills. Language is blossoming during this stage, so respond to their babbles like real conversation, mimic their sounds, and exaggerate facial expressions. Continue reading together, exploring different voices and gestures to bring the story to life. Encourage gestures like waving, pointing, and clapping. These joyful, back-and-forth interactions are not just fun—they're wiring the brain for communication, emotional regulation, and meaningful relationships.

Developmental Milestones: 18–24 months

Gross & Fine Motor	Communication/ Speech	Cognitive	Behavioral/ Emotional
Walks independently, beginning to run	Says 10-50 words by 24 months	Begins to sort shapes and colors	Shows increasing independence, wants to do things by self
Climbs on furniture unassisted	Uses 2-word phrases ("*more juice,*" "*mama go*")	Completes sentences in familiar books	Shows defiant behavior ("*No!*" *is favorite word*)
Walks up stairs step to pattern with help or railing	Repeats word or phrase over and over	Shows interest in pretend play	Strong attachment to caregiver, may show separation anxiety
Kicks ball forward	Begins to say "*my*"	Understands object permanence fully	Interest in routine, may resist change
Builds 4-6 block tower	Uses gestures and words together (*shakes head and says "no"*)	Follows simple directions (*pick up ball and put in baskets*)	May start to show empathy (*try to comfort crying peer or parent*)
Turns page in book (multiple pages at time)	Points to familiar people, objects, and body parts when named	Explores cause and effect through actions (*push button to make sound*)	Imitates others to learn behavior, seeks adult approval
Uses spoon and drinks from cup	Begins to name pictures in books		
Puts objects in/out container			
Scribbles spontaneously			
Begins to show hand preference			

Play with Purpose:

At eighteen to twenty-four months, toddlers are active, opinionated, and full of curiosity. They love to test limits, repeat actions, and explore how things work. Purposeful play during this stage includes building, stacking, climbing, filling, and dumping, and beginning to imitate real-life routines like cooking or cleaning. Pretend play starts to take shape, and it's a powerful tool for social and cognitive growth. Keep on reading, storytelling, singing, and talking—label objects, actions, and feelings, and engage in simple conversation, even if their words aren't clear yet. Every time you respond with interest and warmth, you're strengthening the brain circuits that support language, thinking, and emotional connection.

Developmental Milestones: 2 years

Gross & Fine Motor	Communication/ Speech	Cognitive	Behavioral/ Emotional
Runs with more coordination	Vocabulary of 150-300+ words	Sorting objects by category (*cars, animals*)	Strong sense of independence *"by myself"*
Climbs well (on furniture, playground)	Uses 2- to 4-word sentences ("*want more juice*")	Completes sentences in rhymes/books	Experiences big emotions, tantrums
Walks up and down stairs with support, one step at time	Can name most familiar people and objects	More complex pretend play	Gets excited with other children
Begins to jump with both feet	Uses pronouns (*me, you, mine*)	Matches shapes and begins simple puzzles	Begins to understand and express feelings
Can kick and throw ball	Asks simple questions ("*what's that?*")	Understands time-related concepts (*soon, later, now*)	Does not regulate emotions well
Builds 6-8 block tower	Can be understood by adult half the time	Names basic body parts	Shows affection toward familiar people
Turns individual pages in book	Asks for wants	Understands cause and effect through play	Tests boundaries but also seeks comfort and reassurance
Begins vertical and horizontal lines and circle strokes			Knows gender identity, labels self and others by gender
Uses fork and spoon			May have imaginary friend
Starts to unzip and remove simple cloths			

Play with Purpose:

Welcome to the terrible twos—and the terrific brain-building that comes with them! By age two, a child's brain has already reached about 80 percent of its adult size, and it's busy wiring for movement, language, emotion, and connection. Between twenty-four and thirty-six months, toddlers are gaining independence, testing boundaries, and expanding their abilities across the board. They crave autonomy, yet still rely on adults for support and regulation—so tantrums are a natural (and expected) part of this stage. One of the best ways to ease the power struggles is by offering choices that let them feel in control. Purposeful play should include climbing, jumping, building, matching, sorting, and simple make-believe. They may pretend to cook, care for dolls, or act out daily routines—this kind of imaginative play is essential for both social and cognitive development. Keep the conversation flowing by naming emotions, actions, and options, and encourage back-and-forth dialogue. Continue reading together daily—let them choose the book, turn the pages, and "read" along by repeating favorite lines or telling parts of the story. These shared experiences not only build language and attention, but they also strengthen the relational bonds that fuel all learning. This stage is full of big feelings and even bigger leaps—and play is the perfect way to support both.

Developmental Milestones: 3 years

Gross & Fine Motor	Communication/ Speech	Cognitive	Behavioral/ Emotional
Runs easily, can stop and change direction	Vocabulary of about 900 words	Can work toys with buttons or moving parts	Shows affection without prompting
Jumps forward with both feet	Speaks clear enough to be understood 75% of time	Engages in imaginative and symbolic play	Takes turns in games, shares (*maybe with prompting*)
Begins walking up stairs step over step (*one foot per step*)	Speaks in 3-5 word sentences with short back and forth conversations	Understands "*same*" and "*different*"	Shows empathy and concern (*comfort crying friends*)
Stands on one foot for few seconds	Uses plurals and prepositions (*in, on, under*)	Can complete simple puzzle (3-6 pieces)	Fewer tantrums than age 2, still struggles with emotional regulation
Begins riding tricycle	Asks many "why" and "what" questions	Sorts by shape, size, or color	Shows pride when accomplished ("*I did it*")
Throws and catches with better coordination	Uses pronouns like *I, you, me, he, she* correctly	Understands "*one*" vs. "*many*" and begins counting	Seeks approval and wants to please adults, likes to be helpful
Jumps over small objects	Uses some past tense	Follows 2-3 step instructions	Expresses wide range of emotions
Builds towers 9+ blocks		Recognizes familiar letters, numbers, symbols	Interprets emotions from facial expressions and intonation
Copies shapes like circles and crosses		Understands "*mine*" and "*yours*"	Has no sense of privacy

Turns pages one at a time		Can point to major body parts	Engages in self-genital exploration
Begins using child-safe scissors		Generally understands boy vs. girl differences	Basic understanding of good vs. bad behavior
Draws person with 2 body parts		Helps dress and undress self	Fears imaginary things
Starting to zip and unscrew lids		Feeds self	

Play with Purpose:

If you thought the terrible twos were rough, now you're dealing with a three-nager. At age three, children are full of opinions, emotions, and contradictions. They want independence but still need reassurance, they ask for help then reject it, and they crave connection while demanding control—welcome to the classic push-pull of "need-reject syndrome." The brain is now busy growing wiring for emotion, language, and social understanding. Imaginative play becomes central at this stage—children may assign roles, create storylines, and blur the lines between fantasy and reality. This kind of play isn't just cute—it's how they process emotions, practice problem solving, and begin to understand others. They're also beginning to reason, test limits, and show an eager-to-please side, especially when it earns praise. Reading together is still important and provides for great opportunities to exercise imagination, empathy, problem-solving, and connection. Potty training may also be in progress or recently completed, and cooperative play is emerging as they begin to enjoy interacting with peers. Behavior can still be wildly inconsistent, but that's part of the process. Through imaginative, responsive, and choice-filled play, we give three-year-olds exactly what their developing brains need: structure, freedom, connection, and joy.

Developmental Milestones: 4 years

Gross & Fine Motor	Communication/ Speech	Cognitive	Behavioral/ Emotional
Climbs and descends stairs one foot per step	Vocabulary of about 1500 words	Names/sorts colors, shapes and numbers	Prefers playing with other children over playing alone
Catches a bounced ball by trapping	Sings songs from memory	Understands time concepts ("*soon,*" "*later,*" "*yesterday*")	Often can't tell what's real vs. pretend
Throws ball overhand	Tells stories, recalls past events, asks lots of questions	Counts to 10 or higher	Cooperates with rules
Runs with control, changes speed and direction	Speaks clearly in full sentences (4-8 words), Intelligible to strangers about 90-100%	Engages in pretend play with storylines and roles	May struggle with impulse control and emotional regulation
Kicks ball with direction	Understands and uses "*when,*" "*how,*" "*because*"	Understands fairness and rules	Increasing independence and self-confidence
Balance on one foot 5-10 sec	Can repeat 4-syllable words	Knows familiar animals	Develops strong preference for toys, cloths, routines, etc.
Draws person with 4-6 body parts	Can vocalize most vowels and consonants incl. *p, b, m, w*	Names common objects in books or pictures	Expresses complex emotions like guilt, embarrassment
Copies basic shapes and symbols (*square, triangle, plus*)		Understands difference between under and over	Plays outside with minimal supervision, likes to be trusted
Begins some capital letters (*A, E, T*)			May play with imaginary friend

Uses scissors to cut along straight and curved lines			Starts to demonstrate social problem solving
Dresses, unbuttons, zippers, snaps			Better tolerates delayed gratification
Simple crafting (Play-Doh, LEGO)			Self-esteem reflects opinions of others
Begins hopping on one foot			

Play with Purpose:

At four years old, children are bursting with ideas, opinions, and endless imagination. Their language is more advanced, their questions more persistent ("Why? Why? Why?"), and their play more complex. Make-believe is still central, now with richer storylines, assigned roles, and early rule-following. They love to pretend, perform, and create, using play as a way to explore real-world concepts, relationships, and emotions. Continue to read together and encourage questions and thoughts, to ask how characters may feel. Socially, four-year-olds are learning to cooperate, take turns, and play with—not just alongside—their peers. They still crave autonomy but are often eager to please and thrive with praise and structure. Emotionally, they're starting to identify feelings and may even attempt to manage them (though meltdowns can still happen!). Purposeful play should support their growing confidence with opportunities to build, create, imagine, and collaborate. Whether they're playing house, building a tower, or directing a backyard play, they're not just having fun—they're building the emotional, cognitive, and social skills that will carry them into school and beyond.

Developmental Milestones: 5 years

Gross & Fine Motor	Communication/ Speech	Cognitive	Behavioral/ Emotional
Skips and gallops with good coordination	Generally uses grammatically correct speech	Counts to 20 or more	Enjoys play with others, takes turns, shares
Hops 8-10 times on one foot	Can tell stories with clear beginning, middle, and end	Understands concept of *same/different/opposites*	Strong interest in friendships
Can hit target with ball 10 ft away	Knows and uses positional words (*beside, under, in front*)	Understands concepts of 4 or more	Expresses wide range of emotions with more awareness
Throws overhand with aim, catches with hands	Uses future tense and time (*next week, tomorrow, later, morning, night, day*)	Understands rules and can follow structured games	May have short arguments, but forgets quickly
Improved running coordination and stamina	Participates in conversations, asks thoughtful questions	Responds to why questions	Demonstrates empathy and concern for others
Walks on balance beam or curb	Speaks over 2000 words	Identifies primary colors & shapes	Understands right from wrong
Uses dynamic tripod grip	Expresses vowels and consonants	Knows age, name, address	Apologizes for mistakes
Buttons, zips, snaps, and ties simple knots	Speaks in sentences 8-9 words using all parts of speech	Questions more deeply with meaning and purpose	Is aware of gender differences
Prepares simple breakfast		Accepts that there may be other points of view	Can distinguish fantasy from real

Can cut out shapes with scissors		Responds well to structure and routine	Shows pride in achievements
Can complete more detailed art			Likes to be helpful
Draws person with at least 6 body parts			Seeks approval, sensitive to criticism

Play with Purpose:

Five is a magical age—full of possibility, confidence, and transition. For many children, this is the year they enter kindergarten, and for the first time, a teacher becomes a central figure in their daily life. By this age, the brain has reached nearly 90 percent of its adult size, making it a prime time for learning—but also a time when development still hinges on play, connection, and movement. It's also when the left side of the brain begins to come online, making it a natural entry point for more structured academic skills. But don't make the mistake of replacing play with pressure. This is not the time to drill reading and writing at the expense of joy and curiosity. Phonemic awareness is still developing, and it's common for children to confuse similar-sounding letters (like B, P, and D) or reverse letters in writing—this is not dyslexia; it's normal, age-appropriate development. The most powerful predictor of future reading success is not early decoding—it's the number of books in the home. Read together, visit the library, and let them fall in love with language.

At five, purposeful play is more important than ever. Children are becoming more social, empathetic, and collaborative. Their play becomes more organized, often mimicking real-life roles, routines, and responsibilities. Cooperative, rule-based games support attention, planning, self-control, and the foundation of executive functioning. Pretend play, storytelling, peer interaction, physical activity, and time in nature continue to build confidence, creativity, and connection. This is a pivotal year—don't rush it. When we preserve play, we preserve the magic.

Developmental Milestones: 6 years

Gross & Fine Motor	Communication/ Speech	Cognitive	Behavioral/ Emotional
Rides a 2-wheel bike (or begins learning)	Speaks clearly in grammatically correct complex sentences	Understands concepts of time and money	Talks about thoughts and feelings
Runs, jumps, skips, and hops with coordination and control	Understands jokes, riddles, and wordplay	Begins telling time and understands calendar	Develops strong friendships
Balances on one foot 10+ seconds	Engages in conversation, asks thoughtful questions	Sorts and classify objects by multiple characteristics	Seeks approval and wants to do well with peers and in school
Catches a small ball with hands	Understands and uses more abstract and complex vocabulary	Understands concept of conservation (*same amount, different container*)	Wants to be the first and best at everything
Plays hopscotch	Tells detailed stories with clear beginning, middle, and end	Recognizes and produces rhyming words	Develops a strong sense of right and wrong
Jumps rope, uses skates, hits ball with bat	Reads simple books independently and understands them	Attention span and focus growing to 10-15 minutes.	May experience self-doubt, sensitive to others' opinions about self
Shows improved agility, speed, and stamina	Counts to 100	Knows right from left	Expresses pride in achievements
Participates in organized sports with basic rules	Properly pronouncing 2 letters with one sound (*sh, ch, th*)	Rapidly developing mental skills	Learning to express and manage emotions with more maturity

Wrist most letters and numbers clearly	Speaks intelligibly and is socially meaningful	May still consider some fantasy as real	Growing desire to be liked
Accurately cuts out shapes			Begins to understand own uniqueness
Ties shoelaces			Learns self-respect
Completes complex crafts			Develops positive, realistic self-concept
Colors within lines and draws detailed figures			
Uses proper pencil grip, writes simple sentences			

Play with Purpose:

At six years old, children are stepping into the world with more confidence, independence, and curiosity. They're refining physical skills, growing more socially aware, and beginning to think more logically and reflectively. Purposeful play should continue to include physical activity, outdoor exploration, storytelling, creative building, and pretend play that now often mimics real-life roles and rules. Rule-based and cooperative games help strengthen emerging executive function skills like planning, focus, flexibility, and self-control. Social dynamics become more complex—children may start to form best friendships and care deeply about fairness and inclusion. Emotionally, they're developing more empathy and beginning to see things from other perspectives. Reading continues to play a critical role at this stage; offer both independent and shared reading experiences, visit the library together, and talk about characters, feelings, and plot. Reading aloud—even to kids who can read independently—helps build vocabulary, comprehension, and emotional insight. Through play, connection, and reading-rich environments, we support both academic growth and the emotional grounding that makes learning meaningful.

Developmental Milestones: 7 years

Gross & Fine Motor	Communication/ Speech	Cognitive	Behavioral/ Emotional
Demonstrates increasing balance, coordination, endurance	Speaks clearly and confidently with growing vocabulary	Solves problems using logic and reasoning	Desires peer approval and is sensitive to criticism
Rides bike confidently	Uses language for persuasion, reasoning, and explanation	Begins to reason and concentrate	Forms stronger, more emotionally invested friendships
Participates in organized sports	Understands figurative speech, metaphors, idioms, and humor	Grasps time (*minutes, hours, days, weeks, seasons, years*)	Develops clear sense of identity, values, preferences
Performs more complex physical sequences (*skip, jump rope, etc.*)	Tells and retells stories with well-organized structure	Understands place value and can perform basic mathematic operations	Can regulate emotions with more independence, still needs support
Throws, catches, kicks with more precision	Pronounces words correctly	Tells time to the quarter hour	Capable of empathy, understanding other perspectives
Begins to show preferences to certain physical activities (*soccer, dance, hockey, etc.*)	Has a sense of humor, tells jokes	Begins to plan ahead, organize thoughts and materials	Enjoys structured routines but also begins to handle small changes with greater flexibility
Writes more fluidly with improved pencil grip and control		Understands abstract ideas like fairness, justice, etc.	May become competitive or compare self to others
Forms letters and numbers consistently and legibly		Shows curiosity and asks many "*how*" and "*why*" questions	Takes responsibility of home chores

Draws more detailed pictures		Considers issues and problems, one factor at a time	Cares about fairness and following the rules
Uses scissors to cut out complex shapes		Handles opposites well (*girl-boy, stop-go, up-down*)	Develops a concept of self
Completes puzzles, models, small building sets			Draws moral distinctions based on internal judgement.
Manages daily tasks like *brushing teeth, dressing, utensils, buttoning*			Builds relationships with others

Play with Purpose:

At seven years old, children are growing more independent, socially aware, and eager to master new skills. Their play often shifts toward games with more structure, strategy, and challenge—board games, sports, building sets, and imaginative storylines with rules and goals. Emotionally, they're developing stronger friendships and beginning to understand fairness, empathy, and group dynamics. They may still seek adult approval but also start to compare themselves with peers, which can bring both motivation and moments of self-doubt. Many children at this age begin to worry about getting in trouble or making mistakes. They understand the difference between right and wrong, and they can feel genuine guilt or anxiety over unintentional errors. School, unknown situations, or high expectations may feel stressful, and without the right support, this fear can stifle creativity or discourage risk-taking. As Sir Ken Robinson wisely said, "If you're not prepared to be wrong, you'll never come up with anything original." It's essential that we create spaces where it's safe to try, to fail, and to learn.

Purposeful play should support creativity, collaboration, and confidence, with opportunities for movement, problem solving, and expressive outlets like art, music, dance, and theater. These forms of play help children process emotions, build identity, and communicate in safe, creative ways. Reading remains a cornerstone of development—encourage independent reading, but continue reading aloud, discussing characters, and connecting stories to real life. Through books, play, and self-expression, we nurture not only the developing mind, but the whole child.

Developmental Milestones: 8 years

Gross & Fine Motor	Communication/ Speech	Cognitive	Behavioral/ Emotional
Shows refined coordination and body control	Can converse at almost an adult level	Solves multi-step problems using logic, planning, and strategy	Develops stronger sense of self-esteem and identity
Participates skillfully in team sports, dance, martial arts, etc.	Speaks clearly and articulately, adapting tone and language to audience	Grasps concepts like cause and effect, classification, comparison	Seeks approval and acceptance from peers, sensitive to exclusion
Can throw and catch with accuracy and timing	More complex grammar, figurative language, storytelling structure	Recognizes reversibility (4+2=6 and 6-2=4)	Makes friends easily, may develop close friends of same sex, may be uncomfortable around opp sex
Enjoys challenging physical activities (obstacle courses, monkey bars, bike tricks)	Engages in conversations that include negotiation, reasoning, and reflection	Follows classroom routines, completes homework, manages transitions	Enjoys group work, collaborative play, team-based problem solving
Improved balance, agility, endurance	Understands jokes, sarcasm, and subtle social cues	Thinks critically, explains ideas in detail	May compare abilities to others
Coordinates movements across body parts (dribbling basketball while moving)	Writes short stories, reports, and journal entries with logical sequencing and detail	May develop personal opinions on real-world issues, but often has a black-and-white perspective	Manages most emotions independently but still needs guidance with frustration or disappointment

Writes in complete sentences with legible handwriting	Reads fluently with comprehension, makes predictions and inferences	May read as a major interest	Understands nuanced social rules (fairness, loyalty, honesty)
Draws with detail, creativity, and planning	Fears speaking in front of class or group of people	Can count by 2, 5, 10…	Shows pride in achievements, sets personal goals
Uses tools with precision (scissors, ruler, glue)			Still may seek immediate gratification, actively seeks praise
Ties shoes, buttons small buttons, opens packages			Wants to be part of a group, influenced by peer pressure
Keyboards and uses digital devices with increased efficiency			May have know-it-all attitude
Increasing interested in skilled hobbies			Shows resiliency, bounces back from mistakes

Play with Purpose:

At eight years old, children are in a powerful stage of transition—stretching toward independence while still deeply needing connection, love, and reassurance. They see the world in black and white: things are either great or awful, right or wrong, beautiful or ugly. One small challenge can ruin an entire day. Emotions can shift rapidly—what starts as confidence can spiral into frustration or even despair. They may be sensitive, dramatic, and deeply impacted by the way others respond to them. Their need for peer approval grows stronger, and they may start to act "cool" or even rude to impress others. Don't take it personally—they're not pushing you away as much as they're trying to figure out where they belong. Beneath that posturing, eight-year-olds are deeply loving, eager to please, and trying really hard. They want to master skills and feel a powerful sense of accomplishment when they do. One of the greatest gifts you can give at this age is the chance to master things on their own—to struggle, try again, and succeed without being rescued too quickly.

Purposeful play remains essential. Team games, group projects, and unstructured exploration help build both collaboration and resilience. Creative outlets like music, dance, theater, art, and journaling give them safe ways to express complex feelings and explore who they are becoming. Reading should continue to be a joyful part of daily life—offer them a wide range of books and let their interests lead the way. Graphic novels, fantasy series, informational books, and silly chapter books all count. Keep reading together, too—those shared moments still matter more than you know. At eight, kids are seeking mastery, belonging, and understanding. Through play, creativity, reading, and patience, we can help them grow with confidence and compassion.

Developmental Milestones: 9 years

Gross & Fine Motor	Communication/ Speech	Cognitive	Behavioral/ Emotional
Continued improved strength, stamina, coordination, reaction time	Speaks with confidence and can explain complex ideas or feelings	Solves more complex problems with logic and mental math	Forms deeper friendships based on shared interests and trust
Engages in organized physical activities with strategy and teamwork	Uses speech patterns similar to adults, speaks at close to adult level	Understands abstract concepts like metaphor, justice, and ethics	Creates exclusive friend groups
Shows greater control in fine-tuned movements like dribbling, throwing, or dance routines	Tells engaging, structured stories with beginning, middle, end	Uses planning and critical thinking to complete school projects and tasks	Shows increased empathy and perspective-taking
Rides bike confidently, swims, participates in complex athletics	Understands tone, sarcasm, idioms, and indirect communication	Compares, contrasts, and evaluates ideas or arguments	Competitive and has a sense of humor
Begins to specialize in a sport or physical hobby	Listens to others, responds thoughtfully, engages in group discussion	Begins to reflect on their own thinking— *metacognition*	Seeks independence, may rebel against authority
Writes clearly and quickly, consistent size, spacing, pressure	Reads independently and analyzes character, themes, and plot	Sees inconsistencies and imperfections in adults	Understands right vs. wrong in more nuanced ways

Uses computer or tablet efficiently for writing, typing, navigating apps or websites	Writes paragraphs and multi-page stories or reports with organization and creativity	Has increased sense of truthfulness, is concerned about rules— fair vs. unfair, complains about fairness	May experience mood swings, anxiety, or self-consciousness as self-awareness increases
Begins cursive writing (if taught)	States things in negatives ("I hate…", "It's not…", "I don't like…")	Develops personal interests and abilities	Prefers same sex friends, secretly curious about relationships between boys and girls
Can use simple tools	Vocabulary of 3000+ words		

Play with Purpose:

Nine is a milestone year—the moment many children quietly begin to shift from little kid to young adolescent. You may notice they suddenly seem more mature, more thoughtful, and more self-aware. They begin to reflect on the world and their place in it, asking deeper questions and expressing more complex emotions. While they still need structure, reassurance, and plenty of play, they also crave more independence, privacy, and respect. This can be a time of increased sensitivity and self-consciousness—children may begin comparing themselves more intensely to peers and worrying about how they're perceived. Confidence may waver, especially if they feel behind academically or socially. Don't underestimate how much encouragement and belief from a trusted adult still matters at this age. It is also important to note that nine-year-olds (*particularly boys*) tend to be somewhat inattentive and unfocused. While their unfocused daydreaming may mimic ADHD, at this age it is really part of normal cognitive development.

Purposeful play should meet them where they are—think hands-on projects, team games with strategy, creative outlets like theater, music, art, or coding, and experiences that allow them to take the lead. They want to feel capable, trusted, and challenged. Reading remains a powerful tool for connection and growth—many nine-year-olds are transitioning into deeper chapter books and may start identifying with characters navigating moral dilemmas, friendships, and big emotions. Encourage independent reading while continuing to read together, especially with books that spark conversation and empathy. This age is a beautiful blend of curiosity and complexity—still playful, but increasingly profound. With freedom to explore, fail, and grow, nine-year-olds are building the foundation for who they are becoming.

Developmental Milestones: 10 years

Gross & Fine Motor	Communication/ Speech	Cognitive	Behavioral/ Emotional
Shows better integrated motor skills	Effectively persuades or negotiates	Solves abstract problems using logic	Interested in teen culture, avoids looking childish
Gross and fine motor skills developed through physical activity	Uses logic to argue with parents and other adults	Has accurate perception of events	Develops a strong sense of identity
Strives to be physically fit	Improves listening and responding skills	Applies knowledge in creative ways	Improves emotional control
Energetic and spirited	Revels in bathroom humor	Eager to master new skills	Is truthful, becomes more dependable
Fascinated with how body works		Is aware of peer and adult expectations	Has improved self-image, accepting of others
Works to fine tune skills of chosen sport or activity		Possesses a surprising scope of interests	Identifies and finds role models in famous figures (*musicians, athletes, actors*)
Begins to undergo physical maturation		Understands concepts of space, time, and dimension	Relates to peer group intensely and abides by group decisions
Becomes more aware of own body as puberty approaches		Is capable of increasing independence	Continues to participate in small groups of same gender, but may become preoccupied with opposite sex

Play with Purpose:

At ten years old, many children are standing at the edge of adolescence—one foot still in childhood and the other stepping into a more grown-up world. They're more confident, responsible, and reflective—but also more aware of peer dynamics, personal strengths and weaknesses, and the pressures that come with growing up. They may begin idolizing athletes, musicians, YouTubers, or actors, and show a growing curiosity about teen culture, relationships, and the adult world. Depending on the child, this curiosity can include questions about topics like alcohol, drugs, or romantic relationships. It's essential that adults remain open, honest, and unshocked—because if they're asking, they're ready for some form of an age-appropriate answer.

Their identity is developing rapidly, and with it may come insecurity, perfectionism, or increased self-criticism. They care deeply about what others think, and friendships are often intense and emotionally charged. They may crave independence while still quietly needing reassurance and affection. It's a delicate balance—offering guidance without hovering and trust without letting go too fast.

Purposeful play remains essential at ten, though it may look more mature: collaborative games, creative projects, sports teams, storytelling, building challenges, and experiences that let them test leadership and creativity. Depending on where you live and your child's maturity, this may be the age where freedoms begin to expand—riding bikes around the neighborhood, spontaneous pick-up games at the park, or even outings like a movie or mini-golf with friends. These experiences nurture problem solving, decision making, and growing confidence in social settings. This is also a prime age for diving into personal interests—music, theater, coding, photography, writing, or building. Reading can be a refuge, a mirror, or a bridge—books at this age often touch on friendship struggles, family dynamics, adventure, and self-discovery. Let them explore freely, and continue reading together when you can. Ten is a time of expanding horizons, emotional intensity, and emerging individuality. When we honor their independence while still offering connection, we give them exactly what they need to thrive.

Developmental Milestones: 11-14 years

Physical	Communication/ Speech	Cognitive	Behavioral/ Emotional
Physical changes are influenced by puberty and activity choices	At this stage, they may talk a lot.	Develops personal interests and abilities	Goes through another version of terrible twos
Begins to take responsibility for their own health	They may engage in gossip, talking behind back, or putting down kids outside of group	Can apply concepts to specific examples	Enjoys close interactions with peers
Fine motor dexterity improves based upon chosen activities	May engage in creative expression (*art, poetry, music, abstract thought*)	Can use deductive reasoning and make educated guesses	Takes on more responsibility at home
Puberty changes occur during this period	Displays physical affection in relationship or flirting	May *recognize* current actions have future effects, may not *act* on that	Can adapt behavior to fit situation
Develop body hair under arms, in pubic region	May tease or engage in "*smack talk*," competitive	Starts setting personal goals, thinks about future	Exhibit off-color humor and silliness
May have oily skin or acne	Seeks to talk about interests	Develops a conscience	Enjoys recreational activities
May see significant development in athletic ability, artistic and musical talents, or other	Improved arguing skills, demonstrating them often and with great passion	Evaluates credibility of various sources of information.	Generally cooperative and considerate, but inconsistent and unpredictable
Boys will have voice change, increased appetite, increased sweating, rapid growth		Begins to anticipate consequence of different options	Has little impulse control, seeks immediate gratification

Girls begin menstruating, develop breasts and hips. Girls develop more rapidly than boys		May challenge the assumptions and solutions presented by adults	May feel out of control, can show extremes of emotions
Needs more sleep, may sleep in especially weekends		Smart decision-making does not come easy	May not have adequate coping strategies

Play with Purpose:

Just because they're growing up doesn't mean they're grown. Adolescence is one of the most extraordinary and misunderstood chapters of development—a time when kids may look more mature, sound more articulate, and start asking big questions, but their brains are still under heavy construction. Underneath that new height and emerging independence, they are still very much *children becoming*. This stage mirrors toddlerhood in many ways: rapid growth, emotional intensity, and massive brain rewiring. The brain is pruning old connections and building new ones at a staggering rate—especially in areas related to identity, emotion, and social belonging. Meanwhile, the prefrontal cortex—the part that manages impulse control, long-term planning, and decision making—is lagging behind. This mismatch explains why thoughtful kids can still make reckless choices, and why they need adults who can guide without shaming and set boundaries without pushing them away.

Puberty adds another layer of complexity. While girls often enter this phase earlier and may seem emotionally more mature, both boys and girls experience internal shifts that can be difficult to name or manage. Moods swing, friendships shift, and the quest for independence intensifies. They may act like they don't need you—but they absolutely do. This is a time for honest conversations, flexible structure, and room to explore who they are becoming.

This is also a *pivotal time in education*, a season when children are silently measuring their value against grades, test scores, and comparison to peers. In our current system, there's a perceived hierarchy where talents in math, reading, and science are often rewarded above all else, even if a child's true gifts lie in storytelling, design, music, leadership, humor, or empathy. As the late Sir Ken Robinson warned, this is where education can begin to kill creativity. Kids who don't fit the mold can start to believe they're not smart, not enough, or not destined for success. Don't let them believe that lie. Celebrate their passions. Value their creative energy. Remind them that intelligence comes in many forms—and that the world needs all kinds of minds.

Purposeful play evolves during these years but remains essential. It may take the form of team sports, creative projects, performance, gaming, music, writing, or just hanging out with friends. These outlets help process emotions, test boundaries, and express identity. Depending on the child and the community, this may also be a time for growing independence— like going to the mall, movies, or biking with friends—but these freedoms should come with scaffolding, not total release. Reading is still powerful, especially books that mirror their lives or expand their understanding of the world. Let them read what they love and talk about what they're thinking.

Adolescence is *not* a problem to fix—it's a transformation to support. When we stay connected and curious, we give them the courage to keep becoming.

Developmental Milestones: 15-18 years

Physical	Communication/ Speech	Cognitive	Behavioral/ Emotional
Peak physical coordination and strength (especially late adolescence)	Abstract, persuasive, and analytical communication	Fully capable of abstract, strategic, and reflective thinking	More emotionally stable and self-aware
Capable of adult-level athletic activities	Engages in debates, persuasive writing, and interview	Develops personal ethics, opinions, and world views	Deepened self-identity and personal values
May explore fitness routines	Adapts language based on settings (work vs. friends)	Can analyze complex problems and consider multiple perspectives	Shows concern about body image
Specialization in sports or physical disciplines	Communicates ideas and emotions with more subtlety and confidence	Begins to make independent decisions about future	Peer influence still important, but also individual beliefs form
Mastery of fine motor skills (writing, drawing, typing)			Greater responsibility in relationships, academics, jobs
Capable of managing complex tasks (building, driving, complex fine motor skills including trade skills)			May experience anxiety or pressure related to future goals
Advance use of tools, technology, and design			Still a very vulnerable stage emotionally

Play with Purpose:

They look grown. They sound grown. But their brains are still catching up. By the time teens reach fifteen to eighteen years old, many adults assume they're ready to handle the world. And in some ways, they are—they're driving, working, applying to college, or planning their futures. But beneath all that growing independence is a brain that's still *under construction.* The prefrontal cortex, which manages long-term planning, risk evaluation, and emotional regulation, won't fully mature until the mid-to-late twenties. That means these years are still part of childhood—a critical window for shaping identity, values, confidence, and connection.

This stage is rich with transformation and possibility. Teens are trying to figure out who they are, what matters to them, and how to belong. They crave respect, autonomy, and meaningful roles in the world around them. But they also struggle—under the surface, many are managing stress, pressure, self-doubt, and fears of failure. They may push adults away not because they don't care, but because they're trying to prove they can do it alone. What they really need is space to grow and a safety net to fall back on.

This is also a make-or-break moment in education. These are the years when kids start to believe what the world has told them about their worth. If they haven't found success in traditional academic settings—if they've been labeled as "average," "behind," or "unmotivated"—they may begin to disengage or give up. As Sir Ken Robinson so powerfully said, "We are educating people out of their creative capacities." This is our chance to rewrite that story. We must expand the definition of success, celebrate multiple intelligences, and support the passions that light them up—even if those passions don't come with a GPA.

Purposeful play *still matters* here, though it looks different. Teens need expressive outlets—music, theater, sports, film, writing, coding, activism, design, building, gaming, entrepreneurship. These are not just hobbies—they are bridges to purpose, connection, and future careers. Encourage collaboration, real-world problem solving, and opportunities to lead. Give them space to create, explore, and take risks—*without fear of shame if they fail.* Reading can be a mirror, mentor, and catalyst—books that reflect their experiences, challenge their thinking, or offer escape can help them feel less alone in a very noisy world, as can sports and music.

These years are not just preparation for adulthood—*they are life.* And when we guide with humility, connect with compassion, and protect their spark while it's still flickering, we help them cross the bridge into adulthood not just ready but resilient, creative, and rooted in who they are.

Brain Development Beyond Childhood

While childhood and adolescence are critical periods for brain development, research now confirms that our brains continue to grow and change well into early adulthood—at least into our mid- to late twenties. Even more compelling, studies show that *myelination*, the process of insulating neural pathways for more efficient brain communication, continues long after high school. In fact, emerging research suggests this process may extend well into our forties and possibly even to age fifty. That means development doesn't stop at graduation—or even at parenting. It continues, subtly and powerfully, across the lifespan.

This extended window of brain growth is a call to *remain curious, hopeful,* and *engaged* at every age. We must stop thinking of development as something that ends in childhood and start recognizing it as a lifelong process—one that's shaped by experience, enriched environments, safe relationships, meaningful play, and emotional connection.

The milestone charts you've just explored are more than checklists. They're *maps of potential*—a guide to how brains and bodies build themselves step by step, experience by experience, year by year. When we recognize missed milestones as opportunities rather than failures, when we honor a child's unique rhythm instead of forcing them into a rigid mold, when we create space for creativity, movement, connection, and curiosity, we activate something powerful.

That's what **Kid Magic** is. It's not just about childhood—it's about possibility. It's about building strong foundations early and believing in growth at every stage. It's about unlocking the hidden brilliance in each child—and in ourselves.

Because when we understand how development truly works, when we choose to see behavior as communication, movement as learning, play as essential, and connection as medicine, we don't just support kids.

We **unlock magic** that lasts a lifetime.

A FEW OF MY FAVORITE RESOURCES

Because we are friends now and I trust that you are ready to join the revolution, I am going to share my absolute favorite resources. I encourage you to look into them, read up on them, learn from them as I have. These are other revolutionaries doing amazing things! I am also going to leave you some space to add in your own resources, as I want this book to be your guide. I encourage you to reach out to me with recommendations and your own resources so I may continue to learn and grow my library as well!

Note: I will also be including an up-to-date list on my website (as more may be added over time): howtobeakid.com/library

The Sir Ken Robinson Foundation

Sir Ken Robinson was a globally recognized leader in education, creativity, and human potential. He championed the need for personalized, passion-driven learning and famously argued that schools often stifle creativity. The Sir Ken Robinson Foundation continues his legacy by promoting innovative, inclusive education systems that nurture the diverse talents of every child. Sir Ken Robinson is one of the greatest inspirations behind not only this book, but the How To Be A Kid™ program as well. His influence continues to inspire us all to create an educational system that celebrates creativity, individuality, and children as a whole. To quote the movie *The Sandlot*, "heroes get remembered, but legends never die."

Dr. Robert Melillo

Dr. Robert Melillo is a world-renowned functional developmental neurologist, clinician, researcher, and bestselling author specializing in childhood neurological disorders. With over thirty years of experience, he developed the Brain Balance Program®, a non-pharmaceutical approach combining sensory-motor exercises, cognitive training, and nutritional guidance to address conditions like ADHD, autism, and dyslexia. He currently works with children and adults at the Melillo Center for Developing Minds. Dr. Melillo's work takes a brain-based, highly researched approach that results in meaningful changes and results for both the patient and their families. He works with a wide range of diagnoses from developmental neurological conditions to mental health challenges for children and adults. His influential, best-selling book, *Disconnected Kids,* outlines his methodology, aiming to improve brain connectivity and function in children. Dr. Melillo's passion for children and the pursuit of a better world is felt by all who know him and beyond. His work inspires me as a mom, a practitioner, an educator and is reflected in this very book.

The Creative Revolution

The Creative Revolution is an international community that believes in the incredible potential of our individual and shared creative capacities. Inspired by global creative revolutionary Sir Ken Robinson, we believe in creating a future for us all. We advocate for a richer conception of human imagination, creativity, and intelligence, and celebrate the diversity of human potential. The Creative Revolution functions as an active network and resource hub, where dedicated revolutionaries share ideas, knowledge, work together, and collaborate on projects that create a better future for us all.

"The Revolution I am advocating is based on a belief in the value of the individual, the right to self-determination, our potential to evolve and live a fulfilled life, and the importance of civic responsibility and respect for others." —Sir Ken Robinson

Let Grow

Let Grow is a nonprofit organization co-founded in 2017 by Lenore Skenazy, Jonathan Haidt, Peter Gray, and Daniel Shuchman to promote childhood independence and resilience. Through programs like the Let Grow Experience and Play Club, it encourages parents and schools to foster children's confidence and self-reliance by allowing them more freedom and responsibility. Let Grow's mission is to make it easy, normal, and legal to give kids back the independence they need to grow into capable, confident, and happy adults.

Pink Oatmeal

Pink Oatmeal is an educational platform founded by Dr. Chanda Jothen, a physical therapist and mother of three, dedicated to promoting movement and motor skill development in children from birth through elementary school. Combining her expertise in physical therapy with a passion for design, Chanda offers a wealth of resources—including printable activities, digital games, and a comprehensive video library—tailored for parents, educators, and therapists. Her mission is to make physical activity engaging and accessible, helping children build strength, coordination, and confidence through fun, themed exercises. Pink Oatmeal's offerings are designed to support a wide range of developmental needs, making it a valuable tool for fostering active learning environments.

S'cool Moves

S'cool Moves is an educational program founded by Debra Em Wilson, designed to support students' learning and self-regulation through movement-based strategies. Drawing from her experience as a reading specialist and her personal journey as a parent, Wilson developed S'cool Moves to address the needs of diverse learners by integrating principles from Polyvagal Theory and neurodevelopmental research. The program offers evidence-based tools—such as posters, activity cards, and on-demand training—that help educators and therapists improve focus, coordination, and emotional regulation in students. S'cool Moves emphasizes collaboration between teachers and support staff, aiming to create inclusive, engaging classrooms that nurture every child's potential.

1000 Hours Outside Movement

1000 Hours Outside is a global movement founded by Ginny Yurich, a Michigan-based educator and mother of five, aiming to counteract the imbalance between screen time and outdoor play in children's lives. Inspired by the idea that the average child spends over 1,200 hours annually on screens, the initiative encourages families to match that time with outdoor activities, promoting physical, emotional, and cognitive development. Through resources like printable trackers, a podcast, and a mobile app, 1000 Hours Outside supports families in integrating nature into daily life, fostering resilience and well-being.

Canva

Canva for Education is a free, all-in-one visual learning platform that empowers students and teachers to collaborate, create, and communicate through design. It offers thousands of customizable templates for presentations, posters, videos, and infographics, making it easy to integrate creativity into any subject. With tools like interactive whiteboards, AI-powered writing assistants, and multimedia storytelling features, Canva supports project-based and student-centered learning. It also integrates with popular classroom tools like Google Classroom and Microsoft Teams, helping educators personalize instruction and foster critical thinking, collaboration, and digital literacy in learners of all ages. It is a great way to combine technology and creativity.

Insight Educat

Insight Educat is where education meets real-world empowerment. Founded by educator and entrepreneur Cassandra Chamberlin, the program helps young people (and the adults who guide them) move beyond qualification-driven systems and step into curiosity, creativity, courage, and grit. Drawing on principles of *ikigai*—a Japanese concept of living with purpose—Cassandra's work focuses on purpose-driven entrepreneurship and reimagining education as preparation for thriving in an unpredictable, innovation-driven world. Her approach blends teaching experience, leadership expertise, and business insight to create practical tools for helping students discover their strengths and chart meaningful paths forward. Cassandra is one of those rare educators who knows how to bridge the gap between school and real life. Her program empowers kids to find what lights them up and prepare them to thrive in a future that demands curiosity, adaptability, and entrepreneurial thinking.

Quiet Rebel Coaching (for moms)

Quiet Rebel Coaching is designed for purpose-driven mothers who have made bold, unconventional choices for their children's wellbeing—but somewhere along the way, forgot how to advocate for themselves. The founder, Claire Gillespie, understands that parents who fight fiercely for their kids often put their own needs last. Through her Quiet Rebellion approach, Claire helps mothers reconnect with their authentic selves—without guilt, without apology. And that's an essential part of Kid Magic: caring for children means modeling wholeness, joy, and aliveness. When kids see us living fully—not just sacrificing endlessly—they learn that thriving is possible for them, too.

The Cardboard Shed

The Cardboard Shed is a radical, joy-filled approach to childhood that frees kids from constant adult direction and reconnects everyone with their innate creativity. Founded by Claire Gillespie, it's a low-demand, play-based space where children's natural genius can flourish through open-ended building, experimenting, and creating. Claire doesn't set out to "teach" creativity—she trusts it. The Shed shows us what happens when we step back: profound learning, authentic self-expression, and the kind of imaginative play that reminds us all what childhood is meant to be.

Long Island P.R.E.P.

Long Island P.R.E.P. (Prevention and Resilience Enrichment Program) is an organization founded in 2017 by educator and author Paul Vecchione to address the growing crisis of youth substance abuse and mental health challenges. Based in Babylon, New York, the organization provides prevention education, intervention strategies, and professional development for schools and communities. Through programs like PREP Academy and the Mission Z Podcast, Long Island P.R.E.P. empowers students, parents, and educators with tools to foster resilience and informed decision making.

Applied HOPE

Applied HOPE Foundation (Fundación Esperanza Aplicada) is a non-profit in Costa Rica dedicated to environmental education, green entrepreneurship, and restorative development. The Founder and President, Steven Greenleaf, is an environmentalist and educator originally from California. Their eight-acre campus in Tilarán, Guanacaste, features solar-powered classrooms, gardens, and labs where educators, researchers, and students come together for retreats, courses, internships, and hands-on projects in environmental leadership and problem solving, restorative agriculture, and green building. What makes them one of my favorite resources is their deep commitment to protecting our greatest teacher—nature itself—by showing how learning, innovation, and sustainability all begin with the land beneath our feet.

Bibliography

Alexander, Robin. Improving Oracy and Classroom Talk in English Schools. Cambridge Primary Review Trust, 2012.

American Academy of Pediatrics. "Media and Young Minds." Pediatrics 138, no. 5 (2016): e20162591.

American Psychological Association. "Multitasking: Switching Costs." Washington, DC: APA, 2006. https://www.apa.org/research/action/multitask.

Ayres, A. Jean. Sensory Integration and Learning Disorders. Los Angeles: Western Psychological Services, 1972.

Barrett, Peter, Yufan Zhang, Joanne Moffat, and Khairy Kobbacy. "A Holistic, Multi-Level Analysis Identifying the Impact of Classroom Design on Pupils' Learning." Building and Environment 59 (2013): 678–689.

Bartlett, Frederic C. Remembering: A Study in Experimental and Social Psychology. Cambridge: Cambridge University Press, 1932.

Beebe, Dean W. "Cognitive, Behavioral, and Functional Consequences of Inadequate Sleep in Children and Adolescents." Pediatric Clinics 58, no. 3 (2011): 649–665.

Best, John R. "Effects of Physical Activity on Children's Executive Function: Contributions of Experimental Research on Aerobic Exercise." Developmental Review 30, no. 4 (2010): 331–351.

Brown, Eleanor D., and Kelly L. Sax. "Arts Enrichment and Preschool Emotions for Low-Income Children at Risk." Frontiers in Psychology 10 (2019): 1–12.

Catterall, James S., Susan A. Dumais, and Gillian Hampden-Thompson. The Arts and Achievement in At-Risk Youth: Findings from Four Longitudinal Studies. Washington, DC: National Endowment for the Arts, 2012.

Centers for Disease Control and Prevention. Autism and Developmental Disabilities Monitoring (ADDM) Network. Data and Statistics on Autism Spectrum Disorder. Accessed August 2025. https://www.cdc.gov/autism/data-research/index.html.

Centers for Disease Control and Prevention. Leading Causes of Death Reports, 1981–2021. Atlanta: CDC, 2021. https://www.cdc.gov/injury/wisqars/LeadingCauses.curhtml.

Centers for Disease Control and Prevention. "Developmental Milestones." Atlanta: CDC, 2022. https://www.cdc.gov/ncbddd/actearly/milestones/index.html.

Center on the Developing Child at Harvard University (2011). Building the Brain's "Air Traffic Control" System: How Early Experiences Shape the Development of Executive Function: Working Paper No. 11. http://www.developing child.harvard.edu

Collaborative for Academic, Social, and Emotional Learning (CASEL). "What Is SEL?" Chicago: CASEL, 2020. https://casel.org/what-is-sel/.

Condliffe, Barbara, Janet Quint, Mary G. Visher, et al. Project-Based Learning: A Literature Review. MDRC, 2017.

Craig, A. D. "How Do You Feel? Interoception: The Sense of the Physiological Condition of the Body." Nature Reviews Neuroscience 3, no. 8 (2002): 655–666.

Deasy, Richard J., ed. Critical Links: Learning in the Arts and Student Academic and Social Development. Washington, DC: Arts Education Partnership, 2002.

Diamond, Adele, and Kathleen Lee. "Interventions Shown to Aid Executive Function Development in Children 4 to 12 Years Old." Science 333, no. 6045 (2011): 959–964.

Diamond, Adele. "Close Interrelation of Motor Development and Cognitive Development and of the Cerebellum and Prefrontal Cortex." Child Development 71, no. 1 (2000): 44–56.

Diamond, Adele. "Executive Functions." Annual Review of Psychology 64 (2013): 135–168.

Durlak, Joseph A., Roger P. Weissberg, Allison B. Dymnicki, Rebecca D. Taylor, and Kriston B. Schellinger. "The Impact of Enhancing Students' Social and Emotional Learning: A Meta-Analysis of School-Based Universal Interventions." Child Development 82, no. 1 (2011): 405–432.

Edutopia. Oracy in the Classroom: Strategies for Effective Talk. YouTube video, 7:26. June 4, 2018. https://www.youtube.com/watch?v=2ADAY9AQm54.

Else-Quest, N. M., Hyde, J. S., Goldsmith, H. H., & Van Hulle, C. A. (2006). Gender differences in temperament: A meta-analysis. Psychological Bulletin, 132(1), 33-72.

Fiorella, Logan, and Richard E. Mayer. "The Relative Benefits of Learning by Teaching and Teaching Expectancy." Contemporary Educational Psychology 38, no. 4 (2013): 281–288.

Flook, Lisa, Simon B. Goldberg, Laura Pinger, and Richard J. Davidson.

"Promoting Prosocial Behavior and Self-Regulatory Skills in Preschool Children through a Mindfulness-Based Kindness Curriculum." Developmental Psychology 51, no. 1 (2015): 44–51.

Giedd, Jay N. "Structural Magnetic Resonance Imaging of the Adolescent Brain." Annals of the New York Academy of Sciences 1021, no. 1 (2004): 77–85.

Ginsburg, Kenneth R. "The Importance of Play in Promoting Healthy Child Development and Maintaining Strong Parent-Child Bonds." Pediatrics 119, no. 1 (2007): 182–191.

Gray, Peter. Free to Learn: Why Unleashing the Instinct to Play Will Make Our Children Happier, More Self-Reliant, and Better Students for Life. New York: Basic Books, 2013.

Gray, Peter. "The Decline of Play and the Rise of Psychopathology in Children and Adolescents." Pediatrics 142, no. 3 (2018): e20181512.

Haidt, Jonathan, The Anxious Generation (New York: Penguin Press, 2024).

Hallam, Susan. "The Power of Music: Its Impact on the Intellectual, Social and Personal Development of Children and Young People." International Journal of Music Education 28, no. 3 (2010): 269–289.

Hamre, Bridget K., and Robert C. Pianta. "Early Teacher–Child Relationships and the Trajectory of Children's School Outcomes through Eighth Grade." Child Development 72, no. 2 (2001): 625–638.

Hannaford, Carla. Smart Moves: Why Learning Is Not All in Your Head. Salt Lake City: Great River Books, 2005.

Hannaford, Carla. The Dominance Factor: How Knowing Your Dominant Eye, Ear, Brain, Hand & Foot Can Improve Your Learning. Salt Lake City: Great River Books, 1997.

HeartMath Institute. (n.d.). Science of the Heart: Exploring the Role of the Heart in Human Performance. https://www.heartmath.org/research/science-of-the-heart/

Hillman, Charles H., Kirk I. Erickson, and Arthur F. Kramer. "Be Smart, Exercise Your Heart: Exercise Effects on Brain and Cognition." Nature Reviews Neuroscience 9, no. 1 (2008): 58–65.

Hocking, Claire, The Relationship between Retained Primitive Reflexes and Sensory Integration, Whole Brain Learning, accessed August 1, 2025, https://www.wholebrain.com.au/uploads/1/5/9/5/15956426/the_relationship_between_retained_primitive_reflexes.pdf.

Immordino-Yang, Mary Helen, and Antonio Damasio. "We Feel, Therefore We Learn: The Relevance of Affective and Social Neuroscience to Education."

Mind, Brain, and Education 1, no. 1 (2007): 3–10.

Jones, Stephanie M., and Jennifer Kahn. The Evidence Base for How We Learn: Supporting Students' Social, Emotional, and Academic Development. Washington, DC: The Aspen Institute, 2017.

Kamik Survey, Children Spending 35 Percent Less Time Playing Freely Outside, SGB Online, September 20, 2018, https://sgbonline.com/kamik-survey-childre-spending-35-percent-less-time-playing-freely-outside/.

Kaplan, Stephen, "The Restorative Benefits of Nature: Toward an Integrative Framework," Journal of Environmental Psychology 15, no. 3 (1995): 169–82.

Kaput, Manu. "Productive Failure." Cognition and Instruction 26, no. 3 (2008): 379–424.

Kisida, Brian, and Daniel H. Bowen. "New Evidence of the Benefits of Arts Education." Brookings Institution, 2019.

Kolb, Bryan, and Robbin Gibb. "Brain Plasticity and Behaviour in the Developing Brain." Journal of the Canadian Academy of Child and Adolescent Psychiatry 20, no. 4 (2011): 265–276.

Kolb, David A. Experiential Learning: Experience as the Source of Learning and Development. Englewood Cliffs, NJ: Prentice Hall, 1984.

Lenroot, Rhoshel K., and Jay N. Giedd. "Brain Development in Children and Adolescents: Insights from Anatomical Magnetic Resonance Imaging." Nature Reviews Neuroscience 7, no. 10 (2006): 718–729.

Maslow, Abraham H. "A Theory of Human Motivation." Psychological Review 50, no. 4 (1943): 370–396.

McClelland, M. M., & Cameron, C. E. (2012). Self-Regulation and Academic Achievement in Elementary School Children. New Directions for Child and Adolescent Development, 2012(133), 29-44.

McCraty, Rollin, Mike Atkinson, Dana Tomasino, and Raymond T. Bradley. "The Coherent Heart: Heart–Brain Interactions, Psychophysiological Coherence, and the Emergence of System-Wide Order." Integral Review 5, no. 2 (2009): 10–115.

McCraty, R., Atkinson, M., & Tomasino, D. (2001). Science of the Heart: Exploring the Role of the Heart in Human Performance (Publication No. 01-001). HeartMath Research Center, Institute of HeartMath.

McCraty, R., & Zayas, M. A. (2014). Cardiac coherence, self-regulation, autonomic stability, and psychosocial well-being. Frontiers in Psychology, 5, 1090.

McGaugh, James L. "Making Lasting Memories: Remembering the

Significant." Proceedings of the National Academy of Sciences 110, Supplement 2 (2013): 10402–10407.

Medina, John. Brain Rules: 12 Principles for Surviving and Thriving at Work, Home, and School. Seattle: Pear Press, 2014.

Melillo, Robert. Disconnected Kids, 2nd ed. New York: Penguin, 2016.

Melillo, Robert. Disconnected Kids: The Groundbreaking Brain Balance Program for Children with Autism, ADHD, Dyslexia, and Other Neurological Disorders. New York: Penguin, 2009.

Metcalfe, J. (2017). Learning from Errors. Annual Review of Psychology, 68, 465-489).

Mischel, Walter, Yuichi Shoda, and Monica L. Rodriguez. "Delay of Gratification in Children." Science 244, no. 4907 (1989): 933–938.

Mischel, Walter. The Marshmallow Test: Mastering Self-Control. New York: Little, Brown, 2014.

National Institute of Mental Health. "Mental Illness." Bethesda, MD: NIMH, 2022. https://www.nimh.nih.gov/health/statistics/mental-illness.

National Scientific Council on the Developing Child. "Young Children Develop in an Environment of Relationships." Working Paper No. 1, 2004.

Navon, D. "Forest before Trees: The Precedence of Global Features in Visual Perception." Cognitive Psychology 9, no. 3 (1977): 353–383.

Ophir, E., Nass, C., & Wagner, A. D. (2009). Cognitive control in media multitaskers. Proceedings of the National Academy of Sciences, 106(37), 15583-15587.

Organisation for Economic Co-operation and Development (OECD). PISA 2018 Results. Paris: OECD, 2019.

Patel, Aniruddh D. "Why Would Musical Training Benefit the Neural Encoding of Speech? The OPERA Hypothesis." Frontiers in Psychology 2 (2011): 142.

Penfield, Wilder, and Edwin Boldrey. "Somatic Motor and Sensory Representation in the Cerebral Cortex of Man as Studied by Electrical Stimulation." Brain 60, no. 4 (1937): 389–443.

Penfield, Wilder, and Theodore Rasmussen. The Cerebral Cortex of Man. New York: Macmillan, 1950.

Piaget, Jean. The Origins of Intelligence in Children. New York: International Universities Press, 1952.

Pianta, Robert C., and Martha W. Stuhlman. "Teacher–Student Relationships and Children's Success in School." Developmental Psychology 40, no. 2 (2004): 406–417.

Posner, M. I. and Petersen, S. E., "The Attention System of the Human Brain," *Annual Review of Neuroscience* 13, no. 1 (1990): 25–42.

Ratey, John J. Spark: The Revolutionary New Science of Exercise and the Brain. New York: Little, Brown, 2008.

Riding, R. J., and I. Cheema. Cognitive Styles—An Overview and Integration. Educational Psychology 11, no. 3–4 (1991): 193–215.

Robinson, Ken. Creative Schools. New York: Penguin, 2015.

Robinson, Ken. Out of Our Minds. Capstone, 2011.

Robinson, Ken. The Element. New York: Penguin, 2009.

Robinson, Ken. "Do Schools Kill Creativity?" TED Talk, 2006.

Roorda, Debora L., Helma M. Koomen, Jantine L. Spilt, and Frans J. Oort. "The Influence of Affective Teacher–Student Relationships on Students' School Engagement and Achievement: A Meta-Analytic Approach." Review of Educational Research 81, no. 4 (2011): 493–529.

Sahlberg, Pasi. Finnish Lessons 2.0: What Can the World Learn from Educational Change in Finland? New York: Teachers College Press, 2015.

Shams, Ladan, and Aaron R. Seitz. "Benefits of Multisensory Learning." Trends in Cognitive Sciences 12, no. 11 (2008): 411–417.

Shonkoff, Jack P., and Deborah A. Phillips, eds. From Neurons to Neighborhoods: The Science of Early Childhood Development. Washington, DC: National Academy Press, 2000.

Vygotsky, Lev S. Mind in Society. Cambridge, MA: Harvard University Press, 1978.

Wentzel, Kathryn R. "Teacher–Student Relationships and Adolescent Competence at School." In Handbook of School Violence and School Safety: International Research and Practice, edited by Shane R. Jimerson et al., 434–444. New York: Routledge, 2012.

Winner, Ellen, Thalia R. Goldstein, and Stéphan Vincent-Lancrin. Art for Art's Sake? The Impact of Arts Education. Paris: OECD Publishing, 2013.

Yogman, Michael, Andrew Garner, Jeffrey Hutchinson, Kathy Hirsh-Pasek, and Roberta Michnick Golinkoff. "The Power of Play: A Pediatric Role in Enhancing Development in Young Children." Pediatrics 142, no. 3 (2018): e20182058

Youki Terada and Stephen Merrill, "The Science of Classroom Design: Our Comprehensive, All-in, Research-Based Look at the Design of Effective Learning Spaces," Edutopia, November 2, 2023.

Zablotsky, Benjamin, et al. "Prevalence and Trends of Developmental Disabilities among Children in the United States: 2019–2020." Pediatrics 151, no. 2 (2023): e2022057090.

Zelazo, P. D., & Lyons, K. E. (2012). The Potential Benefits of Mindfulness Training in Early Childhood: A Developmental Social Cognitive Neuroscience Perspective. Child Development Perspectives, 6(2), 154-160.

Zenner, Charlotte, Sarah Herrnleben-Kurz, and Harald Walach. "Mindfulness-Based Interventions in Schools—A Systematic Review and Meta-Analysis." Frontiers in Psychology 5 (2014): 603.

Zhang, L. F., and R. J. Sternberg. A Threefold Model of Intellectual Styles. Educational Psychology Review 17, no. 1 (2005): 1–53.

Endnotes

1   Centers for Disease Control and Prevention, Leading Causes of Death Reports, 1981–2021 (Atlanta: CDC, 2021), https://www.cdc.gov/injury/wisqars/LeadingCauses.curhtml.

2   Centers for Disease Control and Prevention, Autism and Developmental Disabilities Monitoring (ADDM) Network, Data and Statistics on Autism Spectrum Disorder, accessed August 2025, https://www.cdc.gov/autism/data-research/index.html.; National Institute of Mental Health, "Mental Illness," (Bethesda, MD: NIMH, 2022), https://www.nimh.nih.gov/health/statistics/mental-illness.

3   Michael Yogman et al., "The Power of Play: A Pediatric Role in Enhancing Development in Young Children," Pediatrics 142, no. 3 (2018): e20182058, https://publications.aap.org/pediatrics/article/142/3/e20182058/38649/The-Power-of-Play-A-Pediatric-Role-in-Enhancing.

4   Peter Gray, "The Decline of Play and the Rise of Psychopathology in Children and Adolescents," Pediatrics 142, no. 3 (2018): e20181512, https://files.eric.ed.gov/fulltext/EJ985541.pdf.

5   Pasi Sahlberg, Finnish Lessons 2.0: What Can the World Learn from Educational Change in Finland? (New York: Teachers College Press, 2015).

6   Ken Robinson, "Do Schools Kill Creativity?" TED Talk, 2006, https://www.ted.com/talks/sir_ken_robinson_do_schools_kill_creativity.

7   Ellen Winner, Thalia R. Goldstein, and Stéphan Vincent-Lancrin, "Art for Art's Sake? The Impact of Arts Education," Frontiers in Psychology 10 (2019): 1430, https://www.oecd.org/content/dam/oecd/en/publications/reports/2013/06/art-for-art-s-sake_g1g21e09/9789264180789-en.pdf.

8   Albert Einstein, quoted in Goodreads, "Play is the Highest Form of Research," accessed August 2025, https://www.goodreads.com/quotes/10008-play-is-the-highest-form-of-research.

9   Reggio Children, "The Reggio Emilia Approach," accessed August 2025, https://www.reggiochildren.it/en/reggio-emilia-approach/.

10   Maria Montessori, The Absorbent Mind (New York: Holt, 1949).

11   Mary Helen Immordino-Yang and Antonio Damasio, "We Feel, Therefore We Learn: The Relevance of Affective and Social Neuroscience to Education," Mind, Brain, and Education 1, no. 1 (2007): 3–10, https://onlinelibrary.wiley.com/doi/10.1111/j.1751-228X.2007.00004.x.

12   Peter C. Brown et al., Make It Stick: The Science of Successful Learning (Cambridge, MA: Harvard University Press, 2014).

13   Lev Vygotsky, Mind in Society (Cambridge, MA: Harvard University Press, 1978).

14   Debora L. Roorda, Helma M. Koomen, Jantine L. Spilt, and Frans J. Oort, "The Influence of Affective Teacher–Student Relationships on Students' School Engagement and Achievement: A Meta-Analytic Approach," Review of Educational Research 81, no. 4 (2011): 493–529, https://

pure.uva.nl/ws/files/21283991/Affective_Teacher_Student_Relationships_and_Students_Engagement_and_Achievement.pdf.

15   Stephanie M. Jones and Jennifer Kahn, The Evidence Base for How We Learn: Supporting Students' Social, Emotional, and Academic Development (Washington, DC: The Aspen Institute, 2017), https://www.aspeninstitute.org/publications/evidence-base-learn/.

16   Bridget K. Hamre and Robert C. Pianta, "Early Teacher–Child Relationships and the Trajectory of Children's School Outcomes through Eighth Grade," Child Development 72, no. 2 (2001): 625–638, https://www.jstor.org/stable/1132418.

17   Kathryn R. Wentzel, "Teacher-Student Relationships and Adolescent Competence at School," in Handbook of School Violence and School Safety: International Research and Practice, eds. Shane R. Jimerson et al. (New York: Routledge, 2012), 434–444.

18   Center on the Developing Child, Harvard University, "Serve and Return," 2010.

19   Molly Wright, "How Every Child Can Thrive by Five," TED Talk, 2021.

20   Toxic Stress," Pediatrics 129, no. 1 (2012): e232–e246, https://publications.aap.org/pediatrics/article/148/2/e2021052582/179805/Preventing-Childhood-Toxic-Stress-Partnering-With?autologincheck=redirected.

21   Robert C. Pianta and Martha W. Stuhlman, "Teacher-Student Relationships and Children's Success in School," Developmental Psychology 40, no. 2 (2004): 406–417, https://bottemabeutel.com/wp-content/uploads/2014/01/Pianta-teacher-student-relationships.pdf.

22   National Scientific Council on the Developing Child, "Young Children Develop in an Environment of Relationships," Working Paper No. 1 (2004), https://www.academia.edu/44520364/Young_children_Develop_in_an_environment_of_relationships.

23   Suzanna Herculano-Houzel, "The Human Brain in Numbers: A Linearly Scaled-up Primate Brain," Frontiers in Human Neuroscience 3 (2009): 31, https://pmc.ncbi.nlm.nih.gov/articles/PMC2776484/.

24   Harvard University, Center on the Developing Child, "Brain Architecture," accessed August 2025, https://developingchild.harvard.edu/science/key-concepts/brain-architecture/.

25   National Scientific Council on the Developing Child, "The Science of Early Childhood Development," 2007, https://developingchild.harvard.edu/resources/the-science-of-early-childhood-development-closing-the-gap-between-what-we-know-and-what-we-do/.

26   Paul H. Lipkin and Michelle M. Macias, "Promoting Optimal Development: Identifying Infants and Young Children with Developmental Disorders through Developmental Surveillance and Screening," Pediatrics 145, no. 1 (2020): e20193449, https://publications.aap.org/pediatrics/article/145/1/e20193449/36971/Promoting-Optimal-Development-Identifying-Infants; Rhoshel K. Lenroot and Jay N. Giedd, "Brain Development in Children and Adolescents: Insights from Anatomical Magnetic Resonance Imaging," Nature Reviews Neuroscience 7, no. 10 (2006): 718–729, https://www.academia.edu/32430234/Brain_development_in_children_and_adolescents_Insights_from_anatomical_magnetic_resonance_imaging.

27   Sally Goddard Blythe, "School-Age Children and Primitive Reflexes," Education 3-13 49, no. 2 (2021): 189–206, https://www.tandfonline.com/doi/full/10.1080/03004279.2021.1895276.

28   John Medina, Brain Rules: 12 Principles for Surviving and Thriving at Work, Home, and School (Seattle: Pear Press, 2014).; Robert M. Sapolsky, Behave: The Biology of Humans at Our Best and Worst (New York: Penguin, 2017), https://www.sackett.net/sapolsky_behave.pdf.

29   Adele Diamond, "Executive Functions," Annual Review of Psychology 64 (2013): 135–168, https://doi.org/10.1146/annurev-psych-113011-143750.

30   Jay N. Giedd, "Structural Magnetic Resonance Imaging of the Adolescent Brain," Annals of the New York Academy of Sciences 1021, no. 1 (2004): 77–85, https://doi.org/10.1196/annals.1308.009.

31   Stephen W. Porges, The Polyvagal Theory: Neurophysiological Foundations of Emotions, Attachment, Communication, and Self-Regulation (New York: W. W. Norton & Company, 2011).

32   Michael S. Gazzaniga, "Cerebral Specialization and Interhemispheric Communication: Does the Corpus Callosum Enable the Human Condition?" Brain 123, no. 7 (2000): 1293–1326, https://pubmed.ncbi.nlm.nih.gov/10869045/.

33   Robert Melillo, Disconnected Kids (New York: Penguin, 2009).; Robert Melillo and Gerry Leisman, Neurobehavioral Disorders of Childhood: An Evolutionary Perspective (New York: Springer, 2004).

34   Carla Hannaford, The Dominance Factor: How Knowing Your Dominant Eye, Ear, Brain, Hand & Foot Can Improve Your Learning (Salt Lake City: Great River Books, 1997).

35   Centers for Disease Control and Prevention, "Developmental Milestones," 2022, https://www.cdc.gov/ncbddd/actearly/milestones/index.html.

36   Hocking, Claire, The Relationship between Retained Primitive Reflexes and Sensory Integration, Whole Brain Learning, accessed September 1, 2025, https://www.wholebrain.com.au/uploads/1/5/9/5/15956426/the_relationship_between_retained_primitive_reflexes.pdf.

37   Jack P. Shonkoff and Deborah A. Phillips, eds., From Neurons to Neighborhoods: The Science of Early Childhood Development (Washington, DC: National Academy Press, 2000).

38   Sally Goddard Blythe, Reflexes, Learning and Behavior: A Window into the Child's Mind (Eugene, OR: Fern Ridge Press, 2005).

39   Robert Melillo, Disconnected Kids (New York: Penguin, 2009).

40   Carla Hannaford, Smart Moves: Why Learning Is Not All in Your Head (Salt Lake City: Great River Books, 2005).

41   Bryan Kolb and Robbin Gibb, "Brain Plasticity and Behaviour in the Developing Brain," Journal of the Canadian Academy of Child and Adolescent Psychiatry 20, no. 4 (2011): 265–276.

42   Rachel S. Herz and Trygg Engen, "Odor Memory: Review and Analysis," Psychonomic Bulletin & Review 3, no. 3 (1996): 300–313.

43   Ladan Shams and Aaron R. Seitz, "Benefits of Multisensory Learning," Trends in Cognitive Sciences 12, no. 11 (2008): 411–417.

44   A. Jean Ayres, Sensory Integration and Learning Disorders (Los Angeles: Western Psychological Services, 1972).

45   Jean Piaget, The Origins of Intelligence in Children (New York: International Universities Press, 1952).

46   A. D. Craig, "How Do You Feel? Interoception: The Sense of the Physiological Condition of the Body," Nature Reviews Neuroscience 3, no. 8 (2002): 655–666.

47   Frederic C. Bartlett, Remembering: A Study in Experimental and Social Psychology (Cambridge: Cambridge University Press, 1932).; Daniel L. Schacter, "Constructive Memory: Past and Future," Dialogues in Clinical Neuroscience 14, no. 1 (2012): 7–18.

48   James L. McGaugh, "Making Lasting Memories: Remembering the Significant," Proceedings of the National Academy of Sciences 110, Supplement 2 (2013): 10402–10407.

49   Ladan Shams and Aaron R. Seitz, "Benefits of Multisensory Learning," Trends in Cognitive Sciences 12, no. 11 (2008): 411–417.

50   David A. Kolb, Experiential Learning: Experience as the Source of Learning and Development (Englewood Cliffs, NJ: Prentice Hall, 1984).

51   Logan Fiorella and Richard E. Mayer, "The Relative Benefits of Learning by Teaching and Teaching Expectancy," Contemporary Educational Psychology 38, no. 4 (2013): 281–288.

52   Wilder Penfield and Theodore Rasmussen, The Cerebral Cortex of Man (New York: Macmillan, 1950).

53   Wilder Penfield and Edwin Boldrey, "Somatic Motor and Sensory Representation in the Cerebral Cortex of Man as Studied by Electrical Stimulation," Brain 60, no. 4 (1937): 389–443.

54   James E. Zull, The Art of Changing the Brain (Sterling, VA: Stylus, 2002).

55   Robin Alexander, Improving Oracy and Classroom Talk in English Schools (Cambridge: Cambridge Primary Review Trust, 2012).

56   Edutopia, Oracy in the Classroom: Strategies for Effective Talk, YouTube video, 7:26, June 4, 2018, https://www.youtube.com/watch?v=2ADAY9AQm54.

57   Education Endowment Foundation, "Oral Language Interventions," 2017, https://educationendowmentfoundation.org.uk/education-evidence/teaching-learning-toolkit/oral-language-interventions.

58   Alexander Tierney and Nina Kraus, "Music Training for the Development of Reading Skills," Progress in Brain Research 207 (2013): 209–241.

59   Susan Hallam, "The Power of Music: Its Impact on the Intellectual, Social and Personal Development of Children and Young People," International Journal of Music Education 28, no. 3 (2010): 269–289.; Aniruddh D. Patel, "Why Would Musical Training Benefit the Neural Encoding of Speech? The OPERA Hypothesis," Frontiers in Psychology 2 (2011): 142.

60   Nikki S. Rickard et al., "Orchestrating Life Skills: The Effect of Increased School-Based Music Classes on Children's Social Competence and Self-Esteem," International Journal of Music Education 31, no. 3 (2012): 292–309.

61   Carla Hannaford, Smart Moves: Why Learning Is Not All in Your Head (Salt Lake City: Great River Books, 2005).

62   Adele Diamond and Kathleen Lee, "Interventions Shown to Aid Executive Function Development in Children 4 to 12 Years Old," Science 333, no. 6045 (2011): 959–964.

63   John Medina, Brain Rules (Seattle: Pear Press, 2014).

64   Charles H. Hillman et al., "The Effect of Acute Treadmill Walking on Cognitive Control and Academic Achievement in Preadolescent Children," Neuroscience 159, no. 3 (2009): 1044–1054.

65   John J. Ratey, Spark: The Revolutionary New Science of Exercise and the Brain (New York: Little, Brown, 2008).

66   Michael I. Posner and Steven E. Petersen, "The Attention System of the Human Brain," Annual Review of Neuroscience 13, no. 1 (1990): 25–42.

67   American Psychological Association. "Multitasking: Switching Costs." Washington, DC: APA, 2006. https://www.apa.org/research/action/multitask.

68   Ophir, E., Nass, C., & Wagner, A. D. (2009). Cognitive control in media multitaskers. Proceedings of the National Academy of Sciences, 106(37), 15583-15587.

69   Zhang, L. F., and R. J. Sternberg. A Threefold Model of Intellectual Styles. Educational Psychology Review 17, no. 1 (2005): 1–53.

70   Riding, R. J., and I. Cheema. Cognitive Styles—An Overview and Integration. Educational Psychology 11, no. 3–4 (1991): 193–215.

71   Hannaford, Carla. The Dominance Factor: How Knowing Your Dominant Eye, Ear, Brain, Hand & Foot Can Improve Your Learning. Salt Lake City: Great River Books, 1997.

72   Navon, D. "Forest before Trees: The Precedence of Global Features in Visual Perception." Cognitive Psychology 9, no. 3 (1977): 353–383.

73   Melillo, R. Disconnected Kids: The Groundbreaking Brain Balance Program for Children with Autism, ADHD, Dyslexia, and Other Neurological Disorders. New York: Penguin, 2009.

74   Medina, John. Brain Rules: 12 Principles for Surviving and Thriving at Work, Home, and School. Seattle: Pear Press, 2014.

75   Melillo, Robert. Disconnected Kids: The Groundbreaking Brain Balance Program for Children with Autism, ADHD, Dyslexia, and Other Neurological Disorders, 2nd ed. New York: Penguin, 2016.

76   Diamond, Adele. "Executive Functions." Annual Review of Psychology 64 (2013): 135–168.

77   Best, John R. "Effects of Physical Activity on Children's Executive Function: Contributions of Experimental Research on Aerobic Exercise." Developmental Review 30, no. 4 (2010): 331–351.

78   Zenner, C., Herrnleben-Kurz, S., & Walach, H. (2014). Mindfulness-based interventions in schools—a systematic review and meta-analysis. Frontiers in Psychology, 5, 603.

79   Else-Quest, N. M., Hyde, J. S., Goldsmith, H. H., & Van Hulle, C. A. (2006). Gender differences in temperament: A meta-analysis. Psychological Bulletin, 132(1), 33-72.

80   Walter Mischel, The Marshmallow Test: Mastering Self-Control (New York: Little, Brown, 2014).

81   Zenner, C., Herrnleben-Kurz, S., & Walach, H. (2014). Mindfulness-based interventions in schools—a systematic review and meta-analysis. Frontiers in Psychology, 5, 603.

82   Flook, Lisa, Simon B. Goldberg, Laura Pinger, and Richard J. Davidson. "Promoting Prosocial Behavior and Self-Regulatory Skills in Preschool Children through a Mindfulness-Based Kindness Curriculum." Developmental Psychology 51, no. 1 (2015): 44–51.

83   Center on the Developing Child at Harvard University (2011). Building the Brain's "Air Traffic Control" System: How Early Experiences Shape the Development of Executive Function: Working Paper No. 11. http://www.developing child.harvard.edu

84   Melillo, Robert. Disconnected Kids: The Groundbreaking Brain Balance Program for Children with Autism, ADHD, Dyslexia, and Other Neurological Disorders, 2nd ed. New York: Penguin, 2016.

85   Melillo, Robert. Disconnected Kids: The Groundbreaking Brain Balance Program for Children with Autism, ADHD, Dyslexia, and Other Neurological Disorders, 2nd ed. New York: Penguin, 2016.

86   Immordino-Yang, Mary Helen, and Antonio Damasio. "We Feel, Therefore We Learn: The Relevance of Affective and Social Neuroscience to Education." Mind, Brain, and Education 1, no. 1 (2007): 3–10.

87   Collaborative for Academic, Social, and Emotional Learning (CASEL). "What Is SEL?" Chicago: CASEL, 2020. https://casel.org/what-is-sel/.

88   National Scientific Council on the Developing Child. "Young Children Develop in an Environment of Relationships." Working Paper No. 1, 2004.

89   McCraty, R., Atkinson, M., & Tomasino, D. (2001). Science of the Heart: Exploring the Role of the Heart in Human Performance (Publication No. 01-001). HeartMath Research Center, Institute of HeartMath.

90   McCraty, Rollin, Mike Atkinson, Dana Tomasino, and Raymond T. Bradley. "The Coherent Heart: Heart–Brain Interactions, Psychophysiological Coherence, and the Emergence of System-Wide Order." Integral Review 5, no. 2 (2009): 10–115.

91   McCraty, R., & Zayas, M. A. (2014). Cardiac coherence, self-regulation, autonomic stability, and psychosocial well-being. Frontiers in Psychology, 5, 1090.

92   Robinson, Ken. "Do Schools Kill Creativity?" TED Talk, 2006.

93   Youki Terada and Stephen Merrill, "The Science of Classroom Design: Our Comprehensive, All-in, Research-Based Look at the Design of Effective Learning Spaces," Edutopia, November 2, 2023.

94   Barrett, Peter, Yufan Zhang, Joanne Moffat, and Khairy Kobbacy. "A Holistic, Multi-Level Analysis Identifying the Impact of Classroom Design on Pupils' Learning." Building and Environment 59 (2013): 678–689.

95   Kamik Survey, Children Spending 35 Percent Less Time Playing Freely Outside, SGB Online, September 20, 2018, https://sgbonline.com/kamik-survey-childre-spending-35-percent-less-time-playing-freely-outside/.

96   Haidt, Jonathan, The Anxious Generation (New York: Penguin Press, 2024), esp. chap. 3–5.

97   Kaplan, Stephen, "The Restorative Benefits of Nature: Toward an Integrative Framework," Journal of Environmental Psychology 15, no. 3 (1995): 169–82.

98   Gray, Peter. Free to Learn: Why Unleashing the Instinct to Play Will Make Our Children Happier, More Self-Reliant, and Better Students for Life. New York: Basic Books, 2013.

99   Gray, Peter. Free to Learn: Why Unleashing the Instinct to Play Will Make Our Children Happier, More Self-Reliant, and Better Students for Life. New York: Basic Books, 2013.

100 Gray, Peter. "The Decline of Play and the Rise of Psychopathology in Children and Adolescents." Pediatrics 142, no. 3 (2018): e20181512.

101 Kamik Survey, Children Spending 35 Percent Less Time Playing Freely Outside, SGB Online, September 20, 2018, https://sgbonline.com/kamik-survey-childre-spending-35-percent-less-time-playing-freely-outside/.

102 Gray, Peter. Free to Learn: Why Unleashing the Instinct to Play Will Make Our Children Happier, More Self-Reliant, and Better Students for Life. New York: Basic Books, 2013.

103 Condliffe, Barbara, Janet Quint, Mary G. Visher, et al. Project-Based Learning: A Literature Review. MDRC, 2017.

104 Haidt, Jonathan, The Anxious Generation (New York: Penguin Press, 2024.

105 Haidt, Jonathan, The Anxious Generation (New York: Penguin Press, 2024).

106 Metcalfe, J. (2017). Learning from Errors. Annual Review of Psychology, 68, 465-489).

Acknowledgements

I never realized how many people would influence the outcome of this book. This section will only scratch the surface of everyone I have to thank. So, for the purpose of attempting to stay focused, I will acknowledge those who had a significant and direct impact on this book.

First and foremost, this is for my children, Jackson, Zachary, and Cameron. You guys are my actual everything! You are the reason for the book, the mission, and the reason I wake up every day and try to help make this world a better place. Your Kid Magic is a bright light and a beacon for a better world. Jackson, you bring such radiant joy, not only through your cooking and your music, but through your compassion, understanding, and beautiful heart. Your brilliant mind and heart inspire those around you. Zachary, you are always looking at the big picture, not just in sports and on the ice, but in every area of life. You always consider everyone else in everything you do. You are the glue that keeps us all together and your smile lights up the universe. Cameron, your artistic and creative talent bring happiness to everyone around you. You are so very thoughtful, and your silliness and laughter brighten up the world.

To my amazing (and ridiculously handsome) husband, Kevin. There is no one I would rather go through this adventure of parenthood and life with. You are my sunshine.

To my mom, for teaching me how to be the mother I am by being the best mom to ever walk God's great Earth. My childhood is part of my greatest inspiration. I'd like to say my parents did it right (no bias here).

To my dad, for literally everything. For the non-stop life lessons, for listening to my great ideas (and terrible ones), for letting me talk it out, for letting me hide out in the gazebo or in front of the fire and making sure I had food while I wrote and thought and drew and wrote some more.

To my siblings, Lauren, Vinny, Stephie, and Stephen, for constantly listening to every single update, change, question and for giving me your very honest advice and opinions. You have literally been on this crazy journey with me since birth, you are my lifelines and my forever partners in crime (the good kind). I also need to shout out the out-laws, Patrick, Andrew, and very special thank you to my sister-in-love, Liz, who has been exceptionally helpful. To my in-laws, Jenny, Jay, and Jason, for letting me show you all my pictures and talk through this book at every single family event. In addition, thank you all for lending me your children to love (and study). My nieces and nephews are dancing in the pages of this book.

To my grandma terrific for being not only my artistic inspiration, but actually sitting down and helping me to draw all of my images. The time we spent together drawing filled my heart and soul. How many girls get to say they illustrated their first book with their grandma!

To my incredible mother-in-law who has not only been supportive of me, but has been absolutely influential in bringing the love and joy of reading to our children and making books an essential part of our home.

To my amazing friends, especially those who have listened to me talk about this book over and over, every single day for like ever! Lori, you are not just my rock, but my actual brain and the only one who can help me manage me! You always make time for me and help me get out of my own way. Annie, you have been my home since we were little and know me better than I know myself. Crystal, you feed my spirit with a constant flow of positive energy. Kayla, you are my heart. Your words of encouragement keep me going. Marisa, you have listened to me, let me share my thoughts, and taken my kids so many times so that I could write. Lisa, Thad, Christina, Bill, Siobhan, and Bill, you are our inner circle and have heard this book story since the very start.

To all my mom friends who helped with rides and took my kids for me so that I could write, draw, and focus on this book! It takes a village and I have the most special one!

An enormous thank you to Mike Hynes, without you, there is no book. Thank you for believing in me and giving me opportunities no one else would. Thank you for telling me to write a book and then demanding an outline the following week. You held me accountable, gave me your heartfelt honest thoughts, and gave me courage to do something I never thought I could do. Even when you had no time, you made time for me. Again, without you, there is no book! Thank you!

A huge thank you to Dr. Robert Melillo for making the time to write the most incredible foreword for this book. You have not only been my most reliable source for much of the neuroscience and development in this book, but an inspiration to myself and many, a revolutionary changing the world, and my friend!

To Carissa Manza for taking a chance on me. You were the very first person to welcome the How To Be A Kid™ program and gave me the opportunity to take off. To Jeff Haubrich for helping me continue to grow the program that led to this book. You both have demonstrated what true leadership looks like in a school. To Lauren Fretto and Tom Keogh who have implemented the How To Be A Kid™ program into their schools and remain dedicated to the overall well-being of our children.

To Travis Davey, the very first person who listened to my idea and told me I had something that was worth it. For all the coffee dates and hours that you have spent "playing" and helping me grow these ideas into something real. For writing a beautiful, heartfelt foreword that brought tears to my eyes. Your friendship is a gift.

To Emily Moran and Samantha Romeo for being the very first teachers to experience the How To Be A Kid™ philosophy. For the hours of letting me present to you, chatting over lunch and giving me your honest feedback. For always standing behind me and the mission and for being such incredible educators, especially to my own kids.

To my incredible readers, Patty Snider and Ashley Donnelly, who read the very first copy of this book and literally gave me line-by-line feedback! The number of times I have called or texted to run ideas by you up until the very end... you have no idea what your support means to me! Thank you with all my heart.

To the amazing teachers from Babylon Schools, who not only teach and care for my children, but were my first crew to run through and continue to be a part of the How To Be A Kid™ program and philosophy. You are a true inspiration and the future of education!

To my Creative Revolutionaries, especially Kate, Anthony, Cassandra, Claire, Daniel, Chad, Steven, William, Galen, and Katie. You are my people! We are literally changing the world. I have never been a part of something so powerful, creative and beautiful. We represent the best of what this world can be... to the Revolution!

To Sir Ken Robinson, you were among my very first inspirations. Your magic continues to grow and spread throughout the universe. While your absence is painful, your impact will never stop spreading. To quote *The Sandlot*, "heroes get remembered, but legends never die."

To my people at Babylon Bean, especially Kayla, Julia, Isabella, Kate, Vanessa, Ryan, Andrew, and Sal. Most of my writing was done at the Bean. You guys take care of me in ways many don't understand. You give me not just liquid strength, but listen to my daily stories, share your thoughts, and give me encouragement. Never underestimate the power of a barista to change your day!

To my super amazing, incredible, spectacular editor, Megan Tatreau. I literally want to scream your name from the rooftops! I am in awe of your talent! You ripped me apart and put me back together in the most beautiful way and I could not have done this without you!

To David Provolo for designing not just the cover, but the entire inside of this book. Your patience is unmatched. I have to be the world's most difficult person to work with and you were patient and kind. They say don't judge a book by its cover, but you helped make my baby beautiful inside and out and it matters.

To the incredible artist who brought Mr. Homunculus to life, Eszter Czap-Tóth. Your talent is breathtaking. Your art has not just blessed this book, but inspired my creativity throughout my journey. I hope we get to work together on future projects!

To all of my kids, yes, "my kids" who I have worked with throughout the years. You are woven into the very pages of this book and the fabric of my being.

To all of the educators who inspire me!

And perhaps most importantly, to all the kids who deserve better... this is for you!

The better future we imagine starts with the Magic in each and every kid.

Meet Dr. Crystal T. Miller

The founder of How To Be A Kid™, Dr. Crystal T. Miller, PT, DPT, has been practicing as a Doctor of Physical Therapy since 2008 and is an expert in human movement. She has worked across more than a dozen school districts, children's hospitals, and rehabilitation settings, as well as with Broadway performers, professional athletes, and dancers—both in the US and overseas. Much of her expertise lies in making the body and mind central to the human experience, and she brings this perspective to education through her program and her book, *Kid MAGIC Unlocked*.

Dr. Miller is a speaker who runs professional development workshops for teachers and parents, equipping them with strategies to integrate movement, sensory experiences, and emotional connection into the classroom in ways that align with child development. She has served on an elementary school Social-Emotional Learning committee, collaborated with school districts to develop whole-child approaches to learning, and draws inspiration from her unique collegiate background in the Delta College Program, where "real life learning" was the focus.

Beyond her professional expertise, Dr. Miller is a dreamer and out-of-the-box thinker who loves creativity as much as science. At just 4'11", this former gymnast can still walk on her hands. She's a coffee enthusiast (especially when it involves a fancy coffee shop or her own creative concoctions) and has a soft spot for sea turtles and never loses sight of the power of imagination—even the smallest Figment of it. She also loves adventuring, paddleboarding, and reading and proudly claims her place as a true Hufflepuff.

Her greatest inspiration comes from her three children and her supportive husband and family. Dr. Miller is dedicated to bridging the gap between child development and meaningful learning, transforming education into a kid-centric approach that celebrates the creativity, curiosity, and MAGIC in every child.